PAINTERS IN

A NEW LAND

A South East View of Cataraqui on Lake Ontario, taken in August 1783

CONTENTS

Acknowledgements

The creation of this volume would have been impossible without the advice over the years of W. McAllister Johnson. H.A. Taylor, Director of the Historical Branch of the Public Archives of Canada, encouraged me when the project was first suggested. My colleagues in the Paintings, Drawings and Prints Section of the Public Archives of Canada have unwittingly contributed to the content in the discussions we have had over the past five years. W.M.E. Cooke read the text and made valuable suggestions.

The water-colours and drawings illustrating this book are all to be found in the collection of documentary art in the Public Archives of Canada—one of the least known, but best collections of its type in Canada. All the colour photography was done by Ron Vickers.

JAMES S. MERES

View of the harbour at Placentia, Newfoundland,
from the artillery placements   1786

Water-colour, 9½ x 30¼ inches

PREFACE

Until recently, certain parts of our cultural heritage have been known only to a small group of historians and private collectors. One of the most exciting of these areas is the chronicle of eighteenth and nineteenth century Canada that exists in the form of water-colours and drawings. This significant and charming collection forms a cohesive unit that links an artistic phenomenon with the events and social climate of the period. Although these pictures have always been of interest to the sensitive private collector, they are now being recognized as a vital part of our national heritage which must be preserved and made available to all Canadians. We owe a great debt to the early collectors. They saw the importance of these early records of life in Canada, and because of their efforts, we are better able to understand the events and surroundings that led up to and formed the Canadian experience.

During Canada's early years under English rule, exciting cultural developments were taking place in England and Europe. Almost contemporary with the Seven Years' War, England and Europe were enthusiastically reaffirming the roots of Western society. Yet, at the same time, they continuously sought out other societies, lands, and experiences alien to the Mediterranean classical world. It was an expansive period for the English. Englishmen in great numbers travelled extensively all over the world. English colonies, established on a worldwide basis in North America, the East and West Indies, India, and later in Australia and New Zealand, provided a sound economic base for English commerce. Secure in their belief in the moral, spiritual, and philosophical superiority of their society, Englishmen exposed themselves without fear to the influences of alien cultures and permitted the introduction of new themes and attitudes into art and literature. In an era of expansion, exploration, and diversity of new experience, "paintings, drawings and prints were . . . the particular visual arts which made it possible for the . . . individual to enter vicariously into the new worlds of information and emotion."[1]

Pictures multiplied in response to the demand for more and more visual information about fresh areas of activity. The Englishman sought the pictorial record as "tangible evidence of British power and expansionism which in the light of British empiricism, technological advance and the interest in the present could not but motivate the capable artist in far away corners of the Empire to record his nation's success."[2]

In response to the Victorian demand for information, illustrated journalism developed; journals such as the *Penny Magazine* and later the *Illustrated London News* and the London *Graphic* dealt with news and information on a popular level, leaning heavily on the illustrative content. Illustrated journalism generated a demand for a large number of on-the-spot pictures of the events and places in the news. "Special artists" travelled all over the globe, often risking their lives in the process, and sent back to the European and English presses clear, informative pictures of what they encountered.

With the great proliferation of pictures and an increasing ability of the public to "read" them, more and more people began to make their own drawings. The age of the amateur was born. Several conditions combined to encourage this new phenomenon; picture exhibitions became a regular social occurrence, providing an opportunity for the viewing public to learn the grammar and syntax of a common style; a school of engravers, which flourished alongside London publishers and printsellers, made the pictures still more widely available; tuition was available from the many competent but penurious English water-colourists; certain occupational groups saw the advantage of being able to sketch and paint in water-colour; and there was a popular subject in landscape.

The medium of water-colour was particularly favoured in the eighteenth and nineteenth centuries because the means were extremely portable and all of the materials—the colour, the binder that holds the particles of colour on the surface of the paper, and the water—are all easily available anywhere. The paper, handmade until the early nineteenth century, was of high quality and diverse in kind. Eventually, the materials became available in prepackaged form for the amateur who did not want to grind his own colours and cut his paper from large Imperial sheets. By 1781, the Reeves firm was producing the small cakes of colour familiar to schoolchildren, and by 1832 the little Japanned or enamelled tin boxes containing cakes of pigment were on the market in much the same form as they are today.

With his materials in hand, the professional or amateur could travel to the countryside and come back with a sketchbook full of studies direct from nature ready to be made into formal pictures. Before long, the formal pictures were completed in the countryside, with a resulting increase in spontaneity and brilliance, which foreshadowed the later developments in "plein"

1. Philadelphia Museum of Art, *Romantic Art in Britain*, Philadelphia: 1968, p. 17.
2. Public Archives of Canada, *Image of Canada*, Ottawa: 1972, Introduction.

SYDNEY PRIOR HALL   A conference of the Governor-General, Lord Lorne, and the Blackfeet Indians   1881
Chalk pastel, 58 x 94 inches

air painting in the late nineteenth century.

The artists exploited the brilliance of their medium which resulted from the transparent qualities of the colour and the reflective capacity of the paper. The views they sought and delicately rendered in their water-colour sketchbooks were very much a reflection of the popular interest in picturesque landscape for itself. This interest was supported by the philosophical positions revolving around the picturesque, the beautiful, and the sublime, and the trends in literature represented by the poetry of Samuel Coleridge and William Wordsworth. Landscape—not formal portraits and not historical painting in the academic sense — became the main pictorial theme in the popular mind.

The well-travelled Englishman often produced his own visual record of his journeys. Sometimes combined with a diary, these pictures were later reproduced in the form of engravings, aquatints, and lithographs. These illustrated travel narratives, from which most of the contemporary texts in this book are extracted, helped to establish the image of North America in Europe.

In England and elsewhere in Europe, people showed far-reaching interest in the progress of the British colonies in North America. For the English, it was one area, reasonably close to home, where English laws and language pertained, where the land was almost free, and where the opportunities for their children were said to be unlimited. For the Europeans, whose few colonies were

mostly in disease-ridden climates and subject to periodic outbreaks of native violence, British North America was particularly attractive: there were few restrictions, and minorities were tolerated and even encouraged. It was to such an interested public that the illustrated journals appealed.

In order to encourage more immigration to British North America, Lord Lorne, the Governor-General of Canada, in 1881 commissioned a group of English and Scottish journalists to come to Canada to report on the opportunities available. It was only natural that one of the illustrated journals should be represented by Sydney Prior Hall. Hall was well prepared for the task before him. His record of the Prussian war was highly praised by his contemporaries.

JAMES PATTISON COCKBURN   The launching of the Royal William at Quebec, Lower Canada   1831
Water-colour, 6 x 9¼ inches

He had covered Royal Tours so well that he received the direct patronage of Queen Victoria, and he had accompanied Lorne and Princess Louise to Canada. In 1881, Hall and the rest of the journalists made their way to the foothills of the Canadian Rockies via steamer, canoe, wagon, and the completed portions of the Canadian Pacific Railway.

Another group who recorded the earlier experiences in the new land were the officers of the British Army and the Royal Navy. Every officer had to try his hand at water-colour painting and to acquire "a certificate of diligence from the Drawing Master"[3] at the officers' training academies such as the Royal Military Academy at Woolwich, where the acknowledged father of English water-colour painting, Paul Sandby, was once

a drawing master. British North America was one of the colonial outposts. In order to defend it, garrisons of the British Army were established and officers served with their regiments on the periphery of the backwoods, if not in them. It was a peacetime posting, except for brief flurries of activity in 1776, 1812, and 1837, and the officers used the opportunity to indulge in the traditional, and at that time acceptable, diversion of painting their surroundings.

To these officers we owe most of our knowledge of what the colony of Canada looked like in the eighteenth and nineteenth centuries. The best known of them — Thomas Davies, James Peachey, and James Pattison Cockburn — were three of many who travelled throughout the colony recording the towns and villages,

the natural wonders, and sometimes the people. Often nothing is known of these officers but their names; often their pictures come to us without even that. Indeed, very little is known of most of these artists.

James Pattison Cockburn and Philip John Bainbrigge were two typical officer-artists about whom we have some biographical information. From 1793 to 1795, Cockburn attended the Royal Military Academy at Woolwich. The ability to draw was one of the entrance qualifications for the academy since the officer-cadets were required to draw the terrain of a battlefield in order to provide data to establish artillery batteries and fortifications. Commissioned as a 2nd lieutenant

3. *Records of the Royal Military Academy, 1741-1892*, Woolwich: 1892, p. 45.

PHILIP JOHN BAINBRIGGE   Amherstburg from the ferry, Upper Canada   1838
                                         Water-colour, 5¾ x 8¾ inches

of the Royal Artillery upon graduation, Cockburn advanced through the ranks, ending his career as a major-general and the director of the Royal Laboratory at the Royal Arsenal at Woolwich. Posted in Canada from 1822 to 1823 and from 1826 to 1832, Cockburn executed an incredible number of water-colours. He was noted by his contemporaries as being an indefatigable and prolific sketcher, often scrambling over the rugged terrain to get the view he wanted. In 1833, two sets of magnificent and large aquatints were published after his drawings—one of Quebec and another of Niagara Falls. Both are desirable collector's items today. In 1831 Cockburn wrote and illustrated a guide-book to Quebec entitled *Quebec and its Environs*.

Deserving to be better known is Philip John Bainbrigge. He took a commission in the Royal Engineers after graduating from the Royal Military Academy in 1833, and his request for a posting in Canada was granted in 1836. He served in Lower Canada at the time of the Rebellion and remained in Canada until 1842. His extraordinary abilities as a draughtsman were utilized in the preparation of special surveys along the undefined boundaries that were an issue between Britain and the United States. At the same time he painted an impressive series of water-colours ranging over the whole of British North America from the Madawaska Portage in New Brunswick to Amherstburg in Upper Canada. He strived for unusual pictorial effects, often selecting unusual points of view. His

compositions are forerunners of the advances of late-nineteenth-century European art.

If painting in water-colour was a necessity for the successful military officer, it was only recreation for the ladies. Accomplished young women learned to paint, dance, and speak French as the officers did, even in the days before formal education became the rule for both men and women. To these women who came to the colonies with their husbands we owe respect for their courage and gratitude for the paintings they have left us. They recorded the flowers, the interiors of the houses, and many other details that escaped the attention of the officer-artists. Accompanying her husband Thomas, an officer in the Coldstream Guard, Millicent Mary Chaplin

KATHERINE JANE ELLICE

The interior of the seigniory house at Beauharnois, Lower Canada   1838
Water-colour, 6½ x 8¾ inches

recorded such homely and Canadian scenes as removing several feet of fresh fallen snow from the front of her husband's stable, and the house in which they lived while in Quebec. Jane Ellice, the wife of Edward Ellice, and sometime mistress of the Seigneury of Beauharnois where she was held captive by the rebels in 1838, left an interesting series of water-colours to accompany her diary. She described the shipboard crossing on the *Hastings* with Lord Durham's entourage, which included the English water-colourist Coke Smyth who taught the Durham children the secrets of laying a water-colour wash. At Quebec she painted the town from shipboard; at Beauharnois she recorded views of the interior of the old seigneury house. Her attitude to her

drawings is indicative of the widespread feelings that the amateur water-colourists had about their work: "Nothing however but what I call scrabbles — recollections of Beauharnois which I shall like to look at when we go home [to England]!"[4]

Women artists in Canada were attracted by the delicate wildflowers, the butterflies, and the people, all of which they interpreted with the usual Victorian sentiment. The advice given by the editor of Catherine Parr Traill's *The Backwoods in Canada* was a sound and commonly held opinion: "To the person who is capable of looking abroad into the beauties of nature, and adoring the Creator through his glorious works, are opened stores of unmixed pleasure, which will not permit her to be dull or unhappy in

the loneliest part of our Western Wilderness."[5]

In addition to the travellers, the illustrators, and the officers and their wives, there were some artists who immigrated to Canada — a colony mainly concerned with the issues of survival — and daringly attempted to gain their livelihood by teaching art, selling their paintings, and working at various occupations in which they could use their talent to draw. William Armstrong, who immigrated to Canada hoping to find work as a railway engineer, was at one time a practising

4. Public Archives of Canada, *Ellice Papers*, MG 24, A2, Diary of Jane Ellice, Saturday, October 13, 1838.

5. Catherine Parr Traill, *The Backwoods of Canada*, London: Charles Knight, 1836, p. 4.

EDWARD ROPER
Prairie flowers near Broadview,
Assiniboia   1887
Water-colour, 20¼ x 12¼ inches

WILLIAM GEORGE RICHARDSON HIND   Duck hunting on the prairies with an immigrant wagon train in the distance   1862
Water-colour, 9 x 11¼ inches

engineer, an artist, a photographer, a land speculator, and an art teacher at the Toronto Normal School. William G. R. Hind immigrated to Canada and attempted to make a living by his art. He too taught in Toronto and led a somewhat itinerant life travelling to British Columbia with the Overlanders of '62 and accompanying his brother Henry Youle Hind into the interior of Labrador.

But the opportunities for the professional artist were scant and temporary, and it is mainly to the amateur that we owe our knowledge of the life and landscape of early Canadian life. It should be remembered, however, that it was an aspiring amateur artist, William Henry Fox

Talbot, who, in his desire to capture the essence of a scene accurately and permanently, invented the Calotype — an early form of photography. This new invention made the water-colour as a record obsolete. Talbot tells how in 1833, despairing of being able to draw an Italian scene at hand with Dr. Wollaston's *Camera Lucida*, he recalled how much easier it had been with the *camera obscura*. He then reflected "on the inimitable beauty of the pictures of Nature's painting . . . how charming it would be if it were possible to cause these natural images to imprint themselves durably and remain fixed upon the paper!"[6] The photograph as it finally took form was

more accurate, required less skill, and was eventually within the capacity of everyone. In 1858 the first successful photographs of the Canadian West were taken on the Canadian Government Assiniboine and Saskatchewan Exploring Expedition. Photography was used also by the North American Boundary Commission in 1870-75. The use of the water-colour as a recording medium was limited now to the tradition-bound military and the ranks of the professional artists, such as Lucius O'Brien. Even at the Royal

6. Quoted in H. Gernsheim, *The History of Photography*, Toronto: Oxford University Press, 1955, p. 61.

Military Academy at Woolwich, a photography laboratory had been set up. No longer would the accomplished amateur water-colourist flourish as he had in the early nineteenth century.

Fortunately for Canadians, a number of circumstances combined to leave us a record of what the country looked like before the advent of photography. The historical circumstances—the rise of the English amateur, the political dominance of England in British North America, and the increasing familiarity and desirability of the visual image as a personal record—would have been to no avail if an interested group of collectors had not preserved the water-colours and drawings for future generations.

The water-colours and drawings of the type illustrating this volume deteriorate with time and exposure to our pollution-filled environment; the colours are often fugitive, if not already faded to a shadow of their earlier state by continuous display in the nineteenth and early twentieth centuries. The short-sighted viewpoint that if something is collected it must be continuously displayed has already lost us a goodly portion of our heritage. We must revise our attitudes in order to guarantee that something is left for our children and grandchildren to experience directly. The decision to prepare this volume was motivated by the need to satisfy these conflicting demands: namely, to provide contact with an important segment of the heritage for as many people as possible, and to ensure that the water-colours and drawings deteriorate as little as possible while in the custody of this generation.

WILLIAM ROEBUCK
Tracking boats up the Long Sault Rapids
on the St. Lawrence River,
near Cornwall,
Upper Canada   1820
Water-colour, 12¾ x 18 inches

NEW FOUND LANDS

The early explorers who came to the shores of Newfoundland in search of the Northwest Passage found in its stead the fisheries of the Grand Banks. Although this was not the wealth of the Indies, its value was sufficiently high that the Newfoundland fisheries became the spoil of continental wars.

St. John's, under the direction of the Royal Navy, became the administrative centre of a multi-national trade; so was founded "the fishiest of modern capitals." The conflicts of the nations, although finally resolved in favour of the English, nonetheless left their mark in the form of towns with French origins, like Placentia, and the "French shore."

To these coasts in 1786 came James S. Meres, the keeper of the logbook of the Pegasus, under the command of William IV, the sailor-king. Meres' record of the shorelines and harbours are happily complemented by Edward Chappell's accounts of the society and trade of the colony.

Nearly one hundred years later, when the "special artist" Sydney Prior Hall came to these same shores with Lord Lorne, he also found the fishermen and their activities the most worthy and appropriate subject matter for his pencil, and he proceeded to describe them in the London Graphic for his readers.

Because of its inhospitable landscape and inclement climate, Newfoundland did not flourish. It was the first land of what was to become Canada that was touched by Europeans, but in later years it did not attract many immigrants, and was the last province to join Confederation.

JAMES S. MERES
A view of the Seven Islands in
the harbour of Placentia, Newfoundland   1786
From the Logbook of H.M.S. *Pegasus*
Water-colour, 7½ x 15 inches

Water-colour, 9¼ x 30½ inches

Placentia Bay is also full of harbours and islands. It is about sixty miles deep, and about forty-five miles broad from Cape St Mary's to Corbin Head, and from twenty to thirty miles broad at different places farther up. There is excellent cod-fishing in this bay; salmon abound in its rivers, and herring, &c., frequent it, as well as all these bays, periodically. The lands are rugged and barren, and the shores are lined with islands and rocks, among which, however, there are many excellent harbours. There are five or six extensive establishments in this bay.

Placentia, on the east side of the bay, was the chief settlement planted by the French in Newfoundland. They had it strongly fortified, and endeavoured at that time to drive the English altogether out of the fisheries. One hundred and fifty ships can lie in safety within the harbour, the entrance of which only admits one vessel at a time. There is a great strand or beach between two hills, sufficiently extensive for sixty ships to cure and dry their fish on. From the head of Placentia Bay to Trinity, the isthmus which connects the peninsula of Avalon to the main body of Newfoundland is low, and little more than three miles over. The fishermen haul their skiffs across.

J. MCGREGOR
British America 1832

JAMES S. MERES

The town and harbour of Placentia, Newfoundland from the hill back of the town   1786
From the Logbook of H.M.S. *Pegasus*
Water-colour, 9 ¼ x 35 inches

It was about the 14th *June* that we at length sailed from *St. John's*. Our Captain had received directions to proceed to the *Straights of Belle-isle*, in order to protect the fisheries established on the southern *Coast of Labrador*.

When quitting the harbour, we observed an immense mountain of *ice*, lying aground, in forty fathoms' water, off the entrance.

During the remainder of this day, we ran towards the *south*, with a gentle breeze from the *north-west:* and having passed *Petty* Harbour, Bay of *Bulls*, *Witless* and *Momables* Bays, we reached Cape *Broyle* at sun-set. The summit of this majestic headland was now covered with snow, and many small vessels were busily employed fishing along its base.

At daylight, on *June* the 15th, we doubled the promontory of Cape *Race*; but as the wind blew in very light airs from the *north-west*, we had not, at night-fall, reached farther than Cape *Pine*, a low point of land covered with trees. It was here that the *American* privateers were accustomed to lie in wait, to intercept the *English* merchant ships bound

for different ports in the River *St. Lawrence;* until the vigilance of Admiral Sir *Richard Keats* succeeded in clearing the coast of them. The inlet between Cape *Race* and Cape *Pine* is called *Trepassy* Bay, and there is a small fishing town situate near its head.

June the 16th. — In the forenoon, we crossed the mouth of a deep gulf, called *Placentia* Bay. When the *French* had possession of the *southern* parts of *Newfoundland*, they built a town upon the shores of this bay, and made *Placentia* the Capital of their territory. It is still a considerable place, and ranks next to *St. John's* in extent and population.

Towards night-fall, we were off Cape *Chapeau-Rouge*, the *western* extremity of *Placentia* Bay; and we could perceive the islands of *St. Pierre* and *Miquelon*, at a short distance towards the west.

June the 17th. — We were becalmed the whole day off the islands of *St. Pierre* and *Miquelon*; concerning which so much has been said, in the different Treaties between *Great Britain* and *France*.

These islands are small and barren; and are divided by a strait, that is navigable only for small vessels.

There is one peculiarity attending the *fogs of Newfoundland*, unnoticed in any account of the country: although it be very important that mariners navigating this coast should be apprised of the circumstance. It often occurs, that the whole of the ocean around *Newfoundland* is enveloped in so dense a fog, that it is apparently impossible for a ship to proceed on her course, without incurring the most imminent danger of shipwreck: but, at the same time, there is generally a small space, within a mile or two of the shore itself, entirely clear of the vapour, and, as it were, forming a zone of light around the coast: so that a person acquainted with this singular phaenomenon, will, in some cases, be enabled to attain his port; while a stranger, on the other hand, is afraid to approach the island.

E. CHAPPELL
Voyage of His Majesty's Ship Rosamond to New-foundland and the Southern Coast of Labrador 1818

FISHERIES

The fisheries are entitled to a few words of separate consideration in concluding our chapter on Newfoundland. They have ever since the discovery of North America been the theme of the particular solicitude, not of Great Britain alone, but of France, Spain, and Portugal, and subsequently of the United States of America, and have evidently been esteemed a subject of the utmost importance in the negotiation of all treaties involving the British, French, or American interests on the western side the Atlantic. It appears that as early as 1517 about fifty French, Spanish, and Portuguese vessels were engaged in the cod-fishery of the Banks, whilst England had but *one ship* employed in that quarter; and although this unit appears to have, in 1578, increased to fifteen, the fishing trade of the other powers had improved in a far greater degree, France having at that period no less than 150 ships engrossed by it, Spain 100, and Portugal 50. The

British shipping occupied in the Newfoundland fisheries some years afterwards, however, increased apace, and in 1615 it amounted to 250 vessels, whose aggregate burden was 1,500 tons; the total number of French, Biscayan, and Portuguese ships employed at the same date were 400.

Anterior to the Treaty of Utrecht, the extent of the respective rights of those nations who participated in the advantages of the Newfoundland fisheries was never defined, but that treaty placed matters in rather a more distinct light. Newfoundland itself, and the islands adjoining, were thereby exclusively left in the possession of Great Britain, the French retaining, under the thirteenth article, the right of fishing on the banks and using the shores of the islands between particular points, viz. from Point Riche (which the French afterwards pretended to be the same as Cape Ray), round the north extremity of the island, to Cape Bonavista on the eastern coast. By the treaty of peace concluded in 1763, this privilege was confirmed to France, and the right was extended to fishing in the Gulf of St.

Lawrence at the distance of three leagues from all coasts belonging to Great Britain, whether continental or insular. Their fisheries out of the gulf were not to be carried on but at the distance of fifteen leagues from the coast of Cape Breton. By another article of the treaty the islands of St. Pierre and Miquelon are ceded to France as a shelter for French fishermen, under an express stipulation against their being fortified, or guarded by more than fifty men for the police.

J. BOUCHETTE
The British Dominions in North America 1832

JAMES S. MERES   Entrance to the harbour of St. John's, Newfoundland   1786
From the Logbook of H.M.S. *Pegasus*
Water-colour, 6¾ x 14 inches

The entrance to *St. John's* Harbour forms a long and extremely narrow strait, but not very difficult of access. There are about twelve fathoms' water in the middle of the channel, with tolerable good anchorage ground. The most lofty perpendicular precipices rise, to an amazing height, upon the *north side;* and the *southern* shore only appears less striking in its attitude, from a comparison with the opposite rocks. There is a light shewn every night on the left side of the entrance; where there are also a small battery and a signal-post. Other batteries of greater strength appear towering above the rocky eminences towards the *north.* At about two-thirds of the distance between the entrance, and what may properly be termed the harbour itself, there lies a dangerous shelf, called the *Chain Rock;* so named from a chain which extends across the strait at that place, to prevent the admission of any hostile fleet. Mariners, on entering this place, ought to beware of approaching too near the rocks beneath the lighthouse point. At the time we sailed by them, the masts of a large ship were still visible above the water, that had a short time before been forced by the swell upon those rocks, where she immediately foundered. We were afterwards concerned to hear, that the unfortunate

vessel in question was one of the ships that had sailed from *Cork* in our convoy, about six weeks before.

In addition to the fortifications already noticed, there are several other strong fortresses upon the heights around the town, so as to render this place perfectly secure against any sudden attack. *Fort Townshend* is situate immediately over the town, and is the usual residence of the Governor. Forts *Amherst* and *William* are more towards the *north;* and there is also a small battery perched on the top of a single pyramidal mount, which is called the *Crow's Nest.*

At the upper part of the harbour, and upon the *eastern* side of it, there is a small place styled the *King's Dock-yard,* although it can scarcely be said to deserve this title. At the time we were there, the Admiral was very intent upon enlarging and improving its condition. It may not be amiss to add one reflection on the obvious policy of rendering *St. John's* a considerable naval depôt; for notwithstanding that we possess so fine an arsenal as *Halifax* upon the coast of *America,* yet *Newfoundland,* as an island, is not so open to the attacks of an enemy; and it would be an excellent resort for our cruizers during the summer months, should we, by any mischance, be deprived of the former valuable acquisi-

tion. In considering this point, *Bermuda* has not been forgotten; but the dangers manifest in the approach to that island will ever render its utility, as a naval depôt, of precarious advantage to our fleets.

The harbour of *St. John's* is most exposed to heavy gales from the *northwest;* as the wind from that point rushes with extreme violence through a valley to the left of the town.

On first entering the bays and ports of *Newfoundland,* the attention of a stranger is mostly attracted by the remarkable appearance exhibited by the innumerable *stages* erected along the sea-side for the salting and drying of *cod.* The shores around the harbour of *St. John's* are entirely covered with them, and their construction is particularly simple. Numerous supporters, exactly resembling *Kentish* hop-poles, are first fixed in the ground: over these is placed a horizontal platform of similar poles; and the whole is finally overspread with a covering of dry fern. This sort of structure is called, by the fishermen, a *Fish Flake:* but there are other stages, erected in a similar manner, although standing partly in the water, with a hut at their extremity, for the reception and salting of the *cod,* previous to its final removal to the *Flakes,* for the purpose of being dried in the sun.

JAMES S. MERES

The town of St. John's and Fort Townshend, Newfoundland   1786
From the Logbook of H.M.S. *Pegasus*
Water-colour, 5 x 14 ¼ inches

The Capital of *Newfoundland* consists of one very narrow street, extending entirely along one side of the port. The houses are principally built of wood; and there are very few handsome or even good-looking edifices in the place. This street stands upon very irregular ground, and is not paved; therefore, in wet weather, it is rendered almost impassable, by mud and filth. There are a great number of small public-houses, but scarcely one tolerable inn: the *London Tavern,* however, has a good billiard-room attached to it. Shops of all descriptions are very numerous; but most commodities are extravagantly dear, particularly meat, poultry, and vegetables, as the town receives all its supplies of those articles from *Nova Scotia.* The number of wharfs for lading ships is remarkable: almost every petty merchant, indeed, possesses one of his own: and there is, besides these, a fine broad quay, called the Government Wharf, which is open for the accommodation of the public.

The Island of *Newfoundland* is governed by a Vice-admiral of the *British* Navy, whose jurisdiction extends also over the coast of *Labrador,* from Cape *Charles* to *Mount Joli,* together with the small islands of *St. Pierre* and *Miquelon* on the *south,* and *Anticosti* in the mouth of the River *St. Lawrence.* The Governor holds his situation for three years; and he is, during this time, Commander-in-chief of the naval force employed within the limits of his government. He usually resides in a fortress above the town of *St. John's,* and returns to *England* for the winter months. During his absence, the chief power of the island is vested in the hands of the Military Commandant, who is styled the *Lieutenant-Governor* of *Newfoundland.* In the event of the decease of this last personage, the government devolves on the *Chief Justice* of *St. John's....*

The state of society in *St. John's* is such as might be expected, in a place where the majority of the principal inhabitants have risen from the lowest fishermen. The vulgar arrogance of these upstarts is sometimes both ludicrous and offensive. Literature and polished manners are here unknown; and a stranger must not be surprised to observe a constant violation of the most ordinary rules of speech.

The lower classes are generally composed of turbulent *Irishmen,* whose unwearied industry during the *fishing* season in summer is forcibly contrasted with their unbounded licentiousness in winter. Indeed, all ranks of society appear to consider debauchery as the only antidote to the *taedium vitae* which prevails between the month of *December* and the recommencement of the *fishery* in the *May* following.

Having spoken of the industry and licentiousness of the *Irish* fishermen, it will be no more than justice to mention an instance of honesty in one of their class. The author had been making a purchase of some trifling article, upon one of the quays in *St. John's;* when, in consequence of being much hurried, he was so negligent as to leave his purse and gloves upon a log of timber near the place. The towncrier was authorized to offer an adequate reward for the recovery of the property; and in less than half an hour afterwards, the purse and gloves were restored to the owner, by a tattered wretch, as destitute in his appearance as the meanest pauper. The purse contained about ten pounds *sterling,* in the current notes of the island.

The trading commodities of *Newfoundland* are so well known, that it will only be requisite to say, the *exports* consist of *fish, oil,* and a very few *furs*: the *imports* are, *provisions, clothing, salt, fishing-gear,* and some *India* goods.

E. CHAPPELL
Voyage of His Majesty's Ship Rosamond to Newfoundland and the Southern Coast of Labrador 1818

In trying to describe St. John's, there is some difficulty in applying to it an adjective sufficiently distinctive and appropriate. We find other cities coupled with words which at once give their predominant characteristic: — London the richest, Paris the gayest, St. Petersburg the coldest. In one respect the chief town of Newfoundland has, I believe, no rival: we may, therefore, call it the fishiest of modern capitals. Round a great part of the harbour are sheds, acres in extent, roofed with cod split in half, laid on like slates, drying in the sun, or rather the air, for there is not much of the former to depend upon. Those ships, bearing nearly every flag in the world, are laden with cod; those stout weatherly boats crowding up to the wharves have just now returned from fishing for cod; those few scant fields of cultivation with lean crops coaxed out of barren soil, are manured with cod; those trim, snug-looking wooden houses, their handsome furniture, the piano, and the musical skill of the young lady who plays it, the satin gown of the mother, the gold chain of the father, are all paid for in cod; the breezes from the shore, soft and warm on this bright August day, are rich, not with the odours of a thousand flowers, but of a thousand cod. Earth, sea, and air, are alike pervaded with this wonderful fish. There is only one place which appears to be kept sacred from its intrusion, and strange to say, that is the dinner table; an observation made on its absence from that apparently appropriate position, excited as much astonishment, as if I had made a remark to a Northumberland squire that he had not a head-dish of Newcastle coals.

G. D. WARBURTON
Hochelaga; or, England in the New World 1846

ANONYMOUS

A view of the Upper and the harbour
of St. John's, Newfoundland.
From a little below Fort William showing
the packing of cod fish on the wharf   1790

Water-colour, 13¼ x 20½ inches

It is difficult to calculate the population of a town which varies so constantly. At the height of the fishing season it is perfectly crowded, but the greater part of this population returns with the vessels to Europe. The resident population may be fairly rated at about 11,000. This town has suffered frequently and severely by fires: in 1815 a great amount of property was destroyed by a visitation of this sort, which was repeated in November, 1817, with increased severity, 140 houses and property to the amount of 500,000 being then consumed. Within a few days after another conflagration destroyed nearly all the town that was left by the former one, and, in the August of the same year, a fourth calamity of the like kind inflicted another loss upon the town. There are places of public worship of various denominations at St. John's, and two school-houses, one established by Lord Gambier, in 1802, for children of both the protestant and Roman creeds, who attend to the number of 300, and another, erected by the efforts of the Benevolent Irish Society, the benefits of which are extended to 700 or 800 children. There are three weekly newspapers published, and a book society has been established.

J. BOUCHETTE
The British Dominions in North America   1832

SYDNEY PRIOR HALL
Captain Smart, Commodore of the Fisheries Fleet   1878
Pencil drawing, 6 x 4¼ inches

SYDNEY PRIOR HALL
A Newfoundland "Padre"   1878
Pencil drawing, 6¾ x 4¼ inches

The people in both colonies are equally hard worked, and are equally moral; for I believe, as a race, the Newfoundland fisherman to be as moral as any peasantry in the world; and yet, for want of management, or rather from a cause which I propose to treat of at large in a small work on Newfoundland, the poor fishermen there remain more ignorant and more helpless than any other people similarly employed. The inhabitants of Newfoundland, chiefly of the Irish stock, have had, it is true, very improvident habits to contend with; but they are, as a body, not addicted to drunkenness; their women are careful mothers and good wives; and I am persuaded that but little is wanting to render their condition as happy as that of the Guernsey and Jersey men of the Bay of Chaleurs.

Nationalities and animosities must give way; a new race is fast springing up, who pride themselves upon being natives of the island; and, when the blessings of education can be distributed, by the formation of roads, and a more direct intercourse with the distant stations, there will be as excellent a race in Newfoundland as the world can boast of. Inured to toil, hardy, and healthy, having but little idle time, the progenitors of this race now exhibit qualities which only require fostering to be developed and brighten.

R. H. BONNYCASTLE
The Canada in 1841   1841

Pages 29 + 30 missing

J. H. BASTIDE   Annapolis Royal, Nova Scotia   1757
Water-colour, 14 ½ x 21 ½ inches

cipal Magazine for supplying the French Inhabitants and Indians: In these Forts were found a great quantity of Provisions and Stores of all kinds of which Colonel Monckton has not yet had time to transmit me a particular account. I enclose Your Lordships the Terms of Capitulation. Notwithstanding the Fort at Beausejour had twenty-six pieces of Cannon mounted, they surrendered after four Days Bombardment, before we had even mounted a single Cannon upon our Batteries. Our loss upon this occasion is very inconsiderable, not above twenty killed & as many wounded.

Colonel Monckton has new named the Fort and called it Fort Cumberland: he gives the Troops under his Command great praise for their good behaviour and the spirit & resolution with which they acted upon this occasion.

Quoted from a letter by CHARLES LAWRENCE, *Lieutenant-Governor of Nova Scotia, to the Lord Commissioners of Trade and Plantations* June 28, 1755

Annapolis county is bounded on the north and west by the Bay of Fundy. . . . The first European settlements in Nova Scotia were established by the French in this county, who made some very extensive improvements. After the expulsion of the Acadians, their lands became an object of attention to the people of the British colonies, a considerable number of whom removed thither in 1764, and obtained a grant of the township of Annapolis. This township contains a considerable quantity of valuable dike land; and the upland, though stony, is generally good. Annapolis is the county town. It was founded by the French, who called it Port Royale, and was the capital of the province while in their possession. It was also the seat of the British government until 1750, when it was superseded as such by Halifax. The town is built upon a peninsula, which projecting into the river, forms two beautiful basins, one above and one below the town. It has not much increased in size or population since the conquest of the province, but it

is still a respectable town. It contains a government house, a court house, an episcopalian and methodist church, an academy, commodious barracks, and several handsome private buildings. The military works erected at various times for its defence are now in a state of decay. There are several good roads leading to all parts of the province; a stage coach runs through Granville, Wilmot, Aylesford, Cornwallis, Windsor, and Newport, to Halifax; and a steam packet plies constantly to St. John's, New Brunswick. The trade of this town is comparatively insignificant to what it formerly was, business being removed to more convenient and better circumstanced settlements.

J. BOUCHETTE
The British Dominions in North America   1832

CHARLES RANDALL
Charlottetown on the Island of St. John (Prince Edward Island)   ca. 1778
Water-colour, 3 ¼ x 9 ¾ inches

The Principal settlement in this county is Charlotte Town the seat of government and metropolis, if it may be so termed, of the island. . . . It stands nearly in the centre of the island, with all parts of which it has ready communication, either by water or good roads. The ground on which it is built rises with a gentle slope from the river's edge to a moderate height; the streets are regularly laid out in rectangles, in building lots of 80 feet frontage and 160 depth, with vacancies at chosen intervals for squares; the number of houses already built amounts to nearly 400, several of the more recent being of very handsome appearance.

J. BOUCHETTE
The British Dominions in North America   1832

This island was amongst the early discoveries of Cabot; but no claim was ever made by the English on that account. The French afterwards assumed it, as part of the discoveries of Verazani; and in 1663 a grant of it was made by the company of New France; but the anxiety of the government of France to foster the colony of Cape Breton induced them to afford little countenance or encouragement to that of the island of St. John. The natural advantages of the island, in respect of soil and its situation for fishing, however, induced many families both from Cape Breton and Acadia to settle here after the peace of Utrecht. The surrender of Louisbourg to Great Britain in 1758 was followed by the cession of this island: from several appearances observed on the island at this possession, it was inferred that the principal part of it had long been inhabited by tribes of Micmac Indians, with whom the Acadians had, in a

great measure, assimilated. St. John's was associated with the government of Nova Scotia in 1763, and in 1776 the official survey of it under the British government was accomplished by the late Major Holland, then his majesty's surveyor-general in North America, whose family now reside on the island. The island was shortly afterward divided into sixty-seven townships, containing about 20,000 acres each, which were granted severally to such inhabitants as government conceived to have claims upon them. One condition (amongst others) of the grants was, that they should be settled within ten years, in the ratio of one person to each 200 acres, one fourth of such settlement to be effected within the first four years with emigrants from Europe or other parts of America. Many of the original grantees, however, surrendered, or alienated their property, which in a short time became monopolized by a compar-

SYDNEY PRIOR HALL
John James Macdonald of
Prince Edward Island   1878
Pencil drawing, 13¾ x 8¾ inches

atively few individuals; but when the lands of the adjacent colonies became more thickly peopled, the value of the land in this island became more justly appreciated and in greater request. In 1768 the island was erected into a separate government, though at that time it possessed not more than five resident proprietors, nor did its total number of inhabitants exceed 150 families. For the subsequent five years much pains were taken to increase the settlements by importations of Acadians, Highlanders, and other disbanded troops.

Charlotte Town is the only place where people are sufficiently congregated to form any thing that can be termed society, and, this being, the capital, possesses of course persons of every class.

Those who are received at the castle, or government house, being deemed the superiors, have assemblies, balls, dinners amongst themselves, and sometimes amateur theatricals. Others indulge in picnic, or what in England would be termed gipsy parties, in making country excursions, and each taking his own provisions. As almost every housekeeper is the owner of a horse and a carriole, or winter sledge-carriage, they are readily able to procure such indulgencies. The farmers and husbandmen comprise every class — American loyalists, Acadian French, and emigrants from England, Scotland, and Ireland, whose manners, even in this distant but desirable exile, are in a great measure influenced by their national characteristics and peculiarities. English settlers are distinguished by the cleanliness, neatness, and propriety of their establishment; Scotchmen by their patient endurance of the hardship incidental to early settlement, and their persevering pursuit of wealth and substance, with much more neglect of what we term comfort; and the Irish by a more eager desire to secure temporary advantages and the means of present indulgence. All those occupied in husbandry and farming, to which many join some share in the fishery, timber, and ship-building trades (though the advantage of such a multiplicity of pursuits is somewhat more than equivocal) find abundant employment during the year, without seeking to share the amusements of the town, or substituting others of a more rural description.

J. BOUCHETTE
The British Dominions in North America   1832

JAMES S. MERES
The lower end of the harbour by
moonlight, Halifax, Nova Scotia   1786
From the Logbook of H.M.S. *Pegasus*
Water-colour, 6 ½ x 13 ¾ inches

BELOW

JAMES S. MERES
His Majesty's Careening Yard,
Halifax, Nova Scotia   1786
Water-colour, 8 x 19 inches

The harbour of Halifax is one of the finest in America. A thousand vessels may ride in it in safety. . . . It lies nearly north and south, about sixteen miles in length, and terminates in a beautiful sheet of water called Bedford Basin, within which are ten square miles of safe anchorage. The entrance is marked by Sambro Head, on which a lighthouse was erected soon after the settlement was established. Three miles from Halifax, near the mouth of the harbour, lies M'Nabb's Island, on the western side of which stands Sherbrooke Tower, a circular stone batter, on the top of which is a lantern. This island forms two entrances to the harbour – the eastern passage, which is only used by small vessels, and the western, which is used by all ships bound to and from Halifax. Immediately opposite the town is George Island, which is regularly fortified, and forms the chief defence of the place.

J. BOUCHETTE
The British Dominions in North America 1832

Halifax was first settled in the summer of 1749, and it has ever since that period continued to be a place of considerable importance, not only as a rendezvous for His Majesty's Ships, and as the head quarters of the troops on the establishment of the lower American provinces, but also as the centre of a profitable fishery and trade.

On the south-east coast of Nova Scotia, and nearly at an equal distance from its extreme points, Halifax harbour enters the province. It is at all seasons accessible, and its navigation scarcely ever interrupted by ice. . . . The harbour is not only safe to approach, but from having sufficient width to work a ship against a contrary wind, easy to enter: the water is deep enough for the largest ship in the navy, and there is abundance of room for anchorage.

J. MCGREGOR
Historical and Descriptive Sketches of the Maritime Colonies of British America 1828

The admiral's house is a plain stone building, built in 1819, at the north end of the town, on a rising ground, which commands a view of the harbour and shipping. It is appropriated for the residence of the Admiral, for the time being, commanding the squadron on the American station. There is also a large wooden building, apparently uncomfortable, for the military commandant. The north and south barracks, built also of wood, are extensive enough to accommodate three regiments. The other government buildings are the Ordnance and Commissariat Stores, Naval Hospital, Dock Yard. &c.

His Majesty's Dock Yard is the most respectable establishment of the kind out of England. Its plan is extensive, and combines within the stone wall, which surrounds it on the land side, all that is useful and convenient for repairing and refitting the largest ships. Attached to it is the residence of the commissioner; a respectable-looking house. Never was there a more egregious measure entered upon, than that of removing the naval stores from Halifax, for the purpose of establishing a dock yard, for the use of His Majesty's Ships on the American station at Bermuda; the absurdity of which is too palpable, not to be seen into at once, by all who have any knowledge of both places. Halifax has the best harbour in

North America, in a healthy climate, and in the midst of a country abounding in timber, and all kinds of provisions, at low prices. The Bermuda Islands are little better than a cluster of rocks, in the middle of the ocean, of extremely dangerous access, covered only in detached spots with a scanty soil.

J. MCGREGOR
Historical and Descriptive Sketches of the Maritime Colonies of British America 1828

During the war [Halifax] was the great British naval depot of North America, and the dock-yard establishment gave life and employ to the city; but a few years since a great portion of it was transferred to the Bermudas, as being central between the North American colonies and the West Indies, and the harbour not being liable to be closed by the ice during the winter months. There are great objections, however, to Bermuda, on the score of the climate, which destroys more naval stores in one year than Halifax would in half a dozen. The admiral and commissioner divide their time of residence equally between the two stations, and were on the point of sailing for Bermuda when we quitted Halifax.

E. T. COKE
A Subaltern's Furlough 1833

Though our present fortifications have cost large sums of money, at least the Government has given and is charged with immense sums, (how much of it has been misapplied, I will not take upon myself to say), yet I would now engage that two ships of the line would destroy the whole settlement; but that will not be the case, when the citadel is completed, as it overlooks the town, commands the harbour, and is too high for ships to reach or make any impression on it.

T. C. HALIBURTON
An Historical and Statistical Account of Nova Scotia 1829

The town of Halifax is, in point of extent and population, the third town in British North America. It was founded, upon the first permanent settlement of the English in this province, by Governor Cornwallis in 1749. It is situated on the western side of the harbour, on the declivity of a hill 240 feet above the level of the sea. There are eight streets running through the town, intersected by fifteen others, laid out with regularity, some of them paved, and the others macadamized. The town and suburbs are upwards of two miles in length, and about half a mile in width. It has been very much improved within the last five years. There are meat, vegetable,

and fish markets, all extremely well supplied. The fish, in point of quality, variety, and cheapness, may vie with any in the world.

J. BOUCHETTE
The British Dominions in North America 1832

The capital of Nova Scotia looks like a town of cards, nearly all the buildings being of wood. There are wooden houses, wooden churches, wooden wharfs, wooden slates, and, if there are side walks, they are of wood also.

I. L. BISHOP
The Englishwoman in North America 1856

The Seventy-sixth Regiment has pitched its tents here among the evergreens. Yonder you see the soldiers, looking like masses of red fruit amidst the spicy verdur of the spruces. Row upon row of tents, and file upon file of men standing at ease, each one before his knapsack, his little leather household, with its shoes, socks, shirts, brushes, razors, and other furniture open for inspection. And there is Sir John Gaspard le Marchant, with a brilliant staff, engaged in the pleasant duty of picking a personal quarrel with

each medal-decorated hero, and marking down every hole in his socks, and every gap in his comb, for the honor of the service. And this Point Pleasant is a lovely place too, with a broad look-out in front, for yonder lies the blue harbor and the ocean deeps. Just back of the tents is the cookery of the camp, huge mounds of loose stones, with grooves at the top, very like the architecture of a cranberry-pie; and if the simile be an homely one, it is the best that comes to mind to convey an idea of those regimental stoves, with

their seams and channels of fire, over which potatoes bubble, and roast and boiled send forth a savory odor. And here and there, wistfully regarding this active scent, amid the green shrubbery, stands a sentinel before his sentry-box, built of spruce boughs wrought into a mimic military temple, and fanciful enough, too, for a garden of roses.

F. S. COZZENS
Acadia; or, A Month with the Blue Noses 1859

ALEXANDER CAVALIÉ MERCER

The backyards of Halifax, Nova Scotia
from the window of the Halifax Hotel
1842

Water-colour, 9 x 13 inches

ALEXANDER CAVALIÉ MERCER

The Common and the Citadel at sunrise,
Halifax, Nova Scotia   August 22, 1838

Water-colour, 6 ½ x 9 ¾ inches

JAMES FOX BLAND

The Encampment of the Royal Artillery
and the 76th Regiment at Point Pleasant,
Halifax, Nova Scotia   June 1855

Water-colour, 8 ¼ x 18 ½ inches

The citadel, which is raised upon an old fort of smaller dimensions, will not be completed for some years; the work is carried on chiefly by the soldiers of the garrison, who receive 9d. per diem extra while employed during the summer months. The position is a commanding one, and a fine prospect is afforded from the ramparts. The barracks at present oc-cupied by the troops are of wood, with very little to recommend them, except some fine mess-rooms, and a library in-stituted by Lord Dalhousie, when Gover-nor of the province. A fire would prove of infinite service towards beautifying the city, by destroying both them and a great proportion of the private dwelling-houses. Those even which are built of substantial materials are principally of the shaley iron-stone rock of which the peninsula is formed, and which contains such a quantity of the ore that it oozes out in long streaks down the walls, and gives them a most lugubrious and prison-like appearance.

E. T. COKE
A Subaltern's Furlough   1833

It becomes our painful duty to-day to record the most destructive fire that has ever occurred in this city since its foun-dation. On Friday night last, about nine o'clock, the building in Hollis Street, oc-cupied by Mr. Alderman Wills, paper manufacturer, was discovered to be on fire. The alarm bells sounded, and by the time any great number of persons as-sembled at the scene of the disaster, the building in which the fire originated was not only completely wrapped in flames, but the fire had communicated with some of the adjoining premises south, and extended back into Granville Street, where the buildings of Mr. John Richard-son, Wetmore, Vaux & McCullouch, Mr. Webb, A. & W. McKinlay, and J. A. Graham, almost simultaneously became enwrapped in flames. The fire, by this time completely baffled all the efforts of the enginemen, and owing to an insuf-ficient supply of water, and the *incapac-ity of the limited number comprising the fire staff*, to check it, the flames spread moving south, and west, and by three o'clock in the morning some forty build-ings, among them some of the finest and handsomest Halifax could boast of, were laid in a heap of ruins, *viz*, the range of buildings west side of Hollis street; east and west sides of Granville street, and east side of Barrington Street, within the limits of Duke and Buckingham Streets, together with the block of buildings on Ordnance Square, owned by James F. Avery, Esq. On Barrington we must ex-cept the premises of Esson & Co.; which were saved through the exertions of the firemen, but mainly by the high brick wall, recently erected by the proprietors of the Woolen Hall, in the rear of their premises. Had this wall not existed no human efforts could have saved Esson's building; and that once enveloped in flames, the opposite corner (occupied by Blockly & Co., piano forte manufac-turers) and Chalmer's Church would no doubt have ignited; and owing to their height, have spread the fire through the block, which, as it was, barely escaped being consumed, the houses on the up-per side of Barrington Street, being fired several times, but luckily put out. — It was thought on three or four occasions that the fire would have extended south into Granville Street, but owing to the strenu-ous efforts to save Mr. Crow's property and from the fact of Mr. Roman's house being built of stone, alone prevented it

The education of the people is provided for as well as in any of the British-American colonies. There is an university, called King's College, at Windsor; Dalhousie College at Halifax; academies at Pictou, Annapolis, and Kentville; grammer-schools at Halifax, Windsor, Pictou, and Kentville. The Society for Propagating the Gospel supports between forty and fifty schoolmasters; and schools have been established in all the townships, aided by a very lib-eral pecuniary grant from the provincial legislature. . . . There are four professors [at the university of King's College]: one of Hebrew and divinity, one of moral science and metaphysics, one of mathematics, astronomy, and natural philosophy, and one of grammar, rhetoric and logic. The students are eligible for matriculation at the age of fourteen, and the course occupies from four to seven years. There are twelve divinity scholarships, endowed by the Society for Propagating the Gospel, each enjoying £301 per annum for seven years. There are also some scholarships on the foundation of less emolument. The college possesses a large well-selected library, and a valuable philosophical apparatus. Subordinate to the college, and under its control, is the collegiate school; the system of education is preparatory to that of the college, for which it is intended.

J. BOUCHETTE
The British Dominions in North America 1832

OPPOSITE

LEFEVRE JAMES CRANSTONE
After the fire,
Halifax, Nova Scotia
1859
Water-colour,
6¾ x 12½ inches

GEORGE HERIOT
Chief Justice
Blower's home and
King's College
near Windsor,
Nova Scotia
1807
Water-colour,
5 x 7 inches

from extending in a southerly direction. Had it done so a large number of fine brick and wooden stores in the opposite block, besides a large amount of valuable goods would have become a prey to the flames. Some idea of the rapidity with which the fire extended may be gathered from the fact that scarcely had property been removed from burning stores to those of their neighbors than they had to be again removed in consequence of many of the premises in which the goods were placed for safety having themselves fallen a prey to the devouring elements. At the time the last edifice (Avery's building, Ordnance Square) was consumed, it seemed doubtful whether the "Muirhead property" opposite, now owned by Mr. James Scott, would not have taken, as although this corner prop-erty is built of stone, it had like the rest of the stone buildings destroyed, wooden shutters and sashes, which it was supposed would have ignited, and consumed the interior of the building. Another very foolish practice in putting up brick buildings is the placing of wooden cornices just below the roof. It seems as though they are put there, instead of stone or iron ones, for the mere purpose of attracting fire. . . .

It is almost certain that the loss of property is fully $1,000,000, but the actual loss, taken as a whole, may be fully estimated at $1,200,000.

Owing to the Commander-in-Chief not being called upon until after a considerable lapse of time, to turn out the military, the fire had gained considerable headway before the troops arrived; and from the time of their arrival upon the ground until the fire was extinguished, they, as well as the men of war sailors and marines, worked like Trojans; and the citizens owe them a deep debt of gratitude for the exertion they put forth to stay the flames.

Some idea of the "awful grandeur" this terrible fire presented may be gleaned from the fact that the reflection was seen some sixty miles distant at sea. Capt. Daly informs us that it was so visible off Cross Island light that at first he supposed it to have been in vicinity of St. Margaret's Bay.

HALIFAX
Evening Express Sept. 12, 1859

The Micmac Indians are an inoffensive, harmless people, who are daily vanishing from the land of their fathers, as they are shut in by the whites, their grant being but six hundred acres, of which they only possess three hundred and fifty fit for cultivation, or, in fact, at all certainly belonging to them. They appear poor, and are, no doubt, much exposed to the chicanery of their neighbours. Their interpreter, who is a half-breed, seemed also a designing fellow; and it was whispered, that they had not much confidence in their religious in-structor, who had very little of the vivacity or *bonhommie* of a Frenchman, and was not very cleanly dressed for such an unusual occasion. But the regularity in which they live, their innocent behaviour, simplicity, and the acknowl-edged merit of their conduct in the country, would, nevertheless, seem to be fostered by the priest.

The tribe consists of not more than three hundred and twenty-six souls, part at the Mission, and the rest at New Rich-mond. Several were hunting up the river, and did not attend. . . .

The Indian women here wear a short body gown, and pointed conic head-dress, peculiar to that people in Canada; and some of these cloth head-dresses were beautifully worked in figures and tracery, with the moose-hair and por-cupines' quills, dyed in bright colours. The younger women were extremely clean; and the papouse, or child, in the cradle on their backs, had a nicely-worked clean cap on, and appeared to be neatly tended by the mother.

R. H. BONNYCASTLE
The Canadas in 1841   1841

JOHN G. TOLER
A Micmac Indian camp near Halifax, Nova Scotia   1808 / Water-colour, 13 x 17 inches

I found the Indians occupying about a dozen lodges built in the usual wigwam style, of poles placed on a circle on the ground, brought to a point, and covered with birch bark. Most of the men were out hunting or fishing, those who were at the lodges seemed a slighter made race than the Indians of the Canadian Lakes. They had light brown complexions, coarse black hair, and though it was hot weather, some of them wore tunics of blankets. The women, some of whom had good-humoured oval faces and good hair and eyes, were mostly in dark petticoats and chintz short gowns, cloth leggings and moccasins, and were mak-ing light baskets for sale; also very hand-some chair bottoms of birch bark, or-namented with dyed porcupine quills, and were embroidering very neatly on cloth with beads and moose hair.

J. E. ALEXANDER
L'Acadie   1849

Still, however, especially in the remoter districts of the province, there are exceptions to this character. I have seen Indians walking about the streets of Halifax, where they had arrived on a visit from the westward, in all the native dignity of their forefathers. Unlike those of their tribe residing round Halifax, and clothed in the cast-off rags of white men, they appear in the showy costume of the tribe, in a dark blue or scarlet flannel coat, ornamented with beads, porcupine's quills, and moose-hair, and their moccasins adorned with similar devices.

Their squaws, generally walking behind the men, have the head covered with a tall conical cap of cloth, bordered with beads, their long cloaks fastened by some glittering ornament, and a neat scarlet or blue handkerchief fastened round the neck. Outcasts, as it were, in their own country, and sensible of their position, they bear themselves with becoming haughtiness towards the mob of staring Europeans in the crowded street; and, hastily purchasing their few necessaries, they retreat, as they came, to their hunting grounds in the interior.

The Micmac is generally well formed, active, and capable of enduring great abstinence and amount of cold. His complexion is of the color of brick-dust, though of a more dingy hue. His hair, long, coarse, and maintaining its jet black hue till an advanced age, falls irregularly over the neck and shoulders. The eye is of the darkest hazel, and the white is more dingy than that of the European. The hands and feet of the Indian are small, and often exquisitely formed. This, in the case of the foot, is rather strange, considering the freedom which is given to it by the yielding moccasin; and the features, though coarse, are extremely expressive.

C. HARDY
Sporting Adventures in the New World 1855

MARY R. MCKIE
A Micmac Indian girl / Water-colour, 8¼ x 8 inches

MARY R. MCKIE
A Negro youth in Nova Scotia / Water-colour, 6¼ x 5 inches

Slavery does not exist in Nova Scotia: the number of free negroes may be equal to 1500; part of whom came from the West India Islands, others from the United States, and the residue were born in the province. A settlement was laid out, a few miles from Halifax, for these people, and every facility afforded them, by the provincial government, yet they are still in a state of miserable poverty; while Europeans, who have settled on woodlands, under circumstances scarcely so favourable, thrive with few exceptions. Whether the wretchedness of these negroes may be attributed to servitude and degradation having extinguished in them the spirit that endures present difficulties and privations, in order to attain future advantages; or to the consciousness that they are an unimportant and distinct race, in a country where they feel that they must ever remain a separate people; or, that they find it more congenial to their habits to serve others, either as domestic servants, or labourers, by which they make sure of the wants of the day, certain it is that they prefer servitude, and generally live more comfortably in this condition, than they usually do when working on their own account. I do not, by this observation, mean to inculcate the revolting doctrine, that slavery is the most happy state in which the unfortunate negroes in the West Indies and America can live; but I am certainly of opinion, that, unless they are gradually prepared for personal liberty, they will, on obtaining their freedom, become objects of greater commiseration than they now are in a state of bondage; and the condition of the free negroes in Nova Scotia will fully substantiate this assertion.

J. MCGREGOR
Historical and Descriptive Sketches of the Maritime Colonies 1828

C. WILLIAMS

Washing gold at the "Ovens" near Lunenburg, Nova Scotia   ca. 1860
Water-colour, 9¾ x 14 inches

With the exception of one locality, "The Ovens," near Lunenburg, seventy miles west from Halifax, where a considerable quantity has been obtained in the sand of the beach, formed by the action of the waves upon the rocky cliffs, placer washings and surface diggings have not proved remunerative in Nova Scotia. On the other hand, the quartz veins, on which the Californian and Australian digger is accustomed to look with suspicion, are here remarkably productive; an instance is upon record where one and a half ton of quartz has produced seventy-two ounces of gold, valued at $1,296.

H. Y. HIND ET AL
The Dominion of Canada 1869

This name ["The Ovens"] has been given to a gold district embracing a peninsula on the western side of the harbor of Lunenburg, and comprises an area of a mile and a half long and three-quarters of a mile wide. Several small caves in the side of a promontory facing the sea have, from their fancied resemblance to ovens, given its name to the district. The rocks here exposed are referred to by Mr. Campbell to the same anticlinal as those of Tangier Harbor, and, like that district, exhibit chiefly the slaty upper members of the gold-bearing series. The strata are here nearly vertical, and have a direction, according to Mr. Poole, fifteen degrees to the south of west. There has as yet been very little quartz mining in this district, though gold-bearing veins have been found, and from recent accounts it appears that a mill is about to be erected there. The official returns from 1861 to 1864, shew 1,282 ounces of gold from the Ovens district, but none since that date; of this the greater part, over 1,000 oz., was from alluvial washings in 1861 and 1862, since which time the washings have been abandoned, though it is said that preparations are being made to work them during the present year.

T. S. HUNT
The Gold Region of Nova Scotia 1868

The magnificent splendour of the forests of North America is peculiar to that vast country. In Europe, in Asia, in Africa, and even in South America, the primeval trees, how much soever their magnitude may arrest admiration, do not grow up in the promiscuous style which prevails in the great general character of the North American woods. Many varieties of the pine intermingled with birch, maple, beech, oak, and numerous other tribes, branch luxuriantly over the banks of lakes and rivers, extend in stately grandeur over the plains, and stretch proudly up to the very summits of the mountains.

J. MCGREGOR
*Historical and Descriptive Sketches of the
Maritime Colonies of British America* 1828

JOSEPH BOUCHETTE
Mars Hill, New Brunswick   ca. 1815
Water-colour, 5 ½ x 12 inches

As Mars Hill, however, is invested with a peculiar degree of interest, from the circumstance of its being the point fixed on by the British commissioners as the commencement of the range of highlands, forming the boundary of the United States, we will step a little out of our way to take a rather close survey of it. It is about five and a half miles to the west of the river St. John, about 100 miles above Fredericton. The mountain is about three miles in length, its lower base four and a quarter; it is very narrow and divided by a hollow near the centre; its highest elevation above the level of the sea is about 2000 feet, and about 1200 above the source of the St. Croix. The early part of the ascent is easy to the height of about half a mile, beyond which it becomes much more abrupt, and near the summit almost perpendicular. The prospect viewed from its crest is extensive and commanding, as it is the highest point in its vicinity. Immediately beneath stretches the vast forest of which the adjacent country is composed, whose undulatory swells, clothed with a brilliant green, resemble stupendous waves, the more elevated spots rising from the bosom of the others like towers above the ocean.

J. BOUCHETTE
The British Dominions in North America 1832

When the salmon make their appearance in the Nashwak, fleets of canoes, each containing a couple of Indians, leave Fredericton to spear them by torchlight. The fish, checked by the falls, are collected in great numbers in the pools below. Nothing can be more exciting than this scene—the canoes hurled about in all directions by the foaming tide, the skill displayed by the Indians in forcing them up the rapids, and fending them off the rocks, or allowing them to plunge head-foremost down stream, when they suddenly bring them to, and transfix their fish. The eagerness of the chase, the contrast of the flaming torches with the black masses of the woods, and the fine attitudes of the men, dashing at the salmon with their long spears, form a wild and most animating picture. The spear, which is most destructive, is very simple in its construction, and does not lacerate or spoil the fish. A spike of iron is fastened between two jaws made of rock maple, into the end of a long light fir pole. When the fish is stuck, the jaws open far enough to allow the spike to pierce and break the vertebrae of the spine, and, closing round the fish at the same time, hold it fast.

R. G. A. LEVINGE
Echoes From the Backwoods   1849

RICHARD GEORGE AUGUSTUS LEVINGE
Salmon fishing by torchlight in New Brunswick   ca. 1838
Water-colour, 9½ x 15 inches

ALEXANDER CAVALIÉ MERCER   Fredericton, New Brunswick from the road to St. Johns   1840
Water.colour, 9¼ x 13 inches

The river St. John, at Fredericton, is about a mile wide; the scenery in almost every point of view is as beautiful and luxuriant as in any part of America. Its most striking features are cultivated fields, green islands, a majestic river, winding almost round the town; a back ground, rising into wooded hilly ridges, and clumps of primeval groves, remaining in detached spots among the clearings.

The streets of Fredericton are wide, and cross each other at right angles. Sir Howard Douglas has lately had a public promenade opened along the bank of the river. The Province Building and the Episcopal Church are but humble edifices. This town has frequently had its buildings consumed by fire; but better houses have been built in their place. A residence for the Governor, on the site of the former one burnt in 1825; a college, and a row of barracks are in the progress of building; these will be executed in a substantial and handsome style. One steam boat only plies as yet between Fredericton and St. John. Boats of 20 tons can go up the river from Fredericton to the grand falls, a distance of 230 miles from the sea. . . .

The timber trade has no doubt been one, if not the principal, cause of the rapid growth of St. John. Great gains were at first realized, both by it and ship-building; and although the merchants and others immediately concerned in these pursuits were nearly ruined afterwards by the extent of their undertakings and engagements; yet, it must be recollected, that each of those trades has enabled New Brunswick to pay for her foreign imports, and with the timber trade she has built St. John, Fredericton, and St. Andrew. To the settler on new lands it presented a ready resource; and if he only engaged in it for a few winters it was wise to do so; as by the gains attending it, he was put in possession of the means of stocking his farm and clothing himself and family. The province, therefore, gained great advantage by this trade; and, although it is not less certain that it has been prosecuted to more than double the extent of the demand for timber, it would, notwithstanding, be extreme folly to abandon it altogether.

J. MCGREGOR
Historical and Descriptive Sketches of the Maritime Colonies of British America
1828

QUEBEC

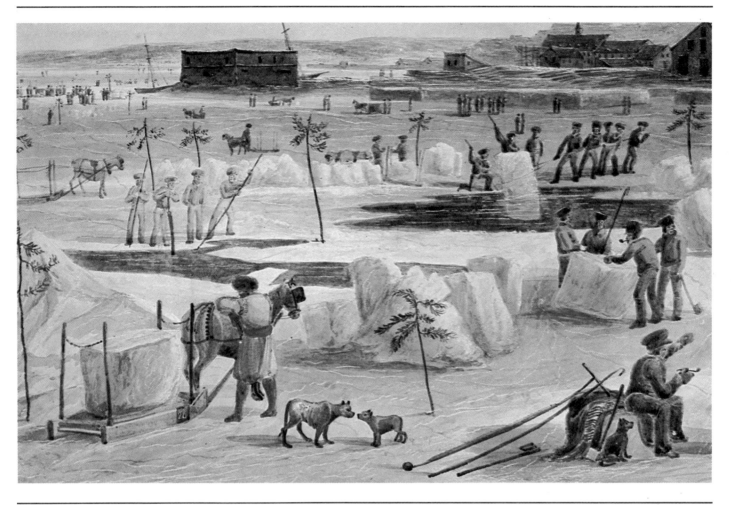

Quebec, the citadel of the St. Lawrence and one of the oldest towns in Canada, was the centre of many of the military and civil activities of the nineteenth-century colony. The British officers and their families who were stationed there after New France became the province of Quebec formed a garrison society surrounded by a subjected French population. Up and down St. Louis Street the red coats marched, as J.P. Cockburn records, often to the rousing accompaniment of a regimental band. The officers like Cockburn and Bainbrigge and their wives portrayed the features of this fortified European town transplanted to North America. These same characteristics were remarked upon by travellers, who always went to Quebec and were struck by its sophistication.

By a unique combination of circumstances, we are well provided with both visual and verbal statements of the everyday environment of French Canada. Some of the artists held official appointments in the civil government of the colony. James Peachey, Deputy Surveyor-General, and George Heriot, Deputy Post-Master General for British North America, have contributed to the most complete pictorial record of the development of any part of the nineteenth-century colony of Canada. Heriot's Travels through the Canadas provides extensive commentary on the topography and the society, but perhaps the most remarkable topographical descriptions are those of Canada's foremost nineteenth-century topographer, Joseph Bouchette, whose book, A **Topographical Description of the Province of Lower Canada**, was published in both English and French.

Montreal derived its advantages from its geographical position. It was a natural terminus of the St. Lawrence shipping route, and was also close to the end of the Richelieu River route. This route was heavily defended in time of war at Ticonderoga, Chambly, and Crown Point by such men as Thomas Davies, who served under General Amherst.

After the war, the French and English lived together with relative ease until the quiet was shattered by the Rebellion of 1837 and 1838. One of the most significant contributions of the artists of this period was their reportage of this rebellion. The fact that many of the officers (Bainbrigge and Levinge, for example) were personally involved lends a peculiar quality of immediacy to the views of the ruins of St. Eustache and St. Denis and the trek of the 43rd Regiment across the snows of eastern Canada. Yet another aspect of the record is the reaction of Jane Ellice at being captured by a "group of the most 'Robespierre' looking ruffians."

Lord Durham's remarkable report analyzed the situation and recommended drastic changes to alleviate what he saw as a conflict between the English and French cultures. However, his solution was doomed to failure because of his insensitivity to the character of the province and its French-speaking population.

HENRY FRANCIS AINSLIE   The quarantine station at Grosse Isle, St. Lawrence River   1838
Water-colour, 9 x 12 ½ inches

August 12 — We reached Gros Isle yesterday evening. It is a beautiful rocky island, covered with groves of beech, birch, ash, and fir-trees. There are several vessels lying at anchor close to the shore; one bears the melancholy symbol of disease, the yellow flag; she is a passenger-ship, and has the smallpox and measles among her crew. When any infectious complaint appears on board, the yellow flag is hoisted, and the invalids conveyed to the cholera hospital or wooden building, that has been erected on a rising bank above the shore. It is surrounded with palisadoes and a guard of soldiers.

There is also a temporary fort at some distance from the hospital, containing a garrison of soldiers, who are there to enforce the quarantine rules. These rules are considered as very defective, and in some respects quite absurd, and are productive of many severe evils to the unfortunate emigrants....

We expect to reach the quarantine ground (Gros Isle) this evening, where the pilot says we shall be detained three days. Though we are all in good health, yet, having sailed from an infected port, we shall be detained on the quarantine ground, but not allowed to land....

These regulations positively forbid the captain and the pilot to allow any person, whether of the crew or passengers, to quit the vessel until they shall have passed examination at the quarantine ground, under the risk of incurring a severe penalty.

C. P. TRAILL
The Backwoods of Canada   1836

S. W. L. S

Quebec from Point Levi. July sixteenth 1818.

SEVERUS STRETTON   Quebec and the mouth of the St. Charles River from Point Lévis, Lower Canada   July 16, 1818
Water-colour, 8 x 13 inches

When viewed from Point Levi, on the opposite coast of the river, an interesting variety of objects is exhibited, by massy rocks, interspersed with shrubbery, by Cape Diamond, boldly rising from the water, by the houses along its base, contrasted with the overhanging cliffs, by a confused cluster of buildings overtopping each other up the side of the hill, and by the fortifications which crown the summit. The Saint Lawrence flowing on one side, and the Saint Charles on the other, give to this spot the appearance of an island.

G. HERIOT
Travels Through the Canadas 1807

It is desirable that strangers arriving in Quebec should so dispose of their time as to be enabled to embrace several objects in a given period. The following remarks will allow them to accomplish this; but it is to be observed that our American friends unfortunately visit Quebec as the last "lion" in their tour, and generally embark in the steamboat from Montreal, remain twenty-four hours, and then return, without seeing any thing except a cursory view of the city; whereas Quebec and the environs abound in the most romantic and charming views, certainly not equalled in the Canadas, and to all admirers of the beauties of nature affording a rich treat. We suppose our friends to have arrived at Quebec preparing to take their first view. It is a good plan to ascend to the highest spot in the neighbourhood; from such a place the whole country lies as a map before you; have a person that is conversant with the site of the towns, villages, and any natural feature of the scenery worthy of remark to accompany you. This gives the spectator a general knowledge of the locality of the neighborhood, and will render more clear his future rambles.

[J. P. COCKBURN]
Quebec and Its Environs 1831

There stands QUEBEC, formerly the seat of the French empire in the west—purchased for England by the blood of the heroic WOLFE, shed in the decisive battle of the Plains of Abraham. A commodious harbor, which can afford a safe anchorage for several fleets—a magnificent river whose banks are secured by steep cliffs—a position on a lofty rock, which bids defiance to external violence, together with extraordinary beauty of scenery, are some of the natural advantages which distinguish the City of QUEBEC. The River St. Lawrence, which flows majestically before the town, is one of the greatest, most noble and beautiful of rivers; and at the same time, the furthest navigable for vessels of a large size of any in the universe.

A. HAWKINS
Hawkins's Picture of Quebec; with Historical Recollections 1834

The street leading to the Upper Town, called Mountain-street, winds in a serpentine direction from the market-place, up the hill; passes through Prescot-gate, and terminates near the French cathedral, within a short distance of the Upper Town market-place. In its present winding form, it is very steep, and requires strength to ascend it. The little Canadian horses have a laborious task to drag up the heavy loads which their masters impose upon them. The carts used in Quebec are light, and usually drawn by one horse; their loads are not excessive, when drawing upon even ground; but the carters seldom make any allowance up Mountain-street, though half the ordinary load is more than their horse can manage; and they are obliged to make frequent stoppages on their way up.

For a pedestrian, it is very fatiguing, if his business requires a frequent intercourse between the upper and lower towns; otherwise, I conceive that two or three excursions up this hill in the course of a day are extremely conducive to health, and I believe the benefit of them is generally felt by the inhabitants. This hill is not paved more than half way, the upper part, I suppose, being thought too steep for that purpose: if that is the case, I do not, however, see the necessity of keeping the foot-paths and the road in such a rugged state: Mountain-street requires more attention than any other in Quebec, yet it is neglected the most. In winter time it is extremely dangerous; the quantity of snow and ice, which accumulate in large masses, renders it absolutely necessary for the inhabitants to provide themselves with outer shoes shod with iron spikes or creepers. These they call goloshoes, and are most frequently used in the fall or spring of the year, when it generally freezes and thaws in succession for two or three weeks. After the snow is well settled on the ground, and it becomes dry walking, they make use of Shetland hose and list shoes, which are worn over their boots and shoes, and have the effect of keeping the feet both warm and dry, while they prevent them slipping about.

J. LAMBERT
Travels Through Canada and the United States
1814

JAMES HUNTER

A bird's eye view of the Lower Town, Quebec from the Bishop's Palace showing also the Chateau St. Louis and the Citadel   1779

Water-colour, 14 x 21 inches

The chateau, wherein the governor resides, is a plain building of common stone, situated in an open place, the houses round which form three sides of an oblong square. It consists of two parts. The old and the new are separated from each other by a spacious court. The former stands just on the verge of an inaccessible part of the rock; behind it, on the outside, there is a long gallery, from whence, if a pebble were let drop, it would fall at least sixty feet perpendicularly. This old part is chiefly taken up with the public offices, and all the apartments in it are small and ill contrived; but in the new part, which stands in front of the other, facing the square, they are spacious and tolerably well finished, but none of them can be called elegant.

This part is inhabited by the governor's family. The chateau is built without any regularity of design, neither the old nor the new part having even a uniform front. It is not a place of strength, as commonly represented. In the garden adjoining to it is merely a parapet wall along the edge of the rock, with embrasures, in which a few small guns are planted, commanding a part of the lower town. Every evening during summer, when the weather is fine, one of the regiments of the garrison parades in the open place before the chateau, and the band plays for an hour or two, at which time the place becomes the resort of numbers of the most genteel people of the town, and has a very gay appearance.

I. WELD
Travels Through the States of North America and the Provinces of Upper and Lower Canada 1799

JAMES PATTISON COCKBURN

The Chateau St. Louis from the gardens and a bird's eye view of Lower Town, Quebec, Lower Canada   June 29, 1831

Pencil drawing, 6 x 9½ inches

The streets of Quebec are, in consequence of its situation, irregular and uneven, many of them are narrow, and but very few are paved. The houses are built of stone, are of unequal heights, and covered, in general, with roofs of boards; the roughness of the materials of which they are constructed, gives them a rugged aspect, and the accommodations are fitted up in a stile equally plain and void of taste. The frequent accidents which have happened, and the extensive damage which the town has repeatedly sustained from conflagrations, have suggested the expediency of covering the public buildings, and many of the dwelling-houses with tin, or painted sheet-iron.

G. HERIOT
Travels Through the Canadas 1807

I am to give a ball to-morrow; Mrs Melmoth is to have the honours of it, but as she is with child, she does not dance. This circumstance has produc'd a dispute not a little flattering to my vanity: the ladies are making interest to dance with me; what a happy exchange have I made! What man of common sense would stay to be overlook'd in England, who can have rival beauties contend for him in Canada? This important point is not yet settled; the *etiquette* here is rather difficult to adjust; as to me, I have nothing to do in the consultation; my hand is destin'd to the longest pedigree; we stand prodigiously on our nobless.

Four o'clock

After a dispute in which two French ladies were near drawing their husbands into a duel, the point of honour is yielded by both to Miss Montague; each insisting only that I should not dance with the other; for my part, I submit with a good grace, as you will suppose.

GEORGE HERIOT
A dance in the Chateau St. Louis,
Quebec, Lower Canada   1801
Water-colour, 9¾ x 14½ inches

Saturday morning

I never passed a more agreeable evening; we have our amusements here, I assure you: a set of fine young fellows, and handsome women, all well dress'd and in humour with themselves, and with each other: my lovely Emily like Venus amongst the Graces, only multiplied to about sixteen. Nothing is, in my opinion, so favourable to the display of beauty as a ball. A state of rest is ungraceful; all nature is most beautiful in motion; trees agitated by the wind, a ship under sail, a horse in the course, a fine woman dancing: never any human being had such an aversion to still life as I have.

I am going back to Melmoth's for a month; don't be alarm'd, Lucy! I see all her perfections, but I see them with the cold eye of admiration only; a woman engaged loses all her attractions as a woman; there is no love without a ray of hope: my only ambition is to be her friend; I want to be the confidant of her passion. With what spirit such a mind as hers must love!

FRANCES BROOKE
The History of Emily Montague   1769

It requires about five thousand soldiers to man the works at Quebec completely. A large garrison is always kept in it, and abundance of stores of every description. The troops are lodged partly in barracks, and partly in blockhouses near Cape Diamond, which is the most elevated part of the point, and is reckoned to be upwards of one thousand feet above the level of the river.

I. WELD

Travels Through the States of North America and the Provinces of Upper and Lower Canada 1799

The court-house on the north side of St. Louis Street is a large modern stone structure, the roof of which is covered with tin; its length is one hundred and thirty-six feet, and breadth forty-four, presenting a regular handsome front, approached by a flight of steps leading to an arched entrance, from whence a vestibule on each side communicates to every part of the building. The ground floor apartments are disposed for holding the quarter sessions, and other inferior courts, offices of clerks of the different courts of law, &c. &c. Above stairs there is a spacious chamber, in which the courts of King's Bench and Common Pleas, the Court of Appeals, and the Admiralty Court are held, with separate offices for the high sheriffs and other magistrates, and a room for the occasional convening of militia courts-martial. In the same building is the hall and offices of the corporation of the Trinity-house of Quebec, established by an act of the Provincial Parliament in the 45th year of George the 3d. The embellishments of this edifice, both interior and external, are in a style of simplicity and neatness; the arrangements for public business methodical and judicious; the whole may be considered a great ornament to the city, and does honour to the liberality of the province, thus to provide for the easy and expeditious administration of justice. It occupies part of the site upon which stood an old monastery, church, and garden of the Recollets, destroyed by fire in the year 1796: it was at one time a very extensive establishment, covering the whole space between the parade, Rue des Jardins, de St. Louis, and de Ste. Anne; the order is now extinct in Canada.

J. BOUCHETTE
A Topographical Description of the Province of Lower Canada   1815

JAMES PATTISON COCKBURN
British troops drilling opposite the Court House, St. Louis Street, Quebec, Lower Canada   1830
Water-colour, 11 1/4 x 15 3/4 inches

Immediately through PALACE-GATE, turning towards the left, and in front of the Ordnance buildings and storehouses, once stood an edifice of great extent, surrounded by a spacious garden looking towards the River St. Charles, and as to its interior decorations, far more splendid than even the Castle of St. Lewis. It was the Palace of the Intendant, so called, because the sittings of the Sovereign Council were held there, after the establishment of the Royal Government in New France. A small district adjoining is still called, *Le Palais,* by the old inhabitants, and the name of the Gate, and of the well proportioned street which leads to it, are derived from the same origin.

The Intendant's Palace was described by La Potherie, in 1698, as consisting of eighty *toises,* or four hundred and eighty feet, of buildings, so that it appeared a little town in itself. The King's stores were kept there. Its situation does not at the present time appear advantageous, but the aspect of the River St. Charles was widely different in those days. The property in the neighborhood belonged to the Government, or to the Jesuits — large meadows and flowery parterres adorned the banks of the rivers, and reached the base of the rock; and as late as the time of CHARLEVOIX, in 1720, that quarter of the city is spoken of as being the most beautiful. The entrance was into a court, through a large gateway, the ruins of which, in St. Valler Street, still remain. The buildings formed nearly a square — in front of the river were spacious gardens, and on the sides the King's store houses. Beyond the Palace, towards the west, were the pleasing grounds of the Jesuits, and of the General Hospital.

This building, like most of the public establishments of QUEBEC, went through the ordeal of fire, and was afterwards rebuilt with greater attention to comfort and embellishment. In September, 1712, M. BEGON arrived as Intendant, with a splendid equipage, rich furniture, plate and apparel befitting his rank. He was accompanied by his wife, a young lady lately married, whose valuable jewels were the general admiration. A fire, which it was found impossible to extinguish, broke out in the night of the 5th January, 1713; and burned so rapidly, that the Indendant and his lady with difficulty escaped in their *robes de chambre.* The latter was obliged to break the panes of glass in her apartment, before she had power to breathe, so as to attempt her escape through the smoke with which the passages were filled. Two young French women, who attended Madame BEGON, perished in the flames — the Intendant's valet anxious to save

GEORGE HERIOT

The ruins of the Intendant's Palace from Grant's Wharf
with the walled town beyond, Quebec, Lower Canada   ca. 1800
Water-colour, 4¼ x 18 inches

some of his master's clothes, ventured imprudently within the burning chambers, and was consumed by the flames — his secretary, desirous of rescuing some valuables, passed several times through the gardens towards the river in front of the house, without shoes, and was frozen. He died in the Hotel Dieu, a few days afterwards. The loss of the Intendant was stated at forty thousand crowns: his lady lost her jewels and rich dresses. Such, however, were the resources of M. BEGON, that he is said to have lived with as much state in the Bishop's Palace, where he established himself, as he had maintained before the fire. On this occasion, the papers and records of the Treasury were lost, as well as the registers of the Council, and other valuable documents belonging to the KING OF FRANCE. The PALACE was afterwards rebuilt in a splendid style by M. BEGON

and the KING's expense. The following is its description, given by CHARLEVOIX, in 1720, a few years afterwards; "The Intendant's house is called the Palace, because the Superior Council assembles in it. This is a large pavilion, the two extremities of which project some feet; and to which you ascend by a double flight of stairs. The garden front which faces the little river, which is very nearly on a level with it, is much more agreeable than that by which you enter. The King's magazines face the court on the right side, and behind that is the prison. The gate by which you enter is hid by the mountain on which the Upper Town stands, and which on this side affords no prospect, except that of a steep rock, extremely disagreeable to the sight. It was still worse before the fire, which reduced some years ago this whole Palace to ashes; it having at that time no outer

court, and the buildings then facing the street which was very narrow. As you go along this street, or to speak more properly, this road, you come first of all into the country."

The Intendant's Palace was neglected as a place of official residence after the conquest in 1759. In 1775, it was occupied by a detachment of the American invading army, and destroyed by the fire of the Garrison. The only remains at present are a private house, the gateway alluded to above, and several stores belonging to Government, formed by repairing some of the old French buildings. The whole is now known by the name of the *King's Woodyard.*

A. HAWKINS

Hawkins's Picture of Quebec; with Historical Recollections 1834

The PARLIAMENT House . . . on the site of the BISHOP'S PALACE. The centre and north-western wing are only completed, so that the whole building, including the old part, now for the first time has assumed the figure intended at the original foundation. The union of the old and the new parts of this building, while it speaks by contrast the great advance of the Province in resources and population, forms an interesting link between its ancient and modern history. The venerable Palace of the BISHOPS, neglected without, but useful and commodious within, rears its modest front by the side of the massive *façade* of its less unpretending, but more durable successor; affording a moral lesson of the rise and decay of buildings, of empires, of man himself, and of the mutability of all sublunary affairs.

It has been stated that the sittings of the PROVINCIAL ASSEMBLY were held in the BISHOP'S Chapel until 1834. It will be remembered, that the HOUSE OF COMMONS in ENGLAND holds its sittings in what was once the small Chapel of ST. STEPHEN, WESTMINSTER. The BISHOP'S Chapel stood upon the site of the central part of the new PARLIAMENT House, the *façade* of which is imposing from its strength and loftiness, and from the dome and spire with which it is crowned. Four massive cut pillars support a pediment, within which will be contained the "Imperial Arms of Great Britain." . . .

Within the *façade* is the new House of Assembly, a spacious Chamber, seventy-nine feet long by forty-six broad, and twenty-eight feet high from floor to ceiling. The interior is not yet finished, but it will, no doubt, be worthy of the building and Province. From the dome there is a splendid view of the picturesque scenery around, which is gained by ascending a staircase until the spectator reaches a small gallery on the outside, and encircling the dome, at the base of the lantern. The whole building is solid and substantial, being of cut stone. The remaining apartments are all for the use of the ASSEMBLY. The Wardrobe and Library are large and in due proportion: the passages and staircase wide and well ventilated. Every care has, in truth, been taken to meet the convenience of the Members, and to expedite the business of the Province. The centre of the NEW PARLIAMENT HOUSE was designed by Mr. Berlinguet, the wings by Mr. Baillargé. The whole was built by Mr. Fortier, Master Mason; and the sums voted by the Legislature to defray the expense amount to £16,000.

It is to be hoped that not long time will elapse, ere the liberality of the Legislature shall have provided for the completion of the NEW PARLIAMENT HOUSE. . . . But in order that the buildings should be seen to advantage, it is highly necessary that the row of houses, which would seem to have intruded themselves between Freemason's Hall and the Seminary, should be removed by an Act of the Legislature, on a fair compensation. When these improvements are made, the PARLIAMENT HOUSE will appear one of the finest buildings in NORTH AMERICA.

A. HAWKINS
Hawkins's Picture of Quebec; with Historical Recollections 1834

ANONYMOUS   The English Cathedral and Place d'Armes,   Water-colour, 5¾ x 9¼ inches
Quebec, Lower Canada   Winter 1835

OPPOSITE

The House of Assembly and the
Point Lévis shore from the ramparts, Quebec, Lower Canada   1842

MILLICENT MARY CHAPLIN   Water-colour, 11 x 14½ inches

It has been stated that the Convent, Church and Garden of the RECOLLET Fathers occupied the site in the front of the CASTLE of ST. LEWIS, as far as the URSULINE Convent in the rear, and contained within St. Lewis, St. Anne and Garden Streets. After the burning of the Church and Convent in 1796, the buildings were razed to the foundation, on the extinction of the order, and the ground appropriated as a site for the new ENGLISH CATHEDRAL. The COURT HOUSE is also built on part of the ground. The area in the centre of the *Place d'Armes* was not always so large. Until a few years ago the foundations of the Récollet Church were to be traced upon the rocky surface, several yards in advance of the present boundary on the western side. On levelling these foundations, and the rock on which they stood, two plates were found. . . . In the month of July, 1834, on sinking one of the posts which surround the area of the *Place d'Armes* some

human bones were discovered very near the surface. As, from their situation, they must have been outside the Convent, it may be fairly supposed that they were the remains of one of the Aborigines, buried there before the coming of the French.

The English Cathedral was built by the bounty of Government, upon the representations of the first Bishop of Quebec, and consecrated in 1804. It is an edifice of regular architecture and very respectable appearance, standing in a spacious area, handsomely enclosed by iron rails and gates, and planted with trees. Its exterior length is 135 feet, its breadth 73; the height of the spire above the ground, 152; from the floor to the centre of the arch within, 41. The communion plate of this Church is very magnificent, and persons in London went to see it while making in the hands of Rundell and Bridge. This plate, together with the altar cloth, hangings of the desk and pulpit, which are of crimson velvet and cloth of gold,

and books for divine service, was a private present from King George the Third. A good peal of eight bells, of which the tenor bell is about 16cwt., was procured some few years ago, by the subscriptions of the congregation. The Church has an excellent organ and a regular cathedral choir, but no Dean and Chapter. It serves also as the Parish Church until such an edifice shall be erected, with a reservation in favor of the Episcopal rights. Near the altar is an elegant font of white marble.

Two new galleries have been recently constructed in the Cathedral, thrown back on each side of the organ, for the accommodation, respectively, of the children attending the male and female National Schools — the front of each is allotted to the orphans of the Asylums, in their distinctive dresses.

A. HAWKINS
Hawkins's Picture of Quebec; with Historical Recollections 1834

The Roman Catholic Church of the CONGREGATION stands on the hill leading from the Esplanade to St. John's-Gate. It is not of ancient construction, and perfectly plain in its interior. Its spire is seen immediately above the ramparts.

The extent of the ramparts towards the land side, from the south-west angle of the Citadel to the cliff above the River St. Charles, is stated by Colonel Bouchette to be eighteen hundred and thirty-seven yards. Within this rampart is the ESPLANADE, between ST. LEWIS and ST. JOHN'S-GATE. It is a level space covered with grass, two hundred and seventy-three yards long, and of irregular breadth. Here are mounted the several guards on duty at the Citadel and other public buildings, each forenoon, except Sunday, at eleven o'clock; and occasional parades of the garrison take place, particularly on the KING's birthday. The muster of the City Militia is also annually held here. The circuit of the fortifications which enclose the UPPER TOWN is two miles and three quarters: the total circumference outside the ditches and space reserved by government, on which no houses can be built on the west side,

is about three miles. The average diameter is about fifteen hundred yards.

Generally speaking, the city may be said to be entirely surrounded by a strong and lofty wall of hewn stone, constructed with elegance as well as with regard to durability. Its castellated appearance, owing to its ditches, embrasures, round towers, battlements and gates, add much to its grand and imposing effect from without.

A. HAWKINS
Hawkins's Picture of Quebec; with Historical Recollections 1834

The houses in Quebec are, with few exceptions, built of stone; the roofs of the better sort are generally covered with sheets of iron, or tin, and those of an inferior description with clap-boards. Shingles have been prohibited; though many old buildings have them. In case of fire, the burning shingles, scattered about by the wind, spread the destructive flames to a great extent: it was the danger apprehended on this account, that caused the provincial parliament to pro-

hibit, in future, the covering of houses with them; but the boarded roofs which are at present chiefly in use, are equally dangerous in catching fire, though perhaps not so likely to communicate it to distant parts of the town. On the roofs of the houses, two or three ladders are placed near the garret windows, for the purpose of assisting the chimney-sweepers to get on the roof, and clean the chimneys. Boys do not go up as in England, but two men perform the work with a bundle of twigs, or furze, tied to a rope, which they pull up and down till the chimney is sufficiently clean; one man goes upon the roof, and the other remains below: a similar mode is practised in Scotland.

J. LAMBERT
Travels Through Canada and the United States of North America 1814

JAMES PATTISON COCKBURN
The Esplanade from the ramparts showing D'Auteuil Street and the Roman Catholic Church of the Congregation, Quebec, Lower Canada   June 27, 1831
Pencil drawing, 5¾ x 9 inches

It has been stated in the account of the RECOLLET Convent, that this extensive establishment—situate on the River St. Charles, about a mile from the walls, and near the spot where JACQUES CARTIER first wintered in New France—owes its foundation to Monseigneur de Saint Vallier, second Bishop of Quebec, who bought the property of the RECOLLETS at *Notre Dame des Anges,* and procured for them a site opposite the Fort of St. Lewis, on which at present stands the English Cathedral. The Bishop expended a very large sum in those days, one hundred thousand crowns, on the buildings, which were intended for a GENERAL HOSPITAL for invalids, and as an asylum for persons permanently afflicted with disease. The HOTEL DIEU was instituted for the care of incidental maladies. . . .

The GENERAL HOSPITAL is at present a Nunnery, governed by a Superior, having forty-five professed Nuns, a few

Novices and *Postulantes.* The whole appearance, both external and internal, of this Hospital is regular and pleasing; while the general arrangement and economy are highly creditable to the institution. Its front is two hundred and twenty-eight feet long—its form nearly square. The main building is thirty-three feet deep; but on the south-west side, a range of one hundred and thirty feet long has fifty feet in breadth.

The Chapel is very neat, and has a gallery communicating with the Hospital, for the use of the indigent sick. A separate house is appropriated to the reception of the insane: the Province, however, requires an establishment on a larger scale for these unfortunates. At Three-Rivers there is an establishment for the insane under the charge of the Ursulines of the Convent.

The means of the GENERAL HOSPITAL, from its unrestricted character, have been found inadequate to defray the ex-

penses of the establishment, and the deficiency is occasionally supplied by grants from the Provincial Parliament. The Nuns are distinguished for the manufacture of Church ornaments, and for the skill in gilding. The produce of the sale of these works becomes part of the general fund of the Institution.

A. HAWKINS
Hawkins's Picture of Quebec; with Historical Recollections 1834

JAMES PATTISON COCKBURN
The General Hospital, Quebec, Lower Canada   1831
Pencil drawing, 4¾ x 8¼ inches

Esplanade - Quebec

General Hospl - Quebec

The market-place at Quebec presents in winter a curious and busy scene. The French Canadians come from great distances very early in the morning, with their sleighs full of vegetables, poultry, fish, &c., to take up their position, and be ready to begin the sale of their wares as soon as the citizens come forth to cater for the daily wants of their households. The horses are never unyoked; and there they stand for hours amongst the snow, their shaggy hair frozen white, and icicles hanging at their poor patient noses. The habitants are of very picturesque figures, in their rough buffalo coats and caps—most wearing red sashes; the women have comfortable, homespun-looking garments, and many wear fur bonnets. The market-place is on a slope, and it is curious to stand outside the crowd, and look on; the sleighs are so low, they are completely hidden; all you can see being alternate stripes of horses and human beings; the former standing still, the latter in constant motion, pushing, and turning and bending in all directions, for no visible object. Join the multitude, and you find that what interests them is frozen fish, flesh, and fowl of all sorts, heaped about on the ground and in the sleighs, which are now much raised above it. They make streets of sleighs by turning the horses face to face, dovetailing them about the length of their necks so they are quite out of the way; and the people move up and down regular lanes, and find all the delicacies of the season displayed to the right and left. There you see frozen pigs set upon their legs, looking very ugly and uncomfortable; and here are great coarse sturgeons, standing on their heads, and leaning against the

The Jesuits' Convent, which reverted to the Crown some years since, is now occupied by a regiment of infantry, and makes an excellent and capacious barrack. What was the fathers' pleasure-garden in olden times is now the parade ground. In other respects it appears to have undergone very little change (except with regard to its occupants), being surmounted by the old spire, and retaining the strong iron-studded gates, with the sacred devices upon them. On the opposite side of the market-place is the large and ungraceful building of the Roman Catholic Cathedral, where I attended one day at the performance of high mass, but was glad to make my escape again into the open air, such a dense crowd was there in every part of it. As in Montreal, the Catholic clergy possess an extensive property in Quebec. The seminary which adjoins the Cathedral occupies, together with its garden, seven acres of ground in the upper town, the Ursuline Convent possesses as much more, and the Hôtel Dieu even as much as twelve; so that, what with the citadel, convents, churches, barrack, and open squares, the population of the upper town is reduced to a mere cipher compared with its extent.

E. T. COKE
A Subaltern's Furlough 1833

side of the sleigh as stark as sticks. The vendor seized two big haddocks by the tails, and held them out to tempt us; tapping their frozen heads together, with a clinking sound, like stones. Vegetables are at this season very dear: a head of cabbage, 4d., currency; a small stick of celery, 4d.; a tiny bit of horse-radish, 1s. Turkeys are reckoned dear just now; at 5s. and 6s. for large ones—their usual price being 2s., 3s., and 4s.; fowls, 2s. a-pair. It is the custom for ladies to go to market, and make their own purchases; a maid, with a large basket on her arm, or else a boy, who carries it on his head, being in attendance. The scene is amusing and lively; but, I confess, I should be sorry to be obliged to see it every morning at nine o'clock without regard to the state of the atmosphere.

Meat is said to lose its flavour by having been frozen; especially if thawed, as is the ordinary custom, in water. It is better to hang it up in the warm kitchen, and to let it thaw gradually. Potatoes and apples are almost spoilt by being frozen; and oranges, which, of course, only come from abroad, completely wither up it not housed before the frost sets in. Fowls do not suffer so much from being frozen; and fish are in no way the worse for it when they come to table. Some fresh-water species will actually return to life again, if put into water after being frozen.

W. H. G. KINGSTON
Western Wanderings 1856

JAMES PATTISON COCKBURN

The Market and the Jesuit Barracks with the Catholic Cathedral in view, Quebec, Lower Canada 1830

Water-colour, 3¾ x 5½ inches

OPPOSITE

JAMES PATTISON COCKBURN

The Catholic Cathedral of Notre Dame and the Market, Quebec, Lower Canada July 25, 1830

Water-colour, 10½ x 14¾ inches

Having thus made the circuit of the fortifications, it is necessary to notice the different barracks and military buildings for the accommodation of the troops composing the garrison. Besides those contained within the CITADEL, and the Artillery barracks, the spacious building in the market-place, formerly the College of the JESUITS, has long been occupied by the KING'S troops, under the name of the JESUITS Barracks. This edifice is of stone, three stories high, and measures two hundred and twenty-four feet by two hundred, being in shape a parallelogram. The principal entrance into the barracks is from the market-place, opposite to the French Cathedral. Through a lofty passage admittance is gained into a considerable area, the buildings around which are occupied by the soldiers. On the other side is an arch leading to the barrack yard and offices. To the left of the great entrance is a large door opening into a hall. Here is the room set apart for the Garrison library, the property of the military, containing a number of valuable books and maps. The barrack yard is enclosed by a wall two hundred yards long, in St. Ann street, in which is the barrack-gate and main-guard. This was formerly the garden belonging to the College. A little beyond the gate is the barrack office, a neat and substantial stone building standing nearly opposite to the Scottish Church. The JESUITS Barracks are at present occupied as the quarters of that highly distinguished Regiment, the 79th, or CAMERON HIGHLANDERS. This is one of the few which wear the "garb of old Gaul"; and makes a picturesque and highly military appearance in the field, very attractive to the numerous strangers who conclude their summer tour by a visit to the interesting capital of LOWER CANADA. The 79th Regiment is under the command of Lieutenant Colonel DUNCAN MACDOUGALL.

A. HAWKINS
Hawkins's Picture of Quebec; with Historical Recollections 1834

JAMES PATTISON COCKBURN
Ice cutting at the mouth of the St. Charles River, Quebec, Lower Canada   1831
Water-colour, 14¼ x 19¼ inches

We are returned, my Lord, from having seen an object as beautiful and magnificent in itself, as pleasing from the idea it gives of renewing once more our intercourse with Europe.

Before I saw the breaking up of the vast body of ice, which forms what is here called *the bridge,* from Quebec to Point Levi, I imagined there could be nothing in it worth attention; that the ice would pass away, or dissolve gradually, day after day, as the influence of the sun, and warmth of the air and earth increased; and that we should see the river open, without having observed by what degrees it became so.

But I found *the great river,* as the savages with much propriety call it, maintain its dignity in this instance as in all others, and assert its superiority over those petty streams which we honour with the names of rivers in England. Sublimity is the characteristic of this western world; the loftiness of the mountains, the grandeur of the lakes and rivers, the majesty of the rocks shaded with a picturesque variety of beautiful trees and shrubs, and crowned with the noblest of the offspring of the forest, which form the banks of the latter, are as much beyond the power of fancy as that of description: a landscape-painter might here expand his imagination, and find ideas which he will seek in vain in our comparatively little world.

The object of which I am speaking has all the American magnificence.

The ice before the town, or, to speak in the Canadian style, *the bridge,* being of a thickness not less than five feet, a league in length, and more than a mile broad, resists for a long time the rapid tide that attempts to force it from the banks.

We are prepared by many previous circumstances to expect something extraordinary in this event, if I may so call it: every increase of heat in the weather for near a month before the ice leaves the banks; every warm day gives you terror for those you see venturing to pass it in carrioles; yet one frosty night makes it again so strong, that even the ladies, and the timid amongst them, still venture themselves over in parties of pleasure; though greatly alarmed at their return, if a few hours of uncommon warmth intervene.

But, during the last fortnight, the alarm grows indeed a very serious one: the eye can distinguish, even at a considerable distance, that the ice is softened and detached from the banks; and you dread every step will bring death to those who have still the temerity to pass it, which they will continue to do till one or more pay their rashness with their lives.

From the time the ice is no longer a bridge on which you see crowds driving with such vivacity on business or pleasure, every one is looking eagerly for its breaking away, to remove the bar to the continually wished and expected event, of the arrival of ships from that world from whence we have seemed so long in a manner excluded.

The hour is come; I have been with a crowd of both sexes, and all ranks, hailing the propitious moment: our situation, on the top of Cape Diamond, gave us a prospect some leagues above and below the town; above Cape Diamond the river was open, it was so below Point Levi, the rapidity of the current having forced a passage for the water under the transparent bridge, which for more than a league continued firm.

We stood waiting with all the eagerness of expectation; the tide came rushing with an amazing impetuosity; the bridge seemed to shake, yet resisted the force of the waters; the tide recoiled, it made a pause, it stood still, it returned with redoubled fury, the immense mass of ice gave way.

A vast plain appeared in motion; it advanced with solemn and majestic pace: the points of land on the banks of the river for a few moments stopped its progress; but the immense weight of so prodigious a body, carried along by a rapid current, bore down all opposition with a force irresistable.

FRANCES BROOKE
The History of Emily Montague 1769

Independent of what it owes to its fortifications, and situation on the top of a rock, Quebec is indebted for much of its strength to the severity and great length of the winter, as in that season it is wholly impracticable for a besieging army to carry on any works or blockade the town.

I. WELD
Travels Through the States of North America and the Provinces of Upper and Lower Canada 1799

The farmers' wives manufacture for domestic wear, a woollen cloth, generally dyed of a light blue colour; the threads of which are coarse, but closely woven. They make also a cloth something like the Scotch drugget, and a stuff cloth which is wholly of wool. Some of the linens which they make of the flax that grows on their farms are rather of a fine quality, bleached on the grass, and said to be durable. They have lately begun to make a cloth of cotton yarn. Al-

SEMPRONIUS STRETTON

a Canadian man & woman in their winter Dress Quebec Canada Nov? 21. 1805 —

Fashions in Lower Canada
1805-06

Back view of the above —

Water-colour and
pen and ink drawings,
6¼ x 8 inches

most every farmer in the thinly settled districts has a loom in his house; and their wives or daughters not only spin the yarn, but weave the cloth. The quantity, however, manufactured by the farmers, is not more than half what is required to clothe their families.

J. MCGREGOR
Historical and Descriptive Sketches of the Maritime Colonies of British America 1828

JAMES HOPE   The Wolfe and Montcalm Monument, Quebec, Lower Canada   June 17, 1841
                             Water-colour, 8¾ × 12¾ inches

The memorial in honor of the two military chiefs who fell at the head of the opposing armies, in that decisive battle which made these Provinces a portion of the British Empire, is now completed, and is a conspicuous, as it is the only classical, ornament of the city. It was originally designed by Captain, now Major YONGE of the 79th, or CAMERON HIGHLANDERS, (then on the personal Staff of HIS EXCELLENCY the EARL OF DALHOUSIE,) an officer whose taste had been greatly cultivated by foreign travel; and is a combination of various beautiful proportions to be found in some of the celebrated models of antiquity. It stands on the west side of *Des Carrières* Street, leading from the *Place d'Armes* to the glacis of Cape Diamond, within an area taken from the upper garden belonging to the Government. In front is a broad walk, which has become a public promenade, overlooking the CASTLE garden, and commanding a fine view of the harbor, and the beautiful scenery beyond it.

The Monument is a conspicuous object from the River; but on account of the numerous spires which rise around it in a distant view, it is seen to the best advantage from the centre of the channel between the Lower Town and Pointe Lévi. It is strictly classical in the proportions of every part. To the top of the surbase is thirteen feet from the ground. On this rests the Sarcophagus, seven feet three inches high. The obelisk measures forty-two feet eight inches, and the *apex* two feet one inch, making in the whole an altitude of sixty-five feet from the ground. The dimensions of the obelisk at the base are six feet, by four feet eight inches, tapering conically to the *apex*, where the sides are diminished to three feet two inches, by two feet five inches. This classical ornament of our city was finished, with the exception of the inscription, on the 8th September; and its completion was witnessed by the zealous patron of the work, the EARL OF DALHOUSIE. On the morning of that day, not to be forgotten by the numerous friends of that noble Lord, being the day of his departure from the Province, the Government of which he had conscientiously administered for eight years, HIS LORDSHIP, accompanied by his successor in the Administration of the Government, Lieutenant General Sir JAMES KEMPT, G.C.B., and attended by the Staff, several military officers, and a party of ladies and gentlemen of the city and vicinity, proceeded to the walk in front of the Governor's garden, to witness the completion of the Monument. A few minutes after eight o'clock, the *apex*, or cap-stone, was placed upon the summit; and the ceremony of tapping it with the mallet was performed by his nephew and Aide de Camp, Captain FOX MAULE, 79th Highlanders, as proxy for the noble Earl, who ascended to the top of the obelisk for that purpose. Thus was this chaste memorial to WOLFE and MONTCALM, through the exertions of Mr. John Phillips, the builder, completed during the summer of 1828, to the great gratification of HIS EXCELLENCY, who had all along expressed the strongest wish for its completion before his departure from QUEBEC.

A. HAWKINS
Hawkins's Picture of Quebec; with Historical Recollections 1834

THOMAS DAVIES   The Chaudière Falls near Quebec, Lower Canada   1792
Water-colour, 14 × 20½ inches

The situation of the house is enchanting; and with all my passion for the savage luxuriance of America, I begin to find my taste return for the mild and more regular charms of my native country [England].

We have no Chaudières, no Mont- morencies, none of those magnificent scenes on which the Canadians have a right to pride themselves; but we excel them in the lovely, the smiling; in enamelled meadows, in waving corn- fields, in gardens the boast of Europe; in every elegant art which adorns and soft- ens human life; in all the riches and beauty which cultivation can give.

FRANCES BROOKE
The History of Emily Montague   1769

The cataract of Chaudiere may be truly said to form a complete whole. The sce- nery which accompanies it is beautiful and romantic beyond description. In the centre a large fragment of rock, which first divides the water at the summit of the precipice, forms a sort of small island; and a handsome fir-tree which grows upon it is thus placed in a most singular and picturesque situation. The forest on either side the river consists of firs, pines, birch, oak, ash, and a variety of other trees and shrubs intermingled in the most wild and romantic manner. Their dark green foliage, joined with the brown and sombre tint of the rocky fragments over which the water precipitates itself, forms a striking and pleasing contrast to the snowy whiteness of the foaming surge, and the columns of sparkling spray which rise in clouds and mingle with the air.

The gratification on viewing this beau- tiful cataract is considerably enhanced by the journey which the spectator is obliged to take through a wild and gloomy forest; the toil of which is amply repaid when he emerges all at once from Cimmerian darkness into an expansive view of the falls and the light of heaven. It appears like a sudden enchantment, and the imagination is lost in the variety and grandeur of the scene. I could have con- templated it for hours; but our time was short, and we wished to return to Quebec before dark. I quitted this beautiful and romantic spot with the greatest reluc- tance; regretting that in all probability I should never see it again.

J. LAMBERT
Travels Through Canada and the United States
1814

I must now fulfil my promise to describe the sliding down the cone of ice formed of the frozen spray at the foot of the Falls of Montmorency. . . . After making many fruitless attempts to arrive at the top, with my face towards the cone, I at length leaned with my back against it, and by digging with my heels sharply into the spongy surface, made a sufficient dent to sustain my weight on one foot, whilst with the other I made another dent higher up, and so on alternately, until I accomplished my object.

The top was of the shape of a flattened dome and the surface sufficiently level to admit of several persons standing thereon, being about twenty feet in diameter; but beyond that limit the face by which I had ascended was so steep, that it curved under quite out of sight, seemingly to a perfect perpendicular, and then getting down seems impossible without receiving serious injury; yet when I reflected on the position I was in, and that I had no means of descending but by launching myself off on my back, I absolutely shuddered. Satisfied that I had no alternative, I submitted to my fate; and dragging myself to the brink of the precipice, I started with great velocity; and to my inexpressible joy, arrived at the level ice surrounding the bottom, without sustaining the slightest injury. . . .

At length the ice began to perish, and as it is there termed became rotten, so that it will then break through without any kind of notice; yet, willing to have one more slide, on the 23rd of April, we ordered out the sleigh, and reached the falls, not, however, without observing several holes where the feet of horses had broken through the ice, indicating that it was, indeed, preparing to depart. We nevertheless proceeded, and whilst we were sliding, we observed several sleighs containing ladies and gentlemen drive up to the foot of the cone, and the gentlemen immediately commenced ascending and sliding down, to the no small diversion of the ladies.

Amongst the company was a Lieutenant John Caddy, of the Artillery, who arrived on the top whilst I was there, and noticing the crack we had seen on a former occasion, unhesitatingly stepped over it and began dancing upon that portion which, it was evident to me, was partly detached from the more solid and substantial portion; I remonstrated with him on the folly of doing so, entreating him to come back. Caddy, no doubt, felt his position unsafe; and we both instantly launched ourselves off to descend, yet had not reached the bottom when we were stunned by a sound somewhat resembling a heavy clap of thunder, connected with a deafening hissing. As soon as we were able to scramble up and regain our feet, we were petrified at the fact that all that portion of the cone upon which Caddy but twenty seconds before had been dancing so merrily had sunk, and the ice and spray were rushing up in the most awful manner. Our confidence in the security of the ice was instantly dispelled: everyone hastened away towards their respective sleighs not more than two hundred yards from the cone and close to shore; and our course lay exactly over the ice which covered a wide and deep basin formed, as usual, below considerable falls, by the incessant operation of the rushing water into one

ANONYMOUS / The "Natural Steps" on the Montmorency River, Lower Canada   1835 / Water-colour, 5¾ × 9¼ inches

OPPOSITE

JAMES PEACHEY / Montmorency Falls in the spring, Lower Canada   1781 / Water-colour, 15¼ × 22½ inches

spot. Here the height of the cascade was about two hundred and forty-two feet, over which the fall is nearly perpendicular. A slight fall of snow had covered or effaced the marks of our feet in going to the cone, which rendered it necessary to proceed carefully in order to avoid those cracks which indicate a more tender part of the ice.

The party, probably about twenty in number, keeping close together and forming one group, had nearly arrived at the place where the sleighs were standing, when we heard a loud splashing and a strange noise behind us, upon which everyone of the company started round in fear and surprise, when, to our astonishment and terror, we could not perceive the slightest remnant of the cone, nor of the sheet of ice covering the pool over which we had passed but an instant before, yet we could readily trace the marks of our footsteps from the spot on which we were standing, over a space of ice not exceeding twenty yards, where they led the eye into the uncovered and deep water, rushing on with frightful impetuosity. . . .

In the least space of time I was ever able to persuade my horse to perform the distance, I was at Quebec.

G. T. LANDMANN
Adventures and Recollections   1852

The river Montmorenci, which empties itself into the Saint Lawrence, at the distance of eight miles to the north-east of Quebec, was called after a marechal of that name, who was viceroy of New France. Passing through a course from the north-east, of considerable length, the first settlement through which it flows, is called La Motte, situated on the northern extremity of a sloping ground, which gradually descends from the mountains, to the coast of the great river. At La Motte, the waters diffuse themselves into shallow currents, interrupted by rocks, which break them into foam, accompanied by murmuring sounds, tending to enliven the solitude and solemn stillness, which prevail throughout the surrounding forests, and on the desolate hills. The channel of the river, farther down, is bounded by precipitous rocks, its breadth becomes extremely contracted, and the rapidity of its current is proportionably augmented. At a place called the natural steps, there are cascades of the height of ten, or twelve feet. These steps have been gradually formed, by the accession of waters which the river receives in its progress, at the breaking up of winter, and by the melting of snows. From the middle of April, to the end of May, its waters roll along with an increasing height and rapidity. The banks, from the natural steps, downwards to the Saint Lawrence, are composed of a lime slate, placed in horizontal strata, from the depth of five to twenty-four inches each, connected by fibrous gypsum of a whitish colour. The waters, at the season already mentioned, powerfully impelled in their course, insinuate themselves between the strata, dissolve the gypsum, and tear the horizontal rock, which gives way, in fragments of various sizes, yielding to the rushing violence of the sweeping torrent. The regularity displayed in the formation of some of these steps, is well deserving of observation.

G. HERIOT
Travels Through the Canadas   1807

JAMES PATTISON COCKBURN

In the parish of the Chateau Richer on the St. Lawrence River near Quebec, Lower Canada　1830
Water-colour, 6 × 9½ inches

The settlement of Chateau Richer, derives its name from the ruins of an edifice situated on a small rocky point, on the borders of the Saint Lawrence. It was a Franciscan monastery, when the army under General Wolfe encamped on the eastern bank of the Montmorenci. As the monks used their influence among the inhabitants in their vicinity, to impede a supply of provisions for the English army, it was deemed necessary to send thither a detachment to make them prisoners. They had so fortified themselves within their mansion, that field pieces were required to compel them to a surrender. The house was destroyed by fire, and nothing now remains, except a part of the walls, and the ruins of an adjoining tower, which was formerly a wind-mill. By an inscription above the door, it appears to have been built one hundred and twelve years ago. The parish church is placed on a bank, immediately behind the chateau, and has two spires. The

ruins already described, the great river, the island of Orleans, the point of Ange Gardien, and Cape Diamond in the distance, compose an agreeable scene.

Toward the east, a yet happier combination of objects presents itself. On the left, are the ruins of the monastery, the church, banks cloathed with foliage, and the lower grounds studded with white cottages; over which Cape Tourment, and the chain of mountains whose termination it forms, tower with exalted majesty.

G. HERIOT
Travels Through the Canadas　1807

The ruin of Chateau Richer, though only that of a square building, belonging to the Seminary, is interesting not only as an historical relic, but as a picturesque one, being one of the very few ruins in this

country. Canada must wait some ages before she can become a land of recollections and poetry; to make her amends for these associations, she has few wants to complain of. Though she cannot boast of the elegance and refinements of Europe, she can say, in this happy land wretchedness and want are not known. The environs of Chateau Richer, as the favourite resort of snipe shooters, are much celebrated, few places in the country affording a greater abundance of that game.

The falls of La Puce are two miles beyond Chateau Richer, which the traveller must not omit to see, as they are well worth his attention, and may be seen in half an hour without any difficulty.

If the traveller should pass this road on a fine Sunday, he will have an excellent opportunity of seeing the population in their best attire; if he arrives at the pretty village church of St. Ann, situated on the left of the road, under lofty banks, about the time of morning service, when he will find the environs crowded with one-horse calêches, the horse fastened to one of the posts that for this purpose are always planted near the church. The church is generally so crowded, that groups of the *habitants* are to be seen outside and covering the steps on their knees; every person is respectably dressed, the men mostly in grey cloth, the manufacture of their own fire side, as above noticed. This scene alone bespeaks not only of the wants of life being amply supplied, but the numerous carriages clearly show that the substantial comforts are not scantily enjoyed by this happy race. The village churches in Lower Canada are generally six miles asunder, and the Canadians who are particularly zealous in their religious duties, are sure to attend from the most remote cottage in the parish, either on foot or in their neighbour's calêch.

The road continues enlivened by the appearance of numerous and cleanly cottages on either side, till it reaches the village of St. Ann; two miles beyond which, and on the river of that name, accommodations may be procured both comfortable and cleanly, and where he is sure to meet with civility and kindness. If pressed for time he may here procure a horse to ride to the falls of St. Ann, a distance only of three miles; this road ascends a part of the mountain which rises here, from this ascent he has fine and extensive views of Quebec and the surrounding country; he proceeds ascending till he reaches a level spot which continues a mile and a half over a very rough path through a forest, when he suddenly descends and finds himself enclosed in a valley of rocks and trees, through the centre of which rushes the river St. Ann till it forces itself through a narrow chasm of the rocks, when at an angle of forty-five degrees, it continues tumbling and roaring to the river below. The writer of this description would compare it to the falls of Trenton, though they are on a more extensive scale — after descending some rocks, the traveller has a magnificent view of the cataract, as it hurries past. The diversified appearance of the rocks and trees of this sequestered spot will richly reward the lover of romantic scenery.

[J. P. COCKBURN]
Quebec and its Environs 1831

ANONYMOUS
The falls on the St. Anne's River,
Lower Canada   1835
Water-colour, 9¼ × 5¾ inches

JAMES PATTISON COCKBURN

Nets to capture the passenger pigeons near St. Anne's, Lower Canada 1829
Water-colour, 10¼ × 14½ inches

At one period of the year numerous and immense flights of pigeons visit Canada, when the population make a furious war against them both by guns and nets; they supply the inhabitants with a material part of their subsistance, and are sold in the market at Quebec remarkably cheap, often as low as a shilling per dozen, and sometimes even at a less rate. It appears that the pigeon prefers the loftiest and most leafless trees to settle on. In addition to the natural beauty of St. Ann and its environs, the process by which the inhabitants take the pigeons is worth remarking. Upon the loftiest tree, long bare poles are slantingly fixed; small pieces of wood are placed transversely across this pole, upon which the birds crowd; below, in ambush, the sportsman with a long gun enfilades the whole length of the pole, and when he fires, few if any escape—innumerable poles are prepared at St. Ann for this purpose. The other method they have of taking them is by nets, by which means they are enabled to preserve them alive, and kill them occasionally for their own use, or for the market, when it has ceased to be glutted with them. Behind Madame Fontane's this sport may be seen in perfection. The nets, which are very large, are placed at the end of an avenue of trees, (for it appears the pigeons choose an avenue to fly down) opposite a large tree, upon erect poles two nets are suspended, one facing the avenue, the other the tree, another is placed over them, which is fixed at one end, and supported by pullies and two perpendicular poles at the opposite; a man is hid in a small cov-ered house under the tree, with a rope leading from the pullies in his hand—directly the pigeons fly against the perpendicular nets, he pulls the rope, when the top net immediately falls and encloses the whole flock; by this process vast numbers are taken.

The following day an excursion may be made to the falls of St. Ferréole passing through a new settlement; the descent here is rather fatiguing, but the falls have been visited by Lady Dalhousie and several of our fair countrywomen. The view will more than compensate for the fatigue. On his return to St. Ann's, he should, if he has time, visit the Priest's farm called St. Joseph, to admire the scenery, and on the third day to Quebec.

[J. P. COCKBURN]
Quebec and Its Environs 1831

This river, from Montreal to Quebec, exhibits a scene perhaps not to be matched in the world: it is settled on both sides, though the settlements are not so numerous on the south shore as on the other: the lovely confusion of woods, mountains, meadows, corn-fields, rivers (for there are several on both sides, which lose themselves in the St. Lawrence), intermixed with churches and houses breaking upon you at a distance through the trees, form a variety of landscapes, to which it is difficult to do justice.

This charming scene, with a clear serene sky, a gentle breeze in our favour, and the conversation of half a dozen fine women, would have made the voyage pleasing to the most insensible man on earth: my Emily too of the party, and most politely attentive to the pleasure she saw I had in making the voyage agreeable to her.

FRANCES BROOKE
The History of Emily Montague   1769

JAMES PEACHEY

Three Rivers, Lower Canada, from the road leading to Pointe du Lac   1784
Water-colour, 5¼ × 12 inches

The town of Three Rivers is situated upon a point of land, near the confluence with the Saint Lawrence, of the stream from which it derives its name. It extends about three quarters of a mile, along the north bank of the former. The surrounding country is flat, and its soil is composed of sand, mixed with black mould. In the mouth of the stream, there are two islands, which divide it into three branches. On ascending its course, the borders become wild and picturesque. The town was indebted for its original establishment to the profits arising from the commerce for peltry, which in the infancy of the colony was carried on by the natives, through the course of this river, which flows from the north-east, for a distance of three hundred miles. Thither, various tribes of these savages, descended from the vicinity of Hudson's bay, and the country intervening between that and the Saint Lawrence.

Attracted by the advantages which the agreeable situation of the place, and the rendezvous for traffic, presented, several French families here established themselves. The proximity of the Iroquois, a nation which cherished an irreconcilable hostility to the French, suggested the necessity of constructing a fort, and the district of Three Rivers became, at length, a separate government. After a lapse of some years, the natives who traded to this place, harassed and exposed to continual danger, from the frequent irruptions of that warlike nation, discontinued their accustomed visits.

The town contains a convent of Ursulines, to which is adjoined a parochial church, and an hospital. It was founded in 1677 by M. de Saint Vallier, bishop of Quebec, for the education of young women, and as an asylum for the poor and sick. A superior and eighteen nuns now possess it, and discharge the functions of this humane institution.

G. HERIOT
Travels Through the Canadas   1807

ANONYMOUS
Clearing land, Lower Canada   1835
Water-colour, 5¾ × 9¼ inches

To clear lands in lower Canada, they cut down the wood with a hatchet, heap it together, and burn it; the large roots are extirpated by digging into the ground. The soil thus laid open becomes covered with vegetation, and cattle are sent to graze upon it. This mode is tedious and expensive, and costs, including labour, about thirty shillings sterling per acre.

The Americans have introduced into the province a practice much more simple and economical, and attended with equal success. They cut down the trees, burn them, and sow between the trunks, after having turned up the earth with a harrow or hoe. A third method is by setting fire to the growing woods, and cutting around the bark of the larger trees, to prevent the sap from ascending; these dry up during the first year, and cease to re-produce their foliage; the farmer then sows his grain, and removes at leisure the trees that are dead. The cedar and spruce trees, whose roots are incorruptible, and long resist the ploughshare, it becomes necessary to eradicate before the land can be sown.

G. HERIOT
Travels Through the Canadas   1807

MILLICENT MARY CHAPLIN
The forges on the St. Maurice River, Canada East   1841
Water-colour, 8¼ × 17¼ inches

On the banks of the river already mentioned [St. Maurice River], and about nine miles up its course, an iron foundry, which was first worked in 1737, is situated. The manufacture of ore into cast, as well as hammered iron, is here carried on to a considerable extent. The works, and the soil in which the ore is found, are the property of government, and they are rented by a company at Quebec, on lease, at the rate of eight hundred pounds per annum. The ore lies in horizontal strata, and near the surface. It is composed of masses, easily detached from each other, perforated, and the holes filled with ochre. It possesses softness, and friability, and for promoting its fusion, a grey limestone, found in its vicinity, is used. The hammered iron is soft, pliable, and tenacious, and has the quality of being but little subject to the influence of rust. The latter property is probably derived from the materials employed in its fusion. For this purpose, wood only is applied, which is highly preferable to mineral coal.

G. HERIOT
Travels Through the Canadas   1807

The view from hence is grand beyond description. A prodigious expanse of country is laid open to the eye, with the noble river St. Lawrence winding through it, which may be traced from the remotest part of the horizon. The river comes from the right, and flows smoothly on, after passing down the tremendous rapids above the town, where it is hurried over huge rocks with a noise that is heard even up the mountain. On the left below you, appears the town of Montreal with its churches, monasteries, glittering spires, and the shipping under its old walls; several little islands in the river near the town, partly improved, partly overgrown with wood, add greatly to the beauty of the scene. La Prairie with its large church on the distant side of the river, is seen to the greatest advantage, and beyond it, is a range of lofty mountains which terminates the prospect. Such an endless variety and such a grandeur is there in the view from this part of the mountain, that even those who are most habituated to the view, always find it a fresh subject of admiration whenever they contemplate it; and on this part of the mountain it is that the club which I mentioned generally assembles. Two stewards are appointed for the day, who always chuse some new spot where there is a spring or rill of water, and an agreeable shade: each family brings cold provisions, wine, &c.; the whole is put together, and the company, often amounting to one hundred persons, sits down to dinner.

I. WELD
Travels Through the States of North America and the Provinces of Upper and Lower Canada 1799

Montreal, being placed one degree and sixteen minutes south from Quebec, enjoys a more favourable climate. The soil is richer, and the duration of winter is not so long at the former place, as at the latter, by the space of six weeks. This superiority, with respect to climate and soil, renders it preferable to Quebec, as a place of constant residence. The markets are more abundantly supplied, and the articles of living, are sold at a more reasonable price, especially during winter, when the inhabitants of the United States, who reside upon lands bordering on Lower Canada, bring for sale, a part of the produce of their farms; quantities of cod, and of other fish, in a frozen state, are likewise conveyed thither in slays, from Boston. . . .

A natural wharf, very near to the town, is formed by the depth of the stream, and the sudden declivity of the bank. The environs of Montreal are composed of four streets extending in different directions. That of Quebec on the north, Saint Lawrence towards the west, and the Recollet and Saint Antoine towards the south; in the latter is placed the college, which has been lately rebuilt. These, together with the town, contain about twelve thousand inhabitants.

G. HERIOT
Travels Through the Canadas 1807

From the water we perceived no good view of Montreal. High buildings, confusedly massed, and dirty quays, or rather wharfs, appeared to our fancies to give no great promise of the rival of Quebec.

R. H. BONNYCASTLE
The Canadas in 1841 1841

GEORGE HERIOT   Montreal, Lower Canada from St. Helen's Island   ca. 1800
Water-colour, 4½ × 18 inches

A View of the City of Montreal, taken from the Top of the Mountain, the 15th October 1784

JAMES PEACHEY
Montreal, Lower Canada, from the top
of the Mountain   October 15, 1784
Water-colour, 5 × 10 inches

ANONYMOUS

Montreal, Lower Canada, from the citadel showing
Notre Dame Street and Champs de Mars   1824

The streets are all very narrow; three of them run parallel to the river, and these are intersected by others at right angles, but not at regular distances. On the side of the town farthest from the river, and nearly between the northern and southern extremities, there is a small square, called La Place d'Armes, which seems originally to have been left open to the walls on one side, and to have been intended for the military to exercise in; the troops, however, never make use of it now, but parade on a long walk, behind the walls, nearer to the barracks. On the opposite side of the town, towards the water, is another small square where the market is held.

I. WELD
Travels Through the States of North America and the Provinces of Upper and Lower Canada 1799

The length of the island of Montreal is thirty miles, and its mean breadth about seven, its circumference being seventy miles. It may be said to owe its original settlement to the Abbé Quetus, who, in 1657, arrived from France, accompanied by deputies of the seminary of Saint Sulpicius, to take possession of this spot, and here to found a seminary. The other inhabitants of the colony were gratified to find, that a body of men so respectable, had undertaken to clear, and settle an island, the efforts of whose first possessors, had hitherto been too languid. The seignorial rights of that fertile and valuable tract of territory, are still vested in the representatives of the order of Saint Sulpicius, which, in France, was swept away in the revolutionary torrent.

The city of Montreal, in latitude 45° 33′, longitude 73° 37′, is placed on the south side of the island of the same name, whose banks are here from ten to

fifteen feet high, from the level of the water. It is built in the form of a parallelogram, extending from north to south. A deep and rapid current flows between the shore and the island of Saint Helen; a strong north-east wind is therefore necessary, to carry vessels up to the town, and when that is wanting, they remain at anchor, at the lower end of the stream. This inconvenience might have been obviated, had the city been built about a mile below its present site, at a place called the Cross. The original founders were enjoined by the government of France, to make choice of a situation as high up the river, as large vessels could be navigated, and it appears that the injunction was literally obeyed.

The streets are airy, and regularly disposed, one of them extending nearly parallel to the river, through the whole length of the place; they are of sufficient width, being intersected at right angles, by several smaller streets, which

Water-colour, 8¾ × 28 inches
(two sheets)

descend from west to east. The upper street is divided into two, by the Roman Catholic church, adjoining to which, there is a large open square, called the Place d'Armes.

The habitations of the principal merchants are neat and commodious, and their storehouses are spacious, and secured against risque from fires. They are covered with sheet-iron or tin; without this precaution, as the roofs of dwellings in Canada are usually formed of boards, and sometimes with the exterior addition of shingles, they would, in summer, become highly combustible from without, and liable to ignition from a small spark of fire. The houses which are protected in the former manner will last, without need of repairs, for a considerable number of years.

The town was enclosed by a stone fortification, which, having long fallen to ruins, is now in a great measure levelled, or removed. It was thus fortified, to guard its inhabitants against the frequent irruptions of the Iroquois, and the walls were never in a state to resist the attack of a regular army. An act of the colonial legislature, was some time ago passed, for their total demolition. This has in a great degree been carried into effect, and the place is now rapidly improving in extension, as well as in neatness of edifices.

Montreal is divided into the upper and lower towns, although the difference of level between them, exceeds not twelve or fifteen feet. In the latter are the public market, held twice in the week, and the Hotel Dieu. The upper town contains the cathedral, the English church, the convent of Recollets, that of the sisters of Notre Dame, the Seminary, the Government house, and the new Court of Law. The religious edifices are constructed with more solidity than taste, and all of them are possessed of extensive gardens.

G. HERIOT
Travels Through the Canadas 1807

The Catholic is the prevailing Religion in the city, and the Seigniory of the island is held by the clergy of that church, from which, with a heavy percentage upon the transfer by sale of all real estates, a large revenue is derived. Though so many English and Scotch reside in the city, the French language is very generally spoken, and but few of the natives of the lower class speak the English fluently. The shops are very excellent, and I never saw in one place so many for the sale of clothes, the entire street of Notre Dame being occupied by them. The Market-house is not only a shabby, but a dirty building; at the head of it is a monument erected to Nelson, about thirty feet in height, surmounted by his statue, with an inscription and relievos upon the pedestal.

E. T. COKE
A Subaltern's Furlough 1833

The city possesses some fine public buildings, of which the Catholic Cathedral is probably superior to any thing of the kind on the whole American Continent, or any structure of the 19th century. The funds failed before it was completed; the tower, therefore, and some of the exterior ornamental work are unfinished. It is of dark grey stone, and built after the Gothic style of architecture. The dimensions of the interior are 255 by 130 feet, and it is capable of containing 12,000 people, there being two galleries on each side of it. The vaulted roof is supported by eighteen columns, stained in bad imitation of marble, and with great want of good taste, has been chequered with alternate black and white stripes, which detract much from its beauty. At the south end, there is a large stained window, representing the ascension of our Saviour, but in my opinion executed in too gaudy a style to be pleasing: bright greens, and yellow, which are the predominant colours, neither have a good effect, nor do they throw a soft and mellowed shade over the body of the church.

E. T. COKE
A Subaltern's Furlough 1833

JAMES PATTISON COCKBURN

Notre Dame Street and the old cathedral of Notre Dame with the towers of the new cathedral rising behind the Seminary on the right, Montreal, Lower Canada   July 21, 1829

Water-colour, 12¾ × 16¼ inches

The principal mercantile street is St. Paul-street, or that running parallel with the shore, from which short cuts, at right angles, communicate with Notre Dame-street, where the principal merchants reside. These long corsos are rendered still longer by the suburbs of Quebec, and of Recollet and St. Antoine, whilst in the middle of Rue Notre Dame the suburb of St. Lawrence runs in the form of a long street to the west.

I did not perceive any very striking specimens of architecture in Montreal, any more than at Quebec. The principal are the Hotel Dieu, an excellent charity for the destitute sick, served by nuns, which is in St. Paul-street; the Court House, in Notre Dame-street is a plain and good building; the District Jail, and the Government House, are ancient and forlorn-looking edifices of some size. The old monastery of the Recollets finishes the west of Rue Notre Dame. The convent of the Soeurs Gris, or general hospital for the aged and infirm, and the convent of Notre Dame, a religious house of education, are buildings more useful than ornamental.

The Catholic cathedral is a large but not fine church, finished with singular bad taste in the interior; near it, is the Seminaire de St. Sulpice; and in the Recollet suburbs is the Petit Seminaire, or new college, which is an addition to the former establishment, and exhibits some correctness of taste in the plan on which it is laid out.

The old market-place and Post Office are in the lower town, but a new market-place has been built in the upper town. The barracks and other public buildings connected with the government have nothing very striking in their exterior.

The Place d'Armes, the largest open space in the city, offers nothing particular, excepting when filled by the citizens, to listen to the enlivening strains of a military band.

In the town, or rather in the suburbs, the prettiest spot I observed was the neighbourhood of the mouth of the Lachine canal, where the sombreness of the old town is altogether lost sight of; and the European traveller is gratified by seeing a well-finished and apparently well-planned canal send forth the riches of the upper country.

In this city, one is amused by seeing the never-changing lineaments, the long queue, the bonnet-rouge, and the incessant garrulity, of Jean Baptiste, mingling with the sober demeanour, the equally unchanging feature, and the national plaid, of the Highlander; whilst the untutored sons of labour, from the green isle of the ocean, are here as thoughtless, as ragged, and as numerous, as at Quebec. Amongst all these, the shrewd and calculating citizen from the neighbouring republic drives his hard bargains with all his wonted zeal and industry, amid the fumes of Jamaica and gin-sling.

R. H. BONNYCASTLE
The Canadas in 1841 1841

JAMES PATTISON COCKBURN

St. Paul Street looking towards the Bonsecours Church
and the Theatre Royal, Montreal, Lower Canada   July 20, 1829
Water-colour, 10¾ × 17¾ inches

The French cathedral in the Place
d'Armes is a large substantial stone-
building, built with little taste. The interior is, however, plentifully decorated
in the Catholic style, with all the para-
phernalia of that religion; and the size
of the building renders it a very commodious place of worship, and well
adapted for the accommodation of its
numerous congregation. In summer, a
great many people kneel outside the
church in preference to being within.

J. LAMBERT
Travels Through Canada and the United States
1814

PHILIP JOHN BAINBRIGGE

The Protestant and Catholic Cathedrals
of Montreal, Lower Canada
from near Mount Molson   1840
Water-colour, 6 × 10 inches

In the evening the Professor and an old friend of mine in the Engineers called on us. They told us that yesterday "a shove," as it is called, on the St. Lawrence took place; and as it was still moving, we had hopes of seeing it on the next morning. A shove is the ice formed up the river being broken by the force of the current, and driven violently against the sheet which covers the stiller water on the wide expanse opposite Montreal, when the whole mass with terrific crashes breaks up into huge fragments; the sheets which come hurrying down from the Ottawa and the upper part of the St. Lawrence rushing both under and over that which was stationary; when the whole confused mass drives against the island and shores of the river, sometimes sliding two hundred feet over the land, and rising twenty and thirty feet, and sometimes much more, against walls and other impediments in its way. The water from above, at the same time impeded by the mass of ice, rises many feet and floods the country. A large suburb of Montreal to the west of the city was yesterday under water, so that the inhabitants were compelled to move about in canoes; while, at the same time, they were greatly in fear that their dwellings would be completely ruined by the inundation. What with fires and floods the residents in Montreal seem to have an uneasy life of it. Mr. Logan gave me the following very interesting account of the packing of the ice in the St. Lawrence.

"The frost commences about the end of November, and a margin of ice of some strength soon forms along the shores of the river and around every island and projecting rock in it; and wherever this is still water, it is immediately cased over. The wind, acting on this glacial fringe, breaks off portions in various parts, and these proceeding down the stream, constitute a moving border on the outside of

HENRY JAMES WARRE   Montreal, Lower Canada from the frozen St. Lawrence River

the stationary one, which, as the intensity of the cold increases, is continually augmented by the adherence of the ice-sheets, which have been coasting along it; and as the stationary border thus robs the moving one, this still further outflanks the other, until in some parts the margins from the opposite shores nearly meeting, the floating ice becomes jammed up across the river. The first ice-bridge below Montreal is usually formed at the entrance of the river into Lake St. Peter, where the many channels into which the river is split up great assist the process.

"As soon as this wintry barrier is thrown across (generally towards Christmas), it of course rapidly increased by stopping the progress of the downward floating ice, which has by this time assumed a character of considerable grandeur, nearly the whole surface of the stream being covered with it. It moves in solid and extensive fields, and wherever it meets with an obstacle in its course, the momentum of the mass breaks up the striking part into huge fragments that pile over one another; or, if the obstacle be stationary ice, the fragments are driven under it and then closely packed. Beneath the constantly widening ice-barrier mentioned, an enormous quantity is thus driven, particularly where the barrier gains any position, where the current is stronger than usual.

"There is no place on the St. Lawrence

A fresh and most delightful day, with a bright sun and clear sky, while the cold was not too severe to be unpleasant. Accompanied by my old friend N———, we went down to the river to see the effects of the shove. Far as the eye could reach, the surface of the St. Lawrence was covered with blocks of ice, one overlapping the other, at an angle of about 45°. In some places the slabs had

been forced up to form hillocks, some ten to fifteen feet in height, the whole surface being far too rough to allow any person walking over it. Huge masses had been piled up eight or ten feet above the level of the quays, which the water had also covered, but that had much subsided, though still far above its usual height in summer. Further on, another huge pile of ice-blocks had been formed, still higher

than those near us; while beyond it again, to the westward, a long line like a reef of rock extended outward from a point of land running into the river, and which forms what we may properly call a "break-ice" to the quays in front of the city, and which, without the protection of this point, would be overwhelmed, if not completely destroyed. To comprehend fully the immense and destructive

Montreal (continued) (from other page 1840)

1840

Pencil drawing, 8¼ × 21 inches (two sheets)

tains a height of twenty, sometimes twenty-six feet above its summer level. It is at this period that the grandest movements of the ice occur. From the effect of packing and piling and the accumulation of the snows of the season, the saturation of these with water, and the freezing of the whole into a solid body, it attains the thickness of ten to twenty feet and even more; and after it has become fixed as far as the eye can reach, a sudden rise in the water, occasioned by some greater impediment from submerged ice lifting up a wide expanse of covering of the river, so high as to free it from the many points of rest and resistance, the vast mass is set in motion by the whole hydraulic power of this gigantic stream. Proceeding onward with a truly terrific majesty, it piles up over every obstacle it encounters, and when forced into a narrow part of the channel, the lateral pressure it there exerts drives the border ice up the banks, where it sometimes accumulates to the height of forty or fifty feet.

"In front of the town of Montreal, there has lately been built a fine revêtement wall of cut lime-stone, to the height of twenty-three feet above the summer level of the river. This wall is now a great protection against the effects of the ice. Broken by it, the ice piles on the street or terrace above it, and there stops; but before this wall was built, the sloping bank guided the moving mass up to those of gardens and houses in a very dangerous manner, and many accidents used to occur. I have seen it mount a terrace garden twenty feet above the bank, and crossing the garden, enter one of the principal streets of the town."

where all the phenomena of the taking, packing, and shoving of the ice, are so grandly displayed as in the neighbourhood of Montreal. The violence of the currents is here so great, and the river in some places expands to such a width, that whether we consider the prodigious extent of the masses moved, or the force with which they are propelled, nothing can afford a more majestic spectacle or impress the mind more thoroughly with a sense of irresistible power. Standing for hours together on the bank overlooking St. Mary's Current, or wandering up and down like a weary spirit on the shores of the Styx, I have seen league after league of ice crushed and broken against the barrier lower down, and there sub-

merged and crammed beneath; and when we consider that an operation similar to this occurs in various parts from Lake St. Peter upwards, it will not surprise us that the river should gradually swell. By the time the ice has become stationary at the foot of St. Mary's Current, the waters of the St. Lawrence have usually risen several feet in the harbour of Montreal; and as the space through which that current flows, between the island of St. Helen's and shelving ledges of trap, affords a deep and narrow passage for nearly the whole body of the river, it may well be imagined that when the packing here begins, the inundation rapidly increases.

"The water in the harbour usually at-

W. H. G. KINGSTON
Western Wanderings 1856

power of the ice, the scene I have described must be witnessed, and yet engineering science is now attempting to oppose this power in the wonderful bridge which is being thrown across the river.

Among this chaotic mass of ice were a few level spots, on one of which people were skating, in another men were engaged in sawing out slabs of ice to fill

the ice-houses in the city. They first marked a furrow on the ice with an ice-plough, which is in shape not very dissimilar to a common plough, and then with long saws they cut through the ice at right angles to the line marked by the plough. Other men with hooks dragged the slabs thus separated through the water to a spot where sleighs were in readiness to carry them off. The slabs

were under two feet in thickness, and four or five in length. The charge we were told for a hundred such blocks is three dollars; but whether delivered at the ice-house or on the river I know not. The water ran rapidly under the hole thus cut, and rose at once to the level of the ice, but did not overflow it.

W. H. G. KINGSTON
Western Wanderings 1856

HENRY JAMES WARRE   Sleighing in the country, Lower Canada   1842   Water-colour, 8¼ × 10½ inches

Sleighing in Montreal, Lower Canada

I begin not to disrelish the winter here; now I am used to the cold, I don't feel it so much: as there is no business done here in the winter, 'tis the season of general dissipation; amusement is the study of every body, and the pains people take to please themselves contribute to the general pleasure: upon the whole, I am not

sure it is not a pleasanter winter than that of England.

Both our houses and our carriages are uncommonly warm; the clear serene sky, the dry pure air, the little parties of dancing and cards, the good tables we all keep, the driving about on the ice, the abundance of people we see there, for

every body has a carriole, the variety of objects new to an European, keep the spirits in a continual agreeable hurry, that is difficult to describe, but very pleasant to feel.

FRANCES BROOKE
The History of Emily Montague 1769

PHILIP JOHN BAINBRIGGE

The fort at Chambly, Lower Canada   1838
Water-colour, 6 × 8½ inches

The town of William Henry, or Sorel, in latitude 45° 55', longitude 73° 22', is agreeably situated at the confluence of the Sorel or Chambly river, with the Saint Lawrence, and contains a protestant, and a Roman catholic church. The Sorel takes its rise from lake Champlain, and directing its course towards the north, runs through a fertile and pleasant country, where its borders are adorned by several valuable and productive farms. On the site of the town, a fort was constructed in 1665, by M. de Tracy, viceroy of New France, as a defence against the irruption of the Iroquois. M. de Sorel, a captain, superintended its execution, and from him this part of the river received its name. Between Lake Champlain, and the junction of this stream with the Saint Lawrence, there are two forts situated on its banks, the one called Saint John, composed of cedar pickets and earth, the other, Chambly, built of stone in a quadrangular form, and having the appearance of a castle. It is the only edifice in North America, which has any resemblance to that ancient mode of structure. Saint John is a frontier garrison, and a company of infantry, and some artillery, are generally stationed in it. As the channel of intercourse between Montreal and the United States of America, is principally through this post, a collector, and comptroller of the customs, always reside here. The country around Chambly, exhibits a romantic aspect; the river, in this part shallow, broken and diffused, rushes down a declivity, interrupted by rocks; an extensive and elevated mountain, of a pleasing shape, rears itself aloft, in the midst of level lands, and confines between its conical summits, a lake of pure water. In the months of June and July, great quantities of timber and boards formed into rafts, frequently of two or three hundred feet in length, are floated down this river, from the borders of lake Champlain. These materials are used in ship-building, and are also exported to England.

G. HERIOT
Travels Through the Canadas   1807

THOMAS DAVIES

A southeast view of Crown Point on the Richelieu River   1759
Water-colour, 12 × 18 inches

Early the next morning we left Ticonderoga, and pursued our voyage to Crown Point, where we landed to look at the old fort. Nothing is to be seen there, however, but a heap of ruins; for shortly before it was given up by the British, the powder magazine blew up, by which accident a great part of the works was destroyed; since the evacuation of it also, the people in the neighbourhood have been continually digging in different parts, in hopes of procuring lead and iron shot; a considerable quantity was in one instance got out of the stores that had been buried by the explosion. The vaults, which were bomb proof, have been demolished for the sake of the bricks for building chimneys. At the south side alone the ditches remain perfect; they are wide and deep, and cut through immense rocks of limestone; and from being overgrown towards the top with different kinds of shrubs, have a grand and picturesque appearance. The view from this spot of the fort and the old buildings in it overgrown with ivy, of the lake, and of the distant mountains beyond it, is indeed altogether very fine. The fort, and seven hundred acres of good cleared land adjoining to it, are the property of the state of New York, and are leased out at the rate of one hundred and fifty dollars, equal to £.33.10s. sterling per annum, which is appropriated for the use of a college. The farmer who rented it told us, he principally made use of the land for grazing cattle; these, in the winter season, when the lake was frozen, he drove over the ice to Albany, and there disposed of.

Crown Point is the most advantageous spot on the shores of Lake Champlain for a military post, not being commanded by any rising grounds in the neighbourhood, as Ticonderoga is, and as the lake is so narrow here, owing to another point running out on the opposite side, that it would be absolutely impossible for a vessel to pass, without being exposed to the fire of the fort. The Indians call this place Tek-ya-dough-nigarigee, that is, the two points immediately opposite to each other: the one opposite to Crown Point is called Chimney Point; upon it are a few houses, one of which is a tavern.

I. WELD
Travels Through the States of North America and the Provinces of Upper and Lower Canada 1799

JAMES HUNTER   A southwest view of St. John's on the Richelieu River   1779
Water-colour, 16 × 23 inches

St. John's is a garrison town; it contains about fifty miserable wooden dwellings, and barracks, in which a whole regiment is generally quartered. The fortifications are entirely out of order, so much so that it would be cheaper to erect fresh works than to attempt to repair them. There is a king's dock yard here, well stored with timber, at least, when we saw it; but in the course of the summer, after the armed brig which I mentioned was laid up, all the timber was sold off. The old hulks of several vessels of force were lying opposite the yard. In proportion to the increase of trade between New York and Lower Canada this town must improve, as it is the British port of entry on Lake Champlain.

The country about St. John's is flat, and very bare of trees, a dreadful fire in the year 1788 having done great mischief, and destroyed all the woods for several miles: in some parts of the neighbourhood the people suffer extremely during winter from the want of fuel.

I. WELD

Travels Through the States of North America and the Provinces of Upper and Lower Canada   1799

JAMES HOPE
The 7th Hussars in Quebec,
Lower Canada   1838
Water-colour,
6½ × 8¾ inches

The first symptoms of the Rebellion of 1837 showed themselves at Montreal, where it was immediately quashed. At St. Dennis and St. Charles, on the river Richelieu, the rebels made their first stand. At the latter place, Papineau and his self-styled "Sons of Liberty" formed a confederation, planted the tree and raised the cap of liberty. To drive them from these fortified strongholds, two brigades were dispatched from Montreal. The roads were in a wretched state for the transport of the troops: the mud, being frozen at top, but not sufficiently hard to bear the weight of the men, they broke through the crust and sunk deep at every step. The attack upon St. Dennis, under the command of the Honourable Colonel Gore, mis-carried, the troops being led to the attack when worn-out, jaded and dead-beat, after marching the whole of the night of the 22nd of November, over the vilest of Canadian roads, through which they had floundered knee-deep in mud; nor was it until ten o'clock in the morning of the 23rd that they reached St. Dennis, where they found the rebels occupying the village in great force.

The attack was led by Captain Markham, with the light company of the 32nd, and under a heavy fire from some fortified houses. The engagement lasted until near three o'clock in the afternoon, at which time Captain Markham, assisted by Lieutenant Inglis and a small party, in attempting to carry a building, was severely wounded, and brought to the ground; and, although Lieutenant Inglis kept up a fire, he was on the point of being made prisoner, when Sergeant Alcock, of his company, rushed forward and bore him away, the rebels all the time keeping up a murderous fire, from which Captain Markham received another wound whilst in the brave sergeant's arms.

The brigade being then threatened on all sides by the insurgents, who had received numerous reinforcements and seized a bridge in the rear, the largest field-piece being fixed immoveably by the frost in a deep rut, from which it could not be brought to bear, and the ammunition nearly all expended, Captain Markham's part was obliged to retire. Colonel Gore commenced a retrograde movement, leaving many prisoners and the howitzer in the hands of the rebels.

The brigade under Colonel Wetherel was completely successful. They left Montreal on the 18th of November, and had to contend with the same wretched roads and worse weather. He effected the passage of the Richelieu in an incessant downpour of rain, which froze as it fell, and was illuminated, for two hours, by the blue lights of the rebels. On arriving before St. Charles, Colonel Wetherel summoned the rebels to surrender. This was answered by a cheer of contempt. The gallant Colonel deployed his men, and instantly commenced an attack. The breast-works were stormed and carried. Most of the rebels ran, with the exception of about fifty, who knelt down and reversed their arms, thereby intimating that they surrendered themselves as prisoners. No sooner, however, did the troops advance to take them than the traitors opened a fire, by which a sergeant was killed and many men wounded. This act of treachery so exasperated the troops that the officers could not restrain their fury, and a general massacre ensued; and many were drowned in attempting to escape the enraged soldiery. The estimated loss of the rebels was about 300, killed and wounded.

On the first appearance of the troops

JAMES HOPE

The Grenadier Guards in Quebec, Lower Canada   Fall 1838
Water-colour, 9 × 13 inches

before St. Charles, the cowardly rebel leaders deserted, under pretence of procuring reinforcements; while Papineau and O'Callaghan, who had "Fled like crows when they smell powder" preferred viewing the engagement from the opposite side of the river; but the defenders of the village, some 1,500 in number, fought with a spirit worthy of a better leader and a better cause. A hundred stand of arms, a couple of French six-pounders (committed to the safe keeping of Richelieu) were taken; and among the trophies, the rebel standard, upon the pole of which was a wooden tablet, bearing the inscription "A Papineau, par ses concitoyens reconnaissans." On the arrival of the victorious brigade, under Wetherel, at Montreal, Sir John Colborne sent reinforcements to Colonel Gore, with instructions that he should follow up the advantages already gained, and reduce the disaffected country on the Richelieu.

At St. Dennis, the howitzers and wounded men were retaken, and the strongholds of the rebels reduced to ashes.

Upon the first intimation of the chance of rebellion in Lower Canada, Sir John Colborne did everything that a skillful commander could devise to be prepared to meet it; and, being cut off from all chances of succour from home, (the winter having set in) he instantly communicated with the governors of New Brunswick and Nova Scotia, in the event of requiring reinforcements; which reinforcements could only reach him by traversing the woods between those colonies and Quebec. In anticipation, therefore, of their services being required, engineers were despatched with parties of Indians to prepare camps or houses of refuge along the line of their intended route. There were at that time three regiments in Nova Scotia and New Brunswick; the 34th and 85th at Halifax, and the 43rd Light Infantry, divided into

wings, in garrison at St. John and Fredericton.

When affairs assumed a serious character in Lower Canada, and the line about to be taken by the disaffected became sufficiently evident, a despatch was sent to Fredericton, ordering the 43rd Light Infantry to pass "the Portage" of the Madawaska to Quebec; this they accomplished in thirteen days. Their arrival at Quebec was hailed as next to a miracle, and their exploits in performing such a march in the depth of a North American winter were the theme of universal admiration at the time.

They were subsequently followed by the 85th and 34th. The baggages of the regiments, as well as all the women and children, were left behind until the following summer; and it must be remarked of the inhabitants of New Brunswick, that they deserve the greatest credit for their loyalty and generous conduct; for, besides their public exertions to assist in

RICHARD GEORGE AUGUSTUS LEVINGE   The 43rd Regiment marching to Canada from New Brunswick
Arrival at the St. Lawrence River   December, 1837
Water-colour, 8 × 10¼ inches

every way the transport of the troops, the inhabitants of St. John entered into a subscription for the support of the women and children of the 43rd and 34th, who must have suffered severely had it not been for this most timely and charitable relief.

On the 12th of December, the first company of the 43rd Light Infantry left Fredericton in fifteen sleighs; and they were subsequently followed daily by the other five. A jolly Sub writes to his friend in the old country: "It certainly was a curious sight altogether. Our costumes — self, *par example,* wore four pairs of socks, (*i.e.* when I started) then mocassins, over which I had large worsted sort of long boots; P trowsers, thick P P coat, over that a coat made of seal-skin, rather *outré,* but very warm and comfortable; then a buffalo-skin muff, fur cap, ear covers, and lots of gloves, mits, boas, &c., oceans of baccy, and a short Indian pipe; to this we added a buffalo skin, to keep our legs warm, and we were each served out with a couple of blankets." Our friend, after describing the above "weather-proof" garments, adds, "My dog 'Bob' travelled with me, and helped to keep me warm." The officers all had snow-shoes, and twelve or fifteen pair were served out (each man ought to have had a pair) for the men of every company. They had extra socks, mocassins, ear-covers, throat-warmers, extra flannels, and a pair of blankets.

Rations of pork, biscuits, and rum were served out, and the regiment received field allowance.

The officers were allowed a sleigh for themselves and baggage, and a camp-kettle. Each sleigh, drawn by two horses, held eight men, and a camp-kettle was issued to each company. So far as Madawaska, the men were put up in private houses, and the officers at the inns or taverns. On the St. Lawrence they were almost universally put up in the convents, and received much hospitality from the jolly *Padres,* who were merry good fellows,

*"Round fat oily men of God as ever sang a psalm,
Or closed a penitential fee devoutly in their palm."*

On coming to the Arestook river the ice had not "made" sufficiently, and they had to cross in small canoes. This was a tedious operation, but, by lashing two canoes together, and placing the sleds singly or in pairs across them, it was effected after much delay. Some few accidents happened, but the contrivance was excellent, and is well worthy of imitation in the passage of a river; for by means of it immense loads are made capable of transportation, and it is absolutely impossible to uspet them.

After leaving the Madawaska, the troops reached the first camp on the left bank of the river of that name. "We were

PHILIP JOHN
BAINBRIGGE

St. Denis,
Lower Canada
1837

Water-colour,
6 × 8¾ inches

all heartily tired," says our Sub; "but, notwithstanding the snow-storm and cold, we were compelled to remain in the open air all night, it being impossible to stay any time in the camp, as they, and this one in particular, was dreadfully full of smoke. They were constructed with logs, about thirty feet in length by eighteen wide, open at the top and at the doors; and, with three persons only in them, were awfully cold. We had blazing fires, but, when our feet were burning, (which they constantly were) our heads were freezing; the tea froze a foot from the fire, and the thermometer inside the camp was at 29° *below zero*; the men were much better off and more comfortable: they were 'stowed' closer, but on the line of march they constantly had their feet, ears, or fingers frozen, and when we got in at night, we had the agreeable task of rubbing them with snow to restore circulation. The cooking went on outside, where a sentry always was. Well! at last we turned out our buffalo skins, ate our pork and biscuits, drank our tea and hot rum or brandy and water, and fell asleep, from which we usually awoke from the cold, and got up well bestiffened to renew our fires. Camping in the woods in winter in the Indian fashion is perfect 'feather-bed' work in comparison to this, as in the

former one is generally warm, but never suffocated, as in the latter. Worse camps than ours, and worse adapted to the purpose, could not possibly be made. We always had to wait some time for the provision-sleigh's arrival, and it was late at night generally before our and the men's dinners, frugal as they were, could be cooked; in addition to which, visiting the sentries at night, looking after and doctoring the men, were anything but recruiting. But, independently of leaving New Brunswick, I like it very much, and enjoyed the fun excessively."

On entering the Madawaska district, a part of Lower Canada, the troops were hospitably received by the inhabitants, and the officers in many instances were invited to private houses, and experienced much attention. I mention this, as it has been asserted that the inhabitants were disaffected. But their conduct towards the officers and the men of the three regiments, who passed through their country at a time when the population in their immediate neighbourhood were in open rebellion, gives the strongest contradiction to that report. Had they been otherwise than peaceably inclined, a few trees, felled across the route taken by the troops, might have seriously impeded their progress, and they could have done infinite mischief —

with comparatively little danger to themselves. I have adverted to this point, in the hopes of removing any erroneous impressions produced by slanderous reflections on the loyalty of these people.

On arriving at St. André, on the St. Lawrence, the leading company halted for the arrival of the second; and so on from thence to Point Levi, opposite to Quebec: they proceeded two companies at a time, having one hundred "Carioles" to each grand division. On reaching Point Levi, they were cheered tremendously, and the whole town of Quebec turned out to witness the passage of the St. Lawrence, which they accomplished in log canoes. The river was covered with huge masses of floating ice, on which, as it was propelled downwards by the stream, the men landed, hauled the canoe to the other side of the ice, re-embarked, and so on, until they reached the opposite shore. They were received by the Queen's Volunteers in their rough blanket coats, bands playing, and the whole population cheering vociferously. They were almost carried up to the Jesuits' Barracks, and were looked upon as having performed a miracle; and during their stay (for nine days) they were regularly fêted.

R. G. A. LEVINGE

Echoes from the Backwoods 1849

PHILIP JOHN BAINBRIGGE

The ruins of St. Eustache, Lower Canada, after the battle   1838
Water-colour, 6 × 9 inches

Sir John Colborne, after detaching Major Townsend with a part of the 24th, and the Volunteers of St. Andrews to St. Benoit, moved upon St. Eustache, and crossed the North Branch of the Ottawa, near St. Rose, on the 14th December, three miles below the village, with two brigades, and six field pieces; the Montreal Volunteer Cavalry, and the Montreal Rifle Corps, sending Captain Globinsky, with his Volunteer Militia to skirmish.

Colonel Maitland's brigade, consisting of the 32nd and 83rd, with the Montreal Cavalry, followed by Lieutenant-colonel Wetherall's brigade (the 2nd Battalion of the Royal Regiment, the Royal Montreal Rifles, and Globinsky's Volunteers) advanced to the attack, with Major Jackson, and the Royal Artillery under his orders.

Girod, who had the chief command, opened his fire from the houses of the town, which was soon silenced, and he fled; and Major Jackson, taking up a position in front of the fortified church and houses, and the advanced parties of the 32nd, 83rd, and Rifle Corps having cleared the houses and walls, he battered the church and adjoining buildings. The church, crowded with people, was soon rendered untenable; and a scene of slaughter ensued which may be readily imagined, when it is known that the rebels were completely surrounded from the able and cool measures adopted by the Commander-in-chief. The church and houses, including the *presbytere* or priest's house, and the nunnery, and those of Scott and Dr. Chenier, the rebel leaders, were on fire, and those who could not escape fell a prey to the flames. After an hour's firing, at 280 yards distance, and continued volleys of musketry from the Royals and Riflemen in the neighbouring houses, and that owing to the determined resistance made there and in the seignior's house, it was necessary to assault and carry the church and presbytery by the bayonet.

In this action — the most determined of the whole rebellion — the troops lost 1 private killed, 1 corporal and 7 wounded, whilst Major Gugy, the provincial aide-de-camp, received a severe wound whilst engaged in a storming party; 118 prisoners were made — but the number of killed and wounded of the enemy was never ascertained, but must have been enormous. Amongst the killed was Dr. J. O. Chenier, who was found dead in the yard of the church. F. Peltier fled with Girod.

Lieutenant-colonel Eden, Deputy Adjutant-general, Colonel Gore, Deputy Quartermaster-general, the personal staff, Majors Jackson and Macbean of the Royal Artillery, and Captain Foster of the Royal Engineers, received the honour of a most favourable mention of their services in the despatch to the Horseguards; and the Volunteers of Montreal having taken the garrison duty of that city, and thus enabled Sir John Colborne to quell this rebellious district, were most honourably noticed.

R. H. BONNYCASTLE
Canada, As It Was, Is, And May Be   1852

Sunday, November 4, 1838

It's an odd thing, that last night when we went to bed both Tina & I said we thought something was going to happen — Twice I awoke Edward, because we heard the dogs barking & the *Turkeys* making a noise — About 1 o'clock a messenger came saying there was a disturbance at Chateauguai & several British farmers had fled from the Canadian rebels — E. E. [Edward Ellice] had hardly come to bed again when we thought we heard a *hallo* — he opened the window & listened but all was still, & just as he was getting into bed a *yell* like the *Indian war cry*, burst close to the house, & guns fired at the same moment — struck the house, on all sides, breaking the windows &c Edward jumped *into* his clothes, & drag'd Tina & I *en chemise*, without shoes or stockings down stairs & put us thro' a trap door into the cellar — The house was surrounded on all sides, Edward & M! Brown taken prisoners, and were carried off we knew not where, leaving Tina & I alone, *en chemise*, in the middle of a group of the most "*Robespierre*" looking ruffians, all armed with guns, long knives, and pikes, without a single creature to advise us, every respectable person in the village being taken prisoner — What a day we passed sitting hand in hand, in the midst of a heap confusion, comforting each other, & praying for protection to Him who orders all things well. But it was a severe trial — The ruffian looking men coming in every now & then quite drunk — In the evening the priest came to see us, & we got leave to come to his house — What a wretched day & yet how much worse it might have been.

Wednesday, November 7, 1838

The whole house is surrounded by *Guards* — I sketched some of them from the window — picturesque ruffians —

JANE ELLICE
Diary

KATHERINE JANE ELLICE

The rebels at Beauharnois, Lower Canada
1838
Water-colour, 9¼ × 6½ inches

UPPER CANADA

When England terminated the Seven Years' War, it did not pursue an active policy of settlement west of Montreal until the Loyalists began pouring into British North America. Several groups of Loyalists and disbanded regiments occupied the newly surveyed townships forming the nucleus of the communities of Brockville, Cornwall, and Kingston, among others. James Peachey's View of the Loyalist encampment at Johnston (1784) and the Ruins at Fort Frontenac (1783), on the site of what was to become the Loyalist town of Kingston, are but small indications of the feverish activity that took place to create these new towns. Lord Simcoe, the first Lieutenant-Governor of the new province of Upper Canada, was sworn in at Kingston and called the first legislature at Niagara-on-the-Lake. This town was to remain the capital of the province until 1796 when it was moved to York, whose early beginnings Mrs. Hale depicted.

The close proximity of the aggressive new republic to the south after 1776 left the settlements along the St. Lawrence and the means of communication and transportation at the mercy of the Americans. This state of affairs motivated the construction of the Rideau Canal. The British Parliament paid the bills and the Royal Engineers built the canal between Bytown on the Ottawa River, and Kingston on Lake Ontario. The officer-artists who travelled along the canal were particularly struck by the impressive engineering feats that were necessary to construct the locks.

Upper Canada took hold and began to look settled by the 1840's, as Henry James Warre's sketches show. Land companies speculated and brought in immigrants. The shoreline communities of Trenton, Cobourg, Port Hope, and Toronto were jumping-off points for settlers, such as Catherine Parr Traill and her husband, who headed inland to take up cheap land in the backwoods of Perth, Peterborough, and Lindsay. The established community of Peterborough attracted the attention of the artist Edwin Whitefield in 1854 while he was touring the country making his large lithographs of the principal towns.

When General Simcoe moved the capital of Upper Canada to York and began building the road network that is the basis of Ontario's road system today, he determined the pattern of growth for decades to come. His Yonge Street connected with the Indian trails and portages and continued to Lake Huron. George Back travelled over this route on the way to the Arctic, passing through Fort William, which served as a starting point for the trip over what was to become the Dawson Road to the heart of Rupert's Land. Napier's views of Fort William and Slave Falls were taken on an expedition to investigate the feasibility of this route.

To the west, the energetic Simcoe built another road, which opened up the area now known as Western Ontario. Garrison towns, as depicted by Bainbrigge and Warre, protected the population and maintained order. The last half of the nineteenth century was characterized by waves of immigration which rapidly filled up the land contained by the shores of Lakes Ontario, Erie, and Huron. The settlement patterns established during these years determined the face of the future province of Ontario.

HENRY FRANCIS AINSLIE

A bateau descending the Lachine Rapids with the members of the 83rd Regiment and the mascot, a bear   May 24, 1843

Water-colour, 10 × 14 inches

The transport of merchandise, and other articles, from the island of Montreal to Kingston in Upper Canada, is, it has been remarked, conducted by means of bateaux, or flat-bottomed boats, narrow at each extremity, and constructed of fir planks. Each of these being about forty feet in length, and six feet across the widest part, generally contains twenty-five barrels, or a proportionate number of bales of blankets, cloths, or linens, and is capable of conveying, nine thousand pounds weight. Four men and a guide, compose the number of hands allotted for working a bateau. These are supplied with provisions, and with rum, and are allowed from eight to eleven dollars each, for the voyage to Kingston, and from thence down again to La Chine, the

time of performing which, is from ten to twelve days. The wages of the pilot or guide, amount to twelve or fourteen dollars. Each bateau is supplied with a mast and sail, a grappling iron, with ropes, setting poles, and utensils for cooking. The bateaux when loaded, take their departure from La Chine, in number, of from four, to eight or ten together, that the crews may be enabled to afford aid to each other, amid the difficulties, and laborious exertions required in effecting this voyage. About fifty bateaux are employed on this route, and bring down for the objects of commerce which are conveyed up, wheat, flour, salted provisions, peltry and potash.

From twenty to thirty bateaux are like-

wise kept in the service of government, for transporting necessaries for the troops, and stores for the engineer department; likewise articles of European manufacture, which are every year distributed in presents to the Indian tribes. There are thus engaged about three hundred and fifty men, whose occupation it is, during the sultry months of summer, to struggle against the most tremendous rapids. Besides these, near four hundred men ascend in bark canoes, by the grand river of the Outaouais, in a direct course to Saint Joseph's on Lake Huron, and from thence to the new establishment on Lake Superior, called Kamanastigua.

G. HERIOT
Travels Through the Canadas   1807

WILLIAM ROEBUCK

The lock on the Cascade Rapids on the St. Lawrence River, Lower Canada   1820
Water-colour, 11¼ × 17 inches

The cascades are about two miles in length, and flow among three different islands. The rapidity and force of the stream, arising from the great declivity of its bed, and the number of rocks and cavities which it contains, causes it to break into masses of white foam, moving in a direction the reverse of that of waves produced in a troubled ocean, by the agency of storms. They curl their resplendent tops, towards the quarter from whence they are impelled. The mind of a stranger is filled with admiration, on beholding, in the calmest and finest weather, all the noise, effect, and agitation, which the most violent conflict between the winds and waters is capable of exhibiting.

In a branch of these cascades, near the locks on the western shore, several bateaux, loaded with soldiers belonging to the army under the command of the late Lord Amherst, were lost in 1760, through ignorance of the pilots who undertook to conduct them. Somewhat higher up, on the same coast of the river, and not far from the land, is the Split Rock, close to which, the boats pass, in descending. The current sweeps along the side of this rock, and great attention in steering is required, for, on a too near approach, the bateau would be subject to the danger of being lost.

G. HERIOT
Travels Through the Canadas   1807

We now entered the Cornwall Canal, which cost the Government £60,000; it is eleven and a half miles long, and has seven locks. They are worth examining from their size and the solidity of their construction. Close to the canal is the town of Cornwall, a place of some size, with a population of about two thousand.

Opposite Cornwall, on the south bank, is the village of St. Regis, inhabited by Iroquois Indians. Here the boundary-line between Lower Canada and the State of New York strikes the St. Lawrence. Thus the territory going upwards on the left hand is that of the United States, while that on the right is of the Province of Upper or Western Canada.

It is a curious way in which one literally steps up the St. Lawrence by means of these canals. The huge vessel glides into a space between two stone walls, with a gate at the farther end—a gate is closed behind her, the water which comes from above is slowly let into the space, and as gradually she rises a new country is seen from her deck. The front gate is then open, and she having attained an upper level even with another space, the same process is repeated; or, if there is only one lock at that place, she paddles on along the canal, splashing with her paddle-wheels the muzzles of the sage old cows, who look calmly up at her as they crop the grass in the green fields through which she passes, or putting to flight herds of frisky young colts, or innocent lambs, who cannot make out, for their lives, what strange noisy monster has got into their nursery. To be sure, this process of mounting locks is somewhat tedious after the novelty of the thing has worn off; but then again, as one may be walking about, or eating, or sleeping, or reading, or drawing, or talking, it is one's own fault if one cannot find amusement inside the vessel. Thus our huge steamer was carried up a hill some hundred feet in height without any further manual exertion than that employed by the old lock-keepers in turning the windlasses to open the gates and let in the water. They even do not hurry themselves, and I was amused by seeing a fellow munching an apple as he slowly turned his winch.

W. H. G. KINGSTON
Western Wanderings 1856

H. S.

The Long Sault and the canal on the St. Lawrence River near Cornwall, Canada West
1849
Water-colour, 13¼ x 19¼ inches

After so many [legal] authorities directly supporting the Case of the American Loyalists, little more need be said to prove the legality and justice of their claim upon the nation. They were, and yet are as perfectly subjects of the British State, as any man in London or Middlesex. They were as much bound by all the obligations and duties of the society, and consequently as much entitled to the protection and justice of the State; and therefore, the Crown can have no greater right to sacrifice their property to the public safety, than that of any other subject, without compensation. They have been called on by their Sovereign, when surrounded by tumult and rebellion, to defend the Supreme Rights of the Nation, and to assist in suppressing a rebellion, which aimed at their destruction. They have received from the highest authority the most solemn assurances of *protection*, and even *reward*, for their *"meritorious services."* These Calls, and these Assurances, have been repeated again and again, during the times of the greatest danger, and even after many hundred had fallen victims to the unrelenting cruelties of the Rebel States, on no other account but that of their allegiance to their Sovereign, and fidelity to their fellow-subjects in Great Britain. They have, notwithstanding those cruelties, at every hazard, and in the face of the most imminent danger, obeyed those calls, and generously stept forth in defence of the Supreme Authority of the State.

ANONYMOUS
The Case and Claim of the American Loyalists Impartially Stated and Considered   1783

JAMES PEACHEY
Encampment of the Loyalists at Johnston, a New Settlement on the banks of the St. Lawrence River   June 6, 1784
Water-colour, 5½ × 13¾ inches

The village of Johnstown, which is near a mile in length, and designed to extend a mile in breadth, is placed in the township of Edwardsburg. From hence, decked vessels of considerable burthen may be navigated to Kingston, from thence to Niagara, or to any part of Lake Ontario. The islands opposite to this township are numerous; the principal are Hospital island, and Isle du Forte Levy, where the French formerly had a small garrison, to defend the lower settlements, from the irruptions of the Iroquois. La Galotte is a part of the great river, in which the current flows with much rapidity, although the waters are, in very few places, broken.

G. HERIOT
Travels Through the Canadas   1807

We saw little in the town of Prescott to interest or please. After an excellent breakfast we embarked on board the Great Britain, the finest steamer we had yet seen, and here we were joined by our new friends, to our great satisfaction.

C. P. TRAILL
The Backwoods of Canada   1836

HENRY FRANCIS AINSLIE

The steamer *Great Britain*, the largest vessel on Lake Ontario   1839
Water-colour, 9 × 12½ inches

We now once more embarked in a steam-boat on the waters of the St. Lawrence. This vessel was one of the finest we had yet observed on our route. It was called the "Great Britain," was worked by very fine engines, and re-sembled a floating village in its extent, and was so remarkably fast in its motion, that our night transit was scarcely per-ceptible. We left Prescott before mid-night; but having the wind ahead, and a strong current to oppose, we made but little way; and when morning broke, had, therefore, full leisure to gaze upon the majestic flood and its beautiful shores.

R. H. BONNYCASTLE
The Canadas in 1841   1841

On Friday evening, the expedition under Col. Dundas landed near the Windmill below Prescott. He took up a position on a rising ground, about 400 yards from the Houses and Mill occupied by the Brigands. Major MacBean R.A. placed two 18 Pounders advantageously in the field, the one to batter the Houses and the other on the left to act against the Mill. The Brigands not venturing out of the buildings, though they kept up a constant fire. Major MacBean opened his heavy guns upon the Buildings with great effect. The masonry of the Windmill, however, was so strong, that but little impression was made against it. Captain Sandom, R.N., with two Gun Boats and a Steamboat, took up a position in the River below the Mill, which he cannonaded with two 18 Pounders, but could not succeed in effecting a breach in the wall. It being now late and daylight wearing away, Col. Dundas moved closer to the buildings, the Militia acting on both flanks, and so posted as to prevent the escape of the Brigands, and supported by a company of the 93rd Highlanders, under Major Arthur, on march from Cornwall, who joined just as Col. Dundas was taking up his position. A fire of Musketry was opened by the Brigands from the House, which was quickly replied to by our gallant fellows, and a Howitzer being moved down to the left, opened upon the building, which the Pirates evacuated under cover of the darkness, and concealed themselves in the Brushwood on the bank behind the Mill, where they were subsequently captured by the Militia, among whom was one of the leaders, a Pole, named Van Schultz. The Buildings on the left of the Mill being now gained, were set fire to and a white flag having been displayed from the Mill, Col. Dundas, with that humanity always a prominent attribute of the truly brave, accepted an unconditional surrender, when eighty-seven prisoners were marched out of the Mill, and sixteen more wounded, subsequently carried out.

Ten barrels of powder and several stands of arms and ten thousand rounds of ball cartridge were found in the mill. Three pieces of artillery which had been placed in front of the door of the mill on a battery constructed of loose stones, were also captured. All the houses in the possession of the brigands were set on fire, except the mill, which was occupied during the night by a company of Militia.

KINGSTON
Chronicle and Gazette   November 17, 1838

Fort Wellington stands at the eastern end of the town and, viewed from a distance westward, seems to block King street, the highway (the King's Highway as it was wont to be called) taking a bend towards the river at this point. The fort was built during the war of 1812, apparently to hold in check the Americans who were ever on the look-out to pounce upon reinforcements and supplies for the British military points above. The original building was of timber; this was replaced by the present stone erection in 1837-8. It is a substantial square building situated in the centre of an earthwork enclosure. The entrance to the latter is through a massive gateway on the north side. From this entrance a wide dyke runs either way. On the south-front there is an earth-covered stone sally-port extending into the dyke. Its sides are pierced with loopholes to be used for clearing the dyke should a storming party attempt to scale the earthworks. Some distance beyond the walls there is a tall fence of thick poles stuck in the ground close together, and from the steep sides of the earthworks similar poles, with pointed ends, stick out "like quills upon the fretful porcupine." The earthworks enclose a considerable space and are very wide, having broad sloping roads on each side to enable troops to quickly gain the summit, transport cannon, &c. In the old days four pieces of artillery were mounted at the corners of the embankment, but only the iron runways are to be seen now. The fort building, or block-house as it was originally called, has several floors, the first comprising vaulted chambers intended to be used for the storage of arms and ammunition; the upper stories are fitted up as barracks. The top storey is of heavy timber, with an over-hanging covered gallery running entirely round. This gallery is pierced with numerous windows and loopholes. The roof is covered with bright tin. As a military work the fort can hardly be regarded as a success. History fails to record a single instance wherein its utility was demonstrated. When in 1813 Wilkinson desired to get past Prescott he simply had to land his troops on the American shore and march them down a mile or so; the boats being floated down by a few men at night. We are told that "an active bombardment was kept up on them the whole night without, however, doing much damage." It would no doubt have been a stronghold in the days of attacks by Indians, but a very few years after it was built it must have been plain to military men that to coop troops up in such a place would be to ensure their certain destruction. The fort is commanded by high ground in the rear, from whence it would be easy to carry away the wooden roof and complete the work of destruction by dropping a few shells within the walls and enclosure. If captured by an enemy it might be used to destroy the town. So, considering all things, the order for its dismantlement was a wise one. The Royal Canadian Regiment was quartered here for some time. Within the lines there are all necessary buildings, officers' quarters, guard-room, &c., and the fort itself is in good repair.

During Lord Lisgar's sojourn in Canada a very spirited sham fight took place at the fort. An old soldier who was present assured me that it was the most real sham fight he ever took part in. The "garrison" at present consists of one man, Sergt. Press, a veteran artilleryman.
Canadian Illustrated News   January 5, 1878

ABOVE
HENRY FRANCIS AINSLIE

Prescott, Upper Canada. The site of the "Battle of the Windmill"   1839
Water-colour, 9 × 12½ inches

ANONYMOUS

A militia encampment at Fort Wellington, Prescott, Ontario   ca. 1867
Water-colour, 9¼ × 13½ inches

BROCKVILLE

The District Town of the Johnstown District, in the county of Leeds, situated on the St. Lawrence, fifty-six miles east from Kingston; the eastern road passing through it. It was laid out in 1802, and is now incorporated. This is a handsome town, most of the houses and other buildings being constructed of stone, many of which have cut fronts. Being situated on a bed of lime stone, this material is found the cheapest that can be used for building, and its general adoption gives the town a very substantial appearance. Granite is also to be obtained in the immediate neighbourhood of the town, but being harder to work is not at present used. The court house and jail is a handsome stone building. There are six churches and chapels, viz., Episcopal, Catholic, Presbyterian, Methodist, Baptist and Congregational, all of which are of stone. During the season, the steamboats call here regularly, on their passages to and from Montreal and Kingston. A road is constructed from this place to Perth, the capital of the Bathurst District, which is about 40 miles northwest. Two newspapers are published here weekly, the "Statesman," and the "Brockville Recorder." On an island, or rather rock, in the St. Lawrence, opposite the town, is a block house, where are stationed a few rifles.

W. H. SMITH
Smith's Canadian Gazetteer
1846

Population, 2111.

Post Office, post every day.

The following government and district offices are kept in Brockville: Judge of District Court, Sheriff, Treasurer, Clerk of Peace, Registrar of County of Leeds, do. of Surrogate Court, Collector of Customs, Inspector of Licenses, Superintendent of Schools, Clerk of District Court, District Clerk, Deputy Clerk of Crown.

Professions and Trades — Three physicians and surgeons, seven lawyers, one grist mill, eighteen stores, four tanneries, two asheries, one bookseller, one brewery, one foundry, two printers, two saw mills, three chemists and druggists, ten taverns, four waggon makers, four blacksmiths, two tinsmiths, two gunsmiths, two watchmakers, two saddlers, six tailors, eight shoemakers, three cabinet makers, six groceries, two hatters, four bakers, three painters, two bank agencies — "Montreal," and "Commercial."

Forwarders and Commission Merchants. — Sanderson & Murray, H. & S. Jones.

Land Agent. — Andrew N. Buell.

Principal Tavern. — "Wilson's."

ROBERT ACKERMANN
The Court House and jail on the north side of Court House Square, Brockville, Canada West   ca. 1850
Water-colour, 13¼ × 20½ inches

HENRY FRANCIS AINSLIE
Gananoque Mills, Upper Canada   1839
Water-colour, 9 × 12½ inches

A few miles from Kingston, is Gananoqui, a small village at the mouth of a river of the same name, where some of the steam-vessels take in fuel, and where there is now established a set of mills, principally for flour, which are, perhaps, the most valuable in Canada, as well as the best conducted. I was indeed surprised, on a subsequent visit to this interesting spot, to see such an establishment reared, as it were, in the bosom of the forest, and possessing machinery of the most expensive and complicated description, for all the various operations of reducing grain to its different conditions of use and food. This establishment is set in motion by the falling waters of the Gananoqui, and is the property of the Messrs. M'Donell, who are extremely obliging to strangers, and allow a free inspection of the various buildings and machinery. The Gananoqui flour is deservedly celebrated in the Canadian markets, and is, in the finer qualities, quite as good as any manufactured either in the United States, or in Great Britain.

R. H. BONNYCASTLE
The Canadas in 1841   1841

JAMES PEACHEY
The ruins of Fort Frontenac   June 1783
Water-colour, 12¾ × 20¼ inches

Kingston is an ancient settlement. It was first called Cataraqui, and was established by French missionaries, as a post amongst the Iroquois. Father Henessin [Hennepin] gives a short account of its foundation, and informs us that it was soon discovered to be so advantageous a situation for the command of the interior, that a large fort, with four bastions, was erected by order of Count Frontenae, [Frontenac] then governor-general of Canada, as a bulwark against the excursions of the Iroquois, and to interrupt the fur trade carried on between those powerful Indians and the inhabitants of New York and the Hollanders, who had just settled a new colony; and so important did Fort Frontenae appear in the eyes of the French, that it was speedily strengthened and enlarged to the circumference of three hundred and sixty toises, and adorned with freestone, which they found naturally polished by the action of the water upon the brink of Lake Ontario, or Frontenae.

La Galle [La Salle], whose unfortunate adventures in discovering the Mississippi are well known, was the commander under whose directions this fort was finished, and it took two years to complete. Henessin's account of its site is not the most intelligible; but there still remained, in 1830, enough of the old work extant, to show its former strength, in the shape of a tower and a triangular building, which surrounded one of the bastions.

The French had also a small naval establishment at Frontenae; and a few years ago one of their schooners was raised from the bottom of the lake, and shown as a curiosity.

Frontenae, of course, fell into the hands of the British, and soon became a place of the greatest importance in Upper Canada; and the name was again changed to Kingston. From 1784 to the present time, such has been its extension, that it now presents a front of more than a mile in length, along the low shore of Lake Ontario, and the somewhat more rapid bank of the Great Cataraqui River; whilst its extent towards the country is nearly half that distance, and is every year gaining on the fields and woods.

R. H. BONNYCASTLE
The Canadas in 1841   1841

HENRY HIGGINS DONATUS O'BRIEN   Point Henry and Point Frederick from the infantry barracks at Kingston, Upper Canada

The bay adjoining to Kingston affords good anchorage, and is the safest and most commodious harbour on all Lake Ontario. The bay of Great Sodus, on the south side of the lake, and that of Toronto, situated on the north side of the lake, nearly in the same meridian with Niagara, are said to be the next best to that of Kingston; but the entrance into each of them is obstructed by sand banks, which in rough weather cannot be crossed without imminent danger in vessels drawing more than five or six feet water. On the borders of the bay at Kingston there is a King's dock yard, and another which is private property. Most of the British vessels of burthen on Lake Ontario have been built at these yards. Belonging to his Majesty there were on Lake Ontario, when we crossed it, three vessels of about two hundred tons each, carrying from eight to twelve guns, besides several gun boats; the last, however, were not in commission, but laid up in Niagara River; and in consequence of the ratification of the treaty of amity and commerce between the United States and his Britannic Majesty, orders were issued, shortly after we left Kingston, for laying up all the vessels of war, one alone excepted.

I. WELD
Travels Through the States of North America and the Provinces of Upper and Lower Canada   1799

After visiting the English dock-yard at Kingston, where there were two first-rate line-of-battle ships on the stocks, and several frigates nearly ready for launching, I felt anxious to take a look at Sackett's Harbour, the American naval station, which lies also at the eastern end of Lake Ontario. Accordingly, on the morning of the 6th of August, I crossed the northern branch of the River St. Lawrence in a four-oared gig to Long Island, which lies nearly in the middle of this immense stream. Here I got a waggon, and was rattled for about seven miles over a turnpike, as they called it — Corduroy, however — to the southern side of the island, or that which faces the American shore. The ferry-boat had been taken over the water in quest of a doctor. I don't know a more hopeless predicament for a traveller, or one where he feels his resources so completely exhausted, and sometimes also his patience, than at a ferry where there is no boat. When I did get across at last, I had the mortification to learn that the stage had just started.

The waves from Lake Ontario were rolling into Sackett's Harbour quite in oceanic style, and I had the discomfort of getting soundly ducked in crossing to the navy-yard. I had plenty of daylight, however, for examining at leisure the large three-decked ship which is on the stocks there. It is said that she was built in thirty-one days from the time the first tree was cut down; and I met an American gentleman on the spot, who told me he had been present at the time when this singular operation was accomplished. An im-

ca. 1825   Water-colour, 6½ × 24 inches

mense number of shipbuilders, it seems, all expert workmen, were sent from New York, and other seaport towns. These were assisted by an unlimited number of labouring hands, teams of oxen, horses, carts, and so on. In a couple of weeks more, he told me, she might have been launched, and all her guns, masts and sails on board, ready for action. The treaty of Ghent put a stop to these proceedings; and as it was stipulated by an article in that instrument that neither party should have a force on the lakes, these great ships, both at Sackett's and at Kingston, have come to serve no further end, in the meantime, than the innocent purpose of amusing the perennial crowds of Cockney tourists, who escape in autumn from the Malaria of the southern and middle states, and fill up the time by taking the well-beaten round of the Falls, the Lakes, and the Springs of Saratoga.

B. HALL
Travels in North America in the Years 1827 and 1828   1829

On nearing the harbour, the first object is the strong modern fortification which crowns the promontory of Point Henry, about 100 feet above the level of the lake, and commanding an exceedingly narrow entrance between Cedar Island and Hamilton Cove. Here the eye is struck by a very pleasing scene. On a verdant slope facing the picturesque rocks of Cedar Island, and commanding a beautiful view of the opening of the lake, stands the garrison hospital, an extremely neat building of dark blue stone, with a shining tin roof, and ample verandah in front, under which, in the hottest summer days, the patients can walk and enjoy the air. Such evident attention as is manifested by the British Government on all occasions, and in every corner of the globe, towards the well-being and comfort of those who protect and uphold the honour of their country, cannot fail to strike a foreigner with the liveliest impression.

Passing the hospital and the guns of Fort Henry, a noble prospect suddenly

expands. The opening of the lake is seen in the distance; the town of Kingston begins to show itself; and the vessel glides past Navy Bay and Point Frederick, between which the eye rested, in days of yore, on several enormous hulls of first-rate men-of-war and frigates, with the customary appendages of a large royal dock and ordnance wharf.

Every thing now bears a military aspect. The huge ships, the powder magazines, the forts and batteries, the sentries passing their rounds, a fine range of storehouses built of a beautiful white stone, and a long row of neat barracks for the persons in the employ of the navy, are objects concentrated on a spot admirably chosen for the defence of the harbour, and serving as a key to the great inland seas of the interior.

R. H. BONNYCASTLE
The Canadas in 1841   1841

HARRIET CARTWRIGHT   Kingston, Upper Canada   1832   Water-colour, 6¾ × 9¼ inches

Kingston is a place of very considerable trade, and it is consequently increasing most rapidly in size. All the goods brought up the St. Lawrence for the supply of the upper country are here deposited in stores, preparatory to their being shipped on board vessels suitable to the navigation of the lake; and the furs from the various posts on the nearer lakes are here likewise collected together, in order to be laden on board bateaux, and sent down the St. Lawrence. Some furs are brought in immediately to the town by the Indians, who hunt in the neighbouring country, and along the upper parts of the St. Lawrence, but the quantity is not large. The principal merchants resident at Kingston are partners of old established houses at Montreal and Quebec. A stranger, especially if a British subject, is sure to meet with a most hospitable and friendly reception from them, as he passes through the place.

I. WELD
Travels Through the States of North America and the Provinces of Upper and Lower Canada   1799

Kingston, the largest and most considerable town in Upper Canada, though not the seat of government, opens with a fine effect as you pass the Fort and enter the Bay.... The town of Kingston is well laid out, with some handsome churches, &c. and many excellent private mansions, substantially built of stone. Our quarters in Meyers' Hotel were extremely comfortable, and we reached town in time to attend service in the Episcopal Church. It was pleasing again to listen to the peal of the organ, and the solemn liturgy of our church, in a land yet but half emerged from a savage state; and we had a most excellent sermon from Mr. C., the worthy and exemplary clergyman of the place. Kingston is a place of trade, for which it is well situate, and appears to be in a prosperous state. It is also a military and naval station. The population, I believe, is above three thousand souls.

A. FERGUSSON
Practical Notes Made During a Tour in Canada   1831

Kingston, which might just as well have retained its Indian appellation, is laid out with some regularity, the principal streets being sixty-six feet in width, and running towards the cardinal points, and consequently at right angles to each other. The lower part of the town, near the lake and river, is very level and convenient; but the ascent towards the newer part is rather sudden, along the edge of the limestone rocks, which then begin to show themselves, and are but scantily covered with soil. The superior portion of the town is beautifully laid out on a vast plateau of rock, which is singularly even and level, and extends a long way towards the woods.

R. H. BONNYCASTLE
The Canadas in 1841   1841

PHILIP JOHN BAINBRIGGE
Kingston Mills Locks on the Rideau Canal   1841
Water-colour, 7 × 10½ inches (detail)

This military canal will require a considerable sum of money; but probably there never was any expense better bestowed. For the cost of transporting ordnance and other stores by the direct route of the St. Lawrence, up the rapids, is so enormous, that the saving of a few years on this item alone will repay the whole outlay. The essential advantage, however, and one which, in my opinion, we cannot relinquish without risk of national dishonour, is the perfect security it affords of being able to send troops and stores backwards and forwards, in the event of hostilities, with that rapidity which constitutes the chief desideratum in defensive warfare. It must be remembered that we are pledged in a thousand ways to assist the Canadians in defending their country; and, as long as they perform their part of the international contract, we are bound to shrink from no means of rendering them secure. But without the completion of the Rideau Canal, our fellow-countrymen the Canadians can feel none of that security which our superior means enable us to give them. Any hesitation, therefore, on our part, at this stage of the business, will load us with the responsibility of future disasters. Our present duty is most clear — and though its execution be somewhat costly, its imperative character is not altered on that account. There can be no doubt as to what we ought to do, were a war to break out to-morrow. But a moment's reflection will show, that the obligation is equally binding upon us in advance, as it will be in that contingency.

B. HALL
Travels in North America in the Years 1827 and 1828   1829

PHILIP JOHN BAINBRIGGE   Jones Falls on the Rideau Canal, Upper Canada   1838
Water-colour, 6 × 8½ inches

The other prominent works on the canal are, Brewer's Lower Mills Lock, ten miles and a half; Brewer's Upper Mills, two locks, one mile and three quarters; and Jone's Falls, eleven miles. Here the scenery is very wild and striking, and the works are extremely grand, there being a dam sixty-one feet high, 130 yards broad, sixty feet wide at bottom and twelve feet at top, built of sandstone, and backed with clay and rock, so that the base and rock are supposed to be between three and four hundred feet. There is a waste weir cut fifteen feet into the solid granite; a single lock of fifteen feet two inches lift, leads into a natural basin, which connects it with three other combined locks, two having fifteen feet lift each, and the other thirteen. These splendid locks are built of solid sand-

stone masonry, upon inverted archwork, and although with such extraordinary lifts, have hitherto suffered no derangement, and answer perfectly.

R. H. BONNYCASTLE
The Canadas in 1841   1841

In the beginning of June, we embarked in the small steamer, 'Otter,' towing barges containing the men of the detachment of the 14th Regiment, and began the navigation of the Rideau Canal, which connects — by a series of locks and dams, of most expensive workmanship (and which cost upwards of a million) — the waters of the Ottawa with those of Lake

Ontario, and thus avoiding the United States frontier.

We found the Rideau a hot ditch at this season, and beginning to be infested with musquetoes; there was no casing to the hot funnel of the steamer, which also added to our discomfort. It was painful to witness the hundreds of acres, which had unavoidably been drowned by reason of the dams, and to see the dead trees of the forest standing, with their grey trunks and leafless boughs, like ghosts in the water. Sometimes we navigated lakes, and in the evening had an opportunity of fishing for bass, or paddling in a canoe; "a trick" I first acquired among the Burmans of the Irrawaddy.

J. E. ALEXANDER
L'Acadie   1849

GEORGE SETON   The 'drowned land' on the Rideau Canal, Upper Canada   1862
                                Water-colour, 6¼ × 9¾ inches

It may now however experience a re-action from the Rideau Canal communicating with the lake here, and be again restored to its former prosperity. This canal continues up the inlet of the Bay until it reaches the first locks at the mills, five miles distant: the masonry and the whole workmanship connected with them are much superior to those upon the Erie or Chesapeake and Ohio Canals. The total number of locks between Kingston and Bytown, upon the Ottawa River, 136 miles distant, is 47; their length about 140, breadth 33, and depth 16 or 17 feet. Dams, upon a very extensive scale, have been had recourse to throughout the line of canal, instead of excavations as in England. Where such works have been thrown across marshes, or the Rideau River, in order to swell the Rapids and form a navigable stream, so vast an extent of stagnant water (in one place 10,000 acres) has been created as to render the settlements in the vicinity exceedingly unhealthy. I saw many of the workmen at the mills who were perfectly helpless from the marsh fever they had caught. These large inundations, however, in a few years will destroy the drowned forest, and a quantity of valuable land may then be reclaimed by small embankments. The whole work was completed at an expense to the Imperial Government of £700,000. In the event of war with our neighbours, it will be found invaluable for the transportation of military stores and troops from the lower to the upper province, without being subject as heretofore to captures from the American force upon the St. Lawrence, or to running the gauntlet of the batteries upon their bank of the river. Like the Erie, in the State of New York, it will also encourage settlers along the whole line, as an outlet is now opened for the produce of their farms. Two steamers were at this time continually running between the Ottawa and Ontario, and the traffic of heavy boats also appeared considerable.

E. T. COKE
A Subaltern's Furlough 1833

HENRY FRANCIS AINSLIE
Entrance to the Rideau Canal at Bytown, Upper Canada   1839
Water-colour, 6 × 8½ inches

The great mass of work is now approached, which forms the exitus of the canal. A deep cut of three quarters of a mile, commands notice from the traveller; its average depth is twenty-five feet, through stiff clay, and it was executed with infinite trouble and labour. A basin surrounded by an embankment, with flood-gates to drain the canal, merits notice; and the stupendous system of locks, eight in number, cannot be adequately described in a small space. They have a total lift of eighty-one feet from the surface of the lowest summer level of the Ottawa, and are built of a durable limestone hewn out of the surrounding rocks, and cemented with an excellent material discovered on the opposite shores of the Great River, which has been extensively used on the whole line, and is known by the name of Hull cement.

The tourist has now arrived at the Sappers' Bridge, and at By-Town, which is 328 miles distant from Toronto, 157½ from Kingston by the old route, 127½ by the new, in 45° 24' north latitude, 75° 53' west longitude.

If ever any man deserved to be immortalized in this utilitarian age, it was Colonel John By. Difficulties which no one can form any idea of, excepting those who knew him well and watched his progress, were continually in his way; and although the expenditure he made may appear enormous, yet it is to be considered, that the splendid canal he executed, perhaps one of the finest works of the kind in the world, was executed in a very short time, in a country where forest and flood, silence and shadow, had before reigned undisturbed; in a country the seat of pestilential fever and ague, the paradise of water-snakes and reptiles, of mud and marshes — where the best, or indeed the only mode of progress, was in the frail bark canoe of the Indian, and where even that dangerous vehicle was continually subject to be torn asunder in its march over the sullen waters by the submerged trees.

With a department to form, civil engineers to make, workmen to advise and instruct, Colonel By took charge of this important national work, in September 1826, with a view of forming a military winter communication from the Ottawa to Lake Ontario, so as to avoid the tedious, dangerous navigation of the rapids of the St. Lawrence, and the necessity of transporting stores and troops by a line exposed, in the greatest part of its length, to an enterprizing enemy.

R. H. BONNYCASTLE
The Canadas in 1841   1841

HENRY FRANCIS AINSLIE   Chaudière Falls on the Ottawa River at Bytown, Upper Canada, with the collapsed bridge   1839
Water-colour, 9 × 12½ inches

One of the most picturesque, wild, and stormy falls in Canada, is that called the Chaudière, or Cauldron, of the Ottawa. It is situated at By-Town. The River Ottawa, or the Great River, as it is called, divided the ancient province of Lower Canada from its more youthful sister; and here, Colonel By, with his usual energy, undertook to connect the flourishing settlements of Hull, by a series of bridges, with By-Town, in order to obtain supplies of materials and provisions, and to open up a fertile tract of country.

As the falls are divided by rocky islets, and are only broad at one spot, Colonel By formed a series of stone and simple wooden bridges, connecting the shores and islets, until he came to the great space immediately in front of the Cauldron, over which he threw an arch of timber-work two hundred and twelve feet in span. This chasm is in front of a roaring, turbulent cataract, thirty feet in sheer descent, in which it was, of course, vain to look for any support from below, by piles, or other substantial contrivances. The mode he took was, to make a rope-bridge, mixed with chain-cables, upon which a series of trestles was placed, and on these the timber arch was gradually and successfully laid, a large barge having been, with infinite labour, previously moored in the middle of the torrent, upon which a very strong trestle was fixed, to secure the crown of the arch from sinking during the formation of the roadway and work.

The spring of 1828 was remarkable for a heavy flood on the Ottawa, and masses of ice having floated down the falls, struck the barge, with such force, that the bridge, then nearly complete, gave way, and sank into the roaring torrent.

R. H. BONNYCASTLE
The Canadas in 1841   1841

When Colonel By was looking out for a site for his future city he contemplated establishing it on Philemon Wright's property, but the old man asked so high a price that he abandoned the idea, and fixed on the present far grander, if not so convenient, situation, and Upper Canada gained a city which would otherwise have belonged to the Lower Province.

W. H. G. KINGSTON
Western Wanderings   1856

ANONYMOUS

One of the proposed designs for the Houses of Parliament to be built at Ottawa

Water-colour, 36 × 24 inches

Why Ottawa should have been selected as the seat of the great Canadian legislature one can't imagine, except under the hypothesis that every other place wished to get rid of the nuisance. It is simple banishment, for Canada at best is the Siberia of Great Britain. One doesn't know what can induce a man to accept the post of Governor-General, unless he should be a misanthrope, or have hosts of relations at home whom he is anxious to make distant.

"But wait till you see the Parliament buildings, and then you'll be delighted," said my friends, so I went, and found that they are the place of rendez-vous for all the élite of Ottawa.

There is no quarrelling with a man as to his notions of amusement, but any one who could derive pleasure from listening to a debate in the Canadian Parliament is an object for one's deepest commiseration, though we may say of such people, as one does of other idiots, that perhaps they are the happiest of the human race.

The making Ottawa the capital strikes one as either the result of gross jobbery or stupidity on the part of those who suggested it as the seat of government. Her Majesty is said to have selected it, I believe because some one told her that its situation would make it most eligible as a capital for the Canada of future generations, by which I imagine its advocates must have meant the time when Canada shall have been all built over.

Just as good a reason as might be alleged for converting Stonehenge into a parish church against the time that Salisbury Plain is covered with houses.

As to the name, it must surely be a corruption for "Hoot awa," or out of the way, and I should think the whole place must have been some waste lands which had come into the possession of some canny son of Caledonia. This is purely conjecture, and of course I am speaking as an utter outsider, but of all the inconvenient spots for a seat of legislature, Ottawa seems to be entitled to take first rank.

G. ROSE
The Great Country; or Impressions of America
1868

C. WILLIAMS   The Prince of Wales descending the timber slide at Ottawa, Canada West   1860
Water-colour, 11 × 14 inches

Meanwhile, the rain came down faster than ever, still the people continued cheering lustily. Precisely at eleven o'clock next day (September 1st), the weather having cleared up in a most propitious manner, H.R.H. and suite left the Victoria House, under a royal salute, to lay the foundation-stone of the new Parliament Buildings of Canada. The place selected for so doing was perfectly crowded with elegantly-dressed ladies and gentlemen, seated upon platforms erected for the occasion, and the chief dignitaries of the Province stood within a railing, which surrounded a space where the stone (which was of Canadian marble) was placed; to adorn which a neat

arch and massive crown had been erected by the Board of Works. . . .

H.R.H. and suite, with the Governor-General, &c., took their departure from the room shortly after. They then proceeded to the Chaudière Falls, situated near the city; and viewed the slides over which the timber passes, on a raft which had been previously constructed by Mr. Skead. The Prince and the entire party, including Lord Hinchinbrooke, the Hon. Mr. Eliot, and Lord Mulgrave, embarked and swiftly passed over one of the slides; near the bottom of which, a beautiful new barge, constructed by the Clerk of Works for the Government, met

them, and on which they speedily embarked, and were rowed about the river by a party of Ottawa gentlemen. Afterwards the Prince viewed the grand canoe-regatta which there and then took place. There were six races. In each race, only a certain number of paddles and men were allowed, and it was somewhat ludicrous to view it; each one endeavouring to supplant the other, and, in doing so, requiring to be extremely cautious, lest, by a sudden jerk or move, the whole occupants of the canoe should be precipitated into the water.

[H. J. MORGAN]
The Tour of H.R.H. The Prince of Wales Through British America and the United States   1860

MR. FORD

New Edinburgh and Ottawa from the drawing-room window
of Government House, Ottawa, Ontario   ca. 1876
Water-colour, 8 × 10 inches

Thursday, June 27th.

We arrived at Ottawa, the first view of which is magnificent; but once landed there was no time to look at anything! There were nine addresses to be listened to, and after them we drove off to our new home! . . . We have been so very enthusiastic about everything hitherto that the first sight of Rideau Hall did lower our spirits just a little! The road to it is rough and ugly, the house appears to me to be at the land's end, and there is no view whatever from it, though it is near the river — and we have come through hundreds of miles of splendid scenery to get to it! Then I have never lived in a Government

House before, and the inevitable bare tables and ornamentless rooms have a depressing effect: for the first time I realise that I have left my own home for many years — and this is its substitute!

Friday, 28th.

Please forget the above growl. The morning has brought more cheerful reflections. We are not intended to live here at midsummer, and I dare say that in winter this place looks lovely! Our house is, they say, very warm and comfortable, and the Houses of Parliament — which, after all, I do see from my windows — are very beautiful. And I can cover up the

tables and supply the homey look which at present is wanting — so why did I grumble? We have driven in state through the town, and have visited the Government buildings. I was delighted with the Senate, and with the Library — a large, circular room. When the House is sitting I may come and listen to debates, but the Governor-General may not!

The weather is extremely hot, and we are not going to remain here. D. goes tomorrow to inspect militia at Prescott, and I meet him there two days later.

MARCHIONESS OF DUFFERIN AND AVA
My Canadian Journal, 1872-8   1891

WILLIAM DENNY   The covered bridge over the Trent River, Trenton, Canada West   1845
Pencil drawing, 10 × 13¾ inches

Connected with this paramount work is the Trent navigation, by which the interior of fifty surveyed townships will be laid open for settlement, on the finest lands in the province, by opening that river to the Rice Lake, and thence, by works either performed, or projected, through a series of other connected lakes and rivers, into Lake Simcoe, and thence to Lake Huron. So that it is now by no means improbable that vessels may load in London, and deliver their cargoes in Michigan, either by the Welland Canal direct, or by transhipment through the Trent, which latter will be the safest, and the most expeditious, as the navigation may be performed by steam-boats on Lake Huron under cover of the Manitoulin Islands, without exposure to the angry waves and storms of that great fresh-water sea....

Should this ever be completed by the government, the province of Upper Canada will perhaps be the seat of a future nation, whose internal resources may become so vast and preponderating, that some of the neighbouring northern states would sink into comparative insignificance. Surrounded and crossed by canals, lakes, rivers, her industry will command the west and its unfolded wealth. Imagining a belt embraced by the St. Lawrence, the Ottawa, Huron, Erie and Ontario, containing a population of millions, derived principally from Britain, the statist can easily divine the position they might maintain, and how prudent it must be to hold the dominion of England over this fertile empire as long as possible, closing the links of connexion by every act of kindness, and securing in the new world a future British power, unlike that which is advancing to completion in the United States; where, from the great mixture of races, British feelings and British connexion have given way before a flood of undefinable notions about liberty and equality, mixed with aristocratic wealth, slavery, and bigotry in religion.

R. H. BONNYCASTLE
The Canadas in 1841   1841

SUSANNA MOODIE

The first iron mine in Canada West, Marmora, Hastings County
Water-colour, 7¼ × 11½ inches

Inland from Port Hope, on the Rice Lake, in the district of Colborne, is Peterborough, a flourishing town, which will be of great importance when the Trent Canal is completed, as it will be the centre of one of the most fertile and important sections of Canada, the capabilities of which are immense. Surrounded as it is by lakes, rivers, and water communications with Ontario, Simcoe, Huron, and the Ottawa, it requires no great gift of prophecy to foretell that the whole country, recently comprising the districts of Northumberland and Hastings, will become the greatest and most populous portion of Canada, comprising, as it does, in the townships of Marmora, Madoc, and their vicinities, inexhaustible mines of iron.

R. H. BONNYCASTLE
The Canadas in 1841 1841

MARMORA

A Township in the Victoria District; is bounded on the east by the township of Madoc; on the north by Lake; on the west by Belmont; and on the south by Rawdon. In Marmora 8,629 acres are taken up, 1,772 of which are under cultivation. The Marmora River runs through the centre of the township, from north to south. Marmora has been long noted for the excellence and richness of its iron ore, which is said to yield seventy-five per cent of iron of the best quality. There is no doubt that this township alone, under proper management, would be capable of furnishing sufficient iron for the consumption of the whole of British North America. Some years since a large sum was expended in erecting works for the pur-

pose of smelting; but the speculation unfortunately fell through, for want of sufficient capital. There is one grist and one saw mill in the township. Marmora is but little settled, much of the land being unfit for cultivation. Sixteen thousand three hundred and forty-three acres of Crown lands are open for sale in this township, at 8s. currency per acre.

Population in 1842, 317.

Ratable property in the township, £5,368.

W. H. SMITH
Smith's Canadian Gazetteer 1846

EDWIN WHITEFIELD

The bridge across the Otonabee River
at Peterborough, Canada West   1854
Water-colour, 6½ × 12 inches

But the grand work that is, sooner or later, to raise this portion of the district from its present obscurity, is the opening a line of navigation from Lake Huron through Lake Simcoe, and so through our chain of small lakes to Rice Lake, and finally through the Trent to the Bay of Quinte. This noble work would prove of incalculable advantage, by opening a direct communication between Lake Huron and the inland townships at the back of the Ontario with the St. Laurence. This project has already been under the consideration of the Governor, and is at present exciting great interest in the country: sooner or later there is little doubt but that it will be carried into effect. It presents some difficulties and expense, but it would be greatly to the advantage and prosperity of the country,

and be the means of settling many of the back townships bordering upon these lakes.

I must leave it to abler persons than myself to discuss at large the policy and expediency of the measure; but as I suppose you have no intention of emigrating to our backwoods, you will be contented with my cursory view of the matter, and believe, as in friendship you are bound to do, that it is a desirable thing to open a market for inland produce.

Canada is the land of hope; here every thing is new; every thing going forward; it is scarcely possible for arts, sciences, agriculture, manufactures, to retrograde; they must keep advancing; though in some situations the progress may seem slow, in others they are proportionably rapid.

There is a constant excitement on the minds of emigrants, particularly in the partially settled townships, that greatly assists in keeping them from desponding. The arrival of some enterprising person gives a stimulus to those about him: a profitable speculation is started, and lo, the value of the land in the vicinity rises to double and treble what it was thought worth before; so that, without any design of befriending his neighbours, the schemes of one settler being carried into effect shall benefit a great number. We have already felt the beneficial effect of the access of respectable emigrants locating themselves in this township, as it has already increased the value of our own land in a three-fold degree.

C. P. TRAILL
The Backwoods of Canada   1836

Pic. 94, p. 124-125 — 423
EDWIN WHITEFIELD

We were able to explore the lake, as Mr.
C——had two Rice Lake or Peterboro'
canoes. These boats are built by a firm in
Peterboro', Ontario, and are steadier
than birch-bark canoes, though not so
light. They are much used in all parts of
Canada, although the Indians prefer the
birch-bark.

M. FITZGIBBON
A Trip To Manitoba   1880

Sawmills on the Otonabee River at Peterborough, Canada West   1854
Water-colour, 6½ × 24 inches

Peterborough is situated on the Otonabee, a rapid river, falling in less than ten miles down an incline of more than one hundred and fifty feet. There are several saw-mills upon it; lumber and board cutting is the principal industry of the locality, besides farming. It is a very pretty town, though very much like others in Canada. The main street has some fine buildings on it, and prides itself on its display of plate-glass fronted stores.

In one direction the Otonabee River spreads out into a small lake, where there should be ample room for canoeing and boat-sailing; but they allow all the saw-dust from the mills to collect in it, which ferments and is exceedingly disagreeable, if not worse. It is on this river that the

canoes are made which are of world-wide celebrity.

The river about Peterborough is usually dotted in summer with saw-logs floating down with the stream to the mills. There are frequent "jams" of them in narrow or shallow parts, and then the loggers show their wonderful agility, running out over a mass of them, lying in every awkward position, and getting them adrift by means of long spiked poles, which they use as levers to push with. The Otonabee runs out of a chain of lakes which extends back for very many miles to the pine forests. There in winter they cut these logs, usually from twelve feet to twenty feet in length; these are hauled by oxen, or rolled by hand, to the edges of the then frozen streams. When the ice

breaks up they are floated down to the sawmills. It is a most interesting thing to see the operation conducted. It takes the best part of summer to bring them down from the back-country, for they have to pass through many narrow or shallow places: the tows have to be frequently broken up, the logs sent over falls and "chutes" and down rapids; then they have to be caught again and formed into compact groups, sometimes hundreds of thousands of them, surrounded by logs joined together by chains. These are called "tows," and have to be hauled by main force, often by horses or by tugs, across the currentless lakes to the next narrows, where all has to be repeated.

E. ROPER
By Track and Trail   1891

JAMES PATTISON COCKBURN
The road between Kingston and York,
Upper Canada   1830
Water-colour, 15¾ × 10½ inches

[June] 24 [1819] I arose with the sun, and after going 2 miles, I got into what are called the 9 mile woods — A short time ago there was not a house all this distance, but lately there have been three or four log ones built — The cause of there being so few settlers here is not as in many instances, from the barrenness of the soil, which in these woods is very good, but the Proprietors of this have gotten too much land, and will neither clear it themselves, nor sell it to them who would do it — As a law has been lately passed, obliging every person to keep the road in repair opposite his property it is probable that this will induce them to make some better use of this and many other pieces of land than they have hitherto done — The morning being calm, the mosquitoes were extremely numerous, and almost insufferable — After leaving the Wood there are a few miles, cleared along the road after which you come into the five mile woods, which are still unsettled — These places are likely to retain their original appelations however unappropriate, they may be in a short period — I travelled only a few miles further to night and lodged exactly 30 miles from York — The land looks to be considerably better here, than lower down — and if properly cultivated, and manured, would produce luxuriant crops — for three days past I have seen nothing interesting to the Botanist, which circumstance is not calculated to elevate the spirits, and make a person forget the fatigues of travelling — This day was fair, ther. 80.

J. GOLDIE
Diary of a Journey Through Upper Canada, 1819

The blood-root, sanguinaria, or puc-coon, as it is termed by some of the native tribes, is worthy of attention from the root to the flower. As soon as the sun of April has warmed the earth and loosened it from its frozen bonds, you may distin-guish a number of purely white buds, elevated on a naked footstalk, and par-tially enfolded in a handsome vine-shaped leaf, of a pale bluish green, curiously veined on the under side with pale orange. The leaf springs singly from a thick juicy fibrous root, which, on be-ing broken, emits a quantity of liquor from its pores of a bright orange scarlet colour: this juice is used by the Indians as a dye, and also in the cure of rheumatic, and cutaneous complaints. The flowers of the sanguinaria resemble the white crocus very closely: when it first comes up the bud is supported by the leaf, and is folded together with it; the flower, how-ever, soon elevates itself above its pro-tector, while the leaf having performed its duty of guardian to the tender bud, ex-pands to its full size. A rich black vegeta-ble mould at the edges of the clearings seems the favourite soil for this plant . . . .

FANNY BAYFIELD
Bloodroot, Dog's Tooth Violet, and Red Trillium
Water-colour, 14¾ × 11¼ inches

1 Sanguinaria Canadensis
2 Erythronium - or Dog's-tooth Violet
3 Trillium erectum

The lily tribe offer an extensive variety from the most minute to the very largest flowers. The red martagon grows abun-dantly on our plains; the dog's tooth vio-let, Erythronium, with its spotted leaves and bending yellow blossom, delicately dashed with crimson spots within, and marked with fine purple lines on the outer part of the petal, proves a great at-traction in our woods, where these plants increase: they form a beautiful bed; the leaves come up singly, one from each separate tuber. There are two varieties of this flower, the pale yellow, with neither spots nor lines, and the deep yellow with both; the anthers of this last are reddish-orange, and thickly covered with a fine powdery substance.

A very beautiful plant of the lily tribe abounds both in our woods and clear-ings; for want of a better name, I call it the douri-lily, though it is widely spread over a great portion of the continent. The Americans term the white and red varie-ties of this species, the "white" and "red death." The flower is either deep red, or of a dazzling white, though the latter is often found stained with a delicate blush-pink, or a deep green; the latter appears to be caused by the calix running into the petal. Wherefore it bears so for-midable a name has not yet transpired. The flower consists of three petals, the calix three; it belongs to the class and order Hexandria monogynia; style, three-cleft; seed-vessel of three valves; soil, dry woods and cleared lands; leaves growing in three, springing from the joints, large round, but a little pointed at the extremities.

C. P. TRAILL
The Backwoods of Canada   1836

COBOURG

The District Town of the Newcastle District, in the township of Hamilton, is pleasantly situated on a gently rising ground, on the bank of Lake Ontario, 103 miles from Kingston, and 72 miles from Toronto. The town is incorporated, and the corporation limits extend for nearly two miles from the centre of the town. Cobourg is situated on a gravelly soil, and it is consequently dry, clean and healthy. The town is well laid out, possesses good streets, and many excellent buildings, and has a very flourishing appearance. A harbour has been constructed at an expense of £10,381.6s. 3d and a lighthouse erected at the end of the pier. Excellent planked side-walks extend in every direction for a distance of from one to two miles.

During the season, steamboats call daily on their passages to and from Kingston, Toronto, and Rochester (United States); and a stage leaves daily for Rice Lake, where it is met by the steamboat Forester, which conveys passengers to Peterborough; and the Toronto and Kingston stages pass through the town every day. During the winter, a stage leaves daily for Peterborough. A fair is held here on the second Tuesdays in April and October. The merchants have established amongst themselves a "Board of Trade," for the purpose of regulating the commercial affairs of the place; they have a newsroom, where several papers are taken. There is also a Mechanics' Institute. Three newspapers are published here viz., the "Church," "Cobourg Star," and "Canada Christian Advocate." Churches and Chapels six, viz., Episcopal, Presbyterian, Catholic, Congregational, Methodist, and Christian. In the Episcopal church is a very good organ. The Jail and Court House is a handsome stone building, situated about a mile and a-half from the town, on the Toronto road.

Victoria College was founded by the Wesleyan Conference; the institution was chartered in 1835, as an Academy and by Act of Parliament, in 1842, was constituted a College, with power to confer degrees in the several arts and sciences – (the only degree yet conferred has been one in literature); it is supported partly by a legislative grant of £500 per annum, and partly by tuition fees. The building is handsome, and well situated, and cost nearly £10,000; it con-

tains Library, Reading Room, Chapel, Laboratory, Lecture Rooms, &c. &c. Although the institution was founded by the Methodists, there is nothing sectarian in its character. The following periodicals are received at the Reading Room, which are liberally forwarded by their several editors, the College being merely at the expense of postage: Church, Cobourg; British Colonist, Toronto; British Canadian, do.; Banner (Presbyterian) do.; Kingston News; Montreal Gazette; Hamilton Journal and Express; Canada Gazette; Kingston Herald; Port Hope Gazette; Cornwall Observer; Brockville Recorder; Niagara Chronicle; Belleville Intelligencer; Prince Edward Gazette; Woodstock Herald; British American Cultivator; Christian Guardian, Toronto; Methodist Quarterly Review, New York; Anglo American, do.; Spectator, do.; Literary Garland, Montreal; Albion, New York; New Orleans Picayune; Christian Advocate and Journal, New York; Southern Christian Advocate, Charleston; Episcopal Recorder, Philadelphia. The boarders at the College at present number about thirty-five, and the day pupils about twenty.

A large cloth factory has been lately erected, for the manufacture of coarse cloth, tweeds, cassinett, blankets, flannels, &c.; when in full operation it will employ nearly 200 hands, and will be capable of turning out 850 yards of cloth per day. The building is of brick, and is five stories high, including basement.

The following government and district offices are kept in Cobourg: Judge of District Court, Sheriff, Treasurer, Inspector of Licenses, Collector of Customs, Registrar of County of Northumberland, District Clerk, Clerk of District Court. The office of the Clerk of the Peace is kept at Port Hope.

Post Office, post every day.
Population, 3,347
Professions and Trades. – Six physicians and surgeons, seven lawyers, one steam grist-mill, two water do., two saw-mills, one cloth factory, one brewery, three distilleries, one ashery, one soap and candle factory, three tanneries, two foundries, twenty dry-goods stores, ten groceries, two hardware stores, twelve taverns, two druggists, three printers, three booksellers, two surveyors, five waggon makers, one hatter, two livery stables, one veterinary surgeon, two

watch makers, three tinsmiths, five cabinet makers, ten tailors, two saddlers, four bakers and confectioners, eleven blacksmiths, one marble worker, one pail factory, four planing machines, one machine maker, fourteen shoemakers, three merchant tailors, two barbers, four butchers, three schools for boys, three ladies seminaries, two bank agencies – "Commercial," and "Montreal."

Principal Taverns.—''North American,'' and ''Globe.''
Land Agent, S. Armour.
Stage fare to Peterborough during winter, ten shillings c'y.; stage and steamboat fare to do. during summer, seven shillings and six-pence.

W. H. SMITH
Smith's Canadian Gazetteer   1846

ANONYMOUS
The wharf and town of Cobourg
from the harbour, Canada West   1847
Water-colour, 9 × 12¾ inches

ELISABETH FRANCIS HALE
York on Lake Ontario, Upper Canada   1804
Water-colour, 11 × 17½ inches

The trade carried on from Montreal to the lakes is at present very considerable, and increasing every year. Already are there extensive settlements on the British side of Lake Ontario, at Niagara, at Toronto, at the Bay of Canti, and at Kingston, which contain nearly twenty thousand inhabitants; and on the opposite shore, the people of the states are pushing forward their settlements with the utmost vigour. On Lake Erie, and along Detroit River also, the settlements are increasing with astonishing rapidity, both on the British and on the opposite side.

I. WELD
Travels Through the States of North America and the Provinces of Upper and Lower Canada   1799

York, or Toronto, the seat of government in Upper Canada, is placed in forty-three degrees and thirty-five minutes of north latitude, near the bottom of a harbour of the same name. A long and narrow peninsula, distinguished by the appellation of Gibraltar Point, forms, and embraces this harbour, securing it from the storms of the lake, and rendering it the safest of any, around the coasts of that sea of fresh waters. Stores and block-houses are constructed near the extremity of this point. A spot called the garrison, stands on a bank of the main land, opposite to the point, and consists only of a wooden block-house, and some small cottages of the same materials, little superior to temporary huts. The house in which the Lieutenant-governor resides is likewise formed of wood, in the figure of a half square, of one story in height, with galleries in the center. It is sufficiently commodious for the present state of the province, and is erected upon a bank of the lake, near the mouth of Toronto bay. The town, according to the plan, is projected to extend to a mile and a half in length, from the bottom of the harbour, along its banks. Many houses are already completed, some of which display a considerable degree of taste. The advancement of this place to its present condition, has been effected within the lapse of six or seven years, and persons who have formerly travelled in this part of the country, are impressed with sentiments of wonder, on beholding a town which may be termed handsome, reared as if by enchantment, in the midst of a wilderness. Two buildings of brick at the eastern extremity of the town, which were designed as wings to a center, are occupied as chambers for the upper and lower house of assembly. The scene from this part of the basin is agreeable and diversified; a block-house, situated upon a wooded bank, forms the nearest object; part of the town, points of land clothed with spreading oak-trees, gradually receding from the eye, one behind another, until terminated by the buildings of the garrison and the spot on which the governor's residence is placed, compose the objects on the right. The left side of the view comprehends the long peninsula which incloses this sheet of water, beautiful on account of its placidity, and rotundity of form; the distant lake, which appears bounded only by the sky, terminates the whole.

G. HERIOT
Travels Through the Canadas   1807

Toronto is, as a residence, worse and better than other small communities— *worse* in so much as it is remote from all the best advantages of a high state of civilisation, while it is infected by all its evils, all its follies; and *better*, because, besides being a small place, it is a *young* place; and in spite of this affectation of looking back, instead of looking up, it must advance—it may become the thinking head and beating heart of a nation, great, and wise, and happy—who knows? And there are moments when, considered under this point of view, it assumes an interest even to me; but at present it is in a false position, like that of a youth aping maturity; or rather like that of the little boy in Hogarth's picture, dressed in a long-flapped laced waistcoat, ruffles and cocked-hat, crying for bread and butter. With the interminable forests within half a mile of us—the haunt of the red man, the wolf, the bear—with an absolute want of the means of the most ordinary mental and moral development, we have here conventionalism in its most oppressive and ridiculous forms.

A. JAMESON
Winter Studies and Summer Rambles in Canada   1838

The situation of York is far from an inviting one, the inhabitants being subject during certain seasons to the fever and ague, caused by the marshy ground which lies close to the town and around the head of the bay. It is almost to be regretted that a better site could not have been chosen for the capital of an increasing country. Though a more central position than Kingston at the foot of the lake, yet in no other respects does it equal it. The bay is too shallow to admit vessels of even moderate burden, and in time of war it is always exposed to the incursions of American gun-boats, and the town subject to be sacked, as in 1813. Some years since it was proposed that the capital of Upper Canada should be on the borders of Lake Simcoe, and a water communication be opened with Montreal by means of the shallow lakes and Rideau Canal; but I believe all thoughts of removing the seat of Government from York are now entirely laid aside. The

SEMPRONIUS STRETTON
The barracks at York,
Upper Canada   1804
Water-colour, 12 × 21 inches

land in the immediate vicinity is poor and cold, but becomes more fertile as the distance from the lake increases, and good farms are abundant towards Lake Simcoe, and on the sides of the road called Young Street. The place is however only in its infancy as yet, and said to be increasing rapidly, though the comparisons between it and Buffalo, the last American town I had seen, and of a very few years' growth, were much in favour of the latter. There are no places of public amusement, and the chief diversion for the young men appeared to consist in shooting musquito hawks, which hovered plentifully about the streets and upon the margin of the bay in an evening. Upon these occasions the sportsmen made their appearence, equipped in shooting jackets, and attended by their dogs, as if prepared for a 12th of August on the moors of Scotland.

E. T. COKE
A Subaltern's Furlough   1833

PHILIP JOHN BAINBRIGGE   The pier and barracks at York, Upper Canada   1839
Water-colour, 6 × 10 inches

The military works and buildings at this place, having been originally merely temporary erections, are unworthy of notice. New barracks for the troops, at a distance from the town, are in the course of erection.

R. H. BONNYCASTLE
The Canadas in 1841   1841

The value of property here is incredible. On the military reserve, now forming into the new western portion of the city, acre lots sold by government fetched five and six hundred pounds, at some distance from the parts of the city built upon. Building-ground in the populous streets is worth from ten pounds to twenty pounds a foot, and will no doubt be much higher; and thus many persons who were formerly very needy, and who obtained the land as grants when it was of little value, are now amongst the richest.

Until about six or seven years ago, the buildings in Toronto were mostly of wood, as stone is not found in sufficient quantity in the neighbourhood, and consequently fires frequently devastated the town. Brick has since been chiefly employed, as the soil is so good a clay, that the foundation and cellarage of a house often yield the necessary material for the superstructure.

R. H. BONNYCASTLE
The Canadas in 1841   1841

WILLIAM ARMSTRONG

Prince Arthur arriving for the ceremony of the turning of the first
sod of the Toronto, Grey and Bruce Railway, at Weston, Ontario
October 5, 1869
Water-colour, 18¼ × 27¾ inches

Yesterday forenoon the construction of the Toronto, Grey and Bruce Railway was inaugurated with an *eclat* and brilliancy which, perhaps, have not characterized the turning of the first sod of any railway in Canada, for no other railway in the Dominion can boast of having had its first sod turned by a Royal Prince. . . . A few hundred yards west of the village a platform was built close to the track. This led through a beautiful arch decked with evergreens, and surmounted by ensigns and crown and bannerets, bearing appropriate mottoes innumerable, into a quadrangle surrounded on all sides with sloping galleries crowded with schoolchildren and people of the neighbourhood all of whom were evidently in the highest state of expectancy to catch a glimpse of His Royal Highness. . . . The special consta-

bles had a sad time of it. Each was armed with a baton and had a bunch of ribbon in his button hole, but what could they do. Had it been an ordinary crowd it would have been an easy matter for in that case, no doubt, both the batons and the ribbons would have had their proper effect. But then the crowd was composed largely of ladies, and what could Weston special constables do in the circumstances. They tried to coax the fair creatures to stand back; then they attempted to reason them into good behaviour, but of course all without avail. Then some of them got angry and flourished their batons and fumed and told them in good set terms that they must stand back, but the grandeur and Dido-like magnificence with which the Toronto ladies *looked over* the heads of the constables was a caution.

And as Mr. Armstrong was present taking a sketch of the scene, the whole affair will be permanently preserved. . . . It may be mentioned in closing that when the Prince had tumbled his two sods out of the barrow, a most indiscriminate scramble took place as to who should obtain possession of the precious earth. Ladies and gentlemen joined in the melee, and the two sods were soon torn all to pieces, and several parties in the cars homeward were seen to draw from their pockets a good sized tuft, and showing it to their less fortunate fellow travellers with as much gusto as if they had some relics from the ruins of Pompeii or the ancient palace of Thebes.

TORONTO
Globe   October 6, 1869

GEORGE RUSSELL DARTNELL
At Barrie on Lake Simcoe, Upper Canada   1841
Water-colour, 7 × 10¼ inches

BARRIE

So called after Commodore Barrie, the District town of the Simcoe District is beautifully situated at the head of Kempenfeldt Bay, in the township of Vespra, thirty-two miles from Holland Landing, and forty miles from Penetanguishine. Barrie was first settled in the year 1832; in 1837 it contained about twenty-eight families. In 1843 the county of Simcoe, until then part of the Home District, was declared a separate district, with Barrie for its district town. Since then it has increased rapidly. The situation was well chosen and is healthy. Should the contemplated canal from the bay to Lake Huron, through Willow Creek and the Nottawasaga River, ever be formed, Barrie, which is now truly in the woods, will have uninterrupted water communication with the St. Lawrence. At present, the road from Barrie to the Holland Landing, is, in the spring and fall, almost impassable for waggons. The road to Penetanguishine is much better, running for the most part along a stony ridge of land. The mail, during the spring and autumn, is carried on horse-back; and through the summer, partly on horseback, and partly by water. A new steamboat, the "Beaver," was launched during the summer of 1844: she is an excellent boat, and has good accommodation. The banks of the bay have a rather sombre appearance, being almost totally devoid of clearing: most of the timber on the banks is pine. Town lots, of a quarter of an acre, in the old survey (or original town-plot) are in the hands of private individuals, and sell at from £20 to £50, some higher. An addition has lately been made to the town-plot, and the lots in the new survey sell at from £5 to £12 10s. each; they are mostly in the hands of the Crown. The public buildings are the jail and court-house. The jail is a handsome stone building; the court-house is of brick, and has no beauty to boast of; the two cost the district nearly£9,000. There are three churches and chapels: viz. one Episcopal and two Methodist. There is an excellent district school (where private pupils are taken); a mechanics' institute, and a cricket club.

The inhabitants are principally English, Irish and Scotch, and number about 500.

The following government and district offices are kept in Barrie: Judge of District Court, Sheriff, Clerk of Peace, Registrar, Inspector of Licenses, Crown Lands Agent, District Clerk, Clerk of District Court, Deputy Clerk of Crown.

Professions and Trades — One physician and surgeon, one lawyer, six stores, three tanneries, one surveyor, three taverns, four blacksmiths, one waggon maker, one baker, one saddler, one cabinet maker, one watchmaker, six shoemakers, three tailors, two butchers, one bank agency "Upper Canada."

Agent for Home District Mutual Fire Insurance Company — W. B. Smith.

Steamboat Fares: —

To Holland Landing
. . . . 8s.9d. c'y.
To ditto by Orillia
. . . . . 11s.3d.
To Orillia   8s.9d.
Shorter distance in proportion.

Principal Tavern. — "The Queen's Arms."

W. H. SMITH
Smith's Canadian Gazetteer   1846

GEORGE BACK

A Corporal's house on the portage with the Blue
Mountain in the distance, Upper Canada   1825
Water-colour, 5 × 8 inches

Writers on emigration do not take the trouble of searching out these things, nor does it answer their purpose to state disagreeable facts. Few have written exclusively on the "Bush." Travellers generally make a hasty journey through the long settled and prosperous portions of the country; they see a tract of fertile, well-cultivated land, the result of many years of labour; they see comfortable dwellings, abounding with all the substantial necessaries of life; the farmer's wife makes her own soap, candles, and sugar; the family are clothed in cloth of their own spinning, and hose of their own knitting. The bread, the beer, butter, cheese, meat, poultry, &c. are all the produce of the farm. He concludes, therefore, that Canada is a land of Canaan, and writes a book setting forth these advantages, with the addition of obtaining land for a mere song; and advises all persons who would be independent and secure from want to emigrate.

He forgets that these advantages are the result of long years of unremitting and patient labour; that these things are the crown, not the first-fruits of the settler's toil; and that during the interval many and great privations must be submitted to by almost every class of emigrants.

Many persons, on first coming out, especially if they go back into any of the unsettled townships, are dispirited by the unpromising appearance of things about them. They find none of the advantages and comforts of which they had heard and read, and they are unprepared for the present difficulties; some give way to despondency, and others quit the place in disgust.

C. P. TRAILL
The Backwoods of Canada   1836

The waters of Lake Simcoe are discharged into the Georgian Bay by the River Matchedash, through a series of highly romantic and picturesque falls, which, before the bridle road was made, where, by means of portages, the only route practicable to Penetangueshene from the capital.

Of late years military settlers have been located along the path, which has improved it very much. The path is practicable generally for a strong light waggon, but horseback is the more usual mode of proceeding from Penetangueshene to Lake Simcoe. Settlements are gradually spreading along the whole line, and the distance of twelve miles cannot now be passed in these ancient forests without meeting a house or hut.

R. H. BONNYCASTLE
The Canadas in 1841   1841

The British portion of the expedition were ordered to leave Kingston, in Canada West, as early in the year as possible, in a beautiful clinker-built boat for Toronto. From thence we were to transport boat and baggage thirty-seven miles by Yonge Street, in a waggon, to Holland's Landing on Lake Simcoe; then to pass into Lake Huron by the pretty river Notawasaga, and so onwards to Fort William, in Lake Superior. At Fort William we were to find, ready for us, two north canoes manned by six voyageurs each. In these we were to proceed by the Grand Portage along the old commercial route, to the Lake of the Woods, while the American party were to pursue their new route up the River Kaministigua. . . .

Near its lower end we found ourselves overlooking from a lofty bank a vast prospect of marsh and wood, stretching to the south thirty miles or more, and bounded eastward by a long range of blue hills, flat-topped, and running in the direction of Cabot's Head, Lake Huron. This marsh does not go more than three miles northerly, and is succeeded by high forests and occasional lakes towards Penetanguishene.

J. J. BIGSBY
By Shoe and Canoe 1850

GEORGE BACK

On the portage between Lake Ontario and Lake Simcoe, Upper Canada   1825
Water-colour, 5 × 8 inches

Nottawassaga Bay is one of the largest of the numerous indentations of Huron; in fact, it is larger than many of the largest European lakes. Its shores are yet to be inhabited; for not more than two or three adventurous settlers have penetrated its forests.

I encamped with the commandant of the British post of Penetangueshene, Dr. Ingall, at the mouth of the Nottawassaga River, on the 23rd of June, 1835, in order to examine the estuary, and the site of a former naval establishment, with a view to observe if an artificial harbour could be formed. A more solemn or a more desolate abiding place can scarcely be imagined, as it cannot always be approached from the bay, on account of the terrible violence with which the sea sets in on this long line of shallow and exposed shore. An unhappy wreck had happened just before we were there, and a pole with a board placed on the sands, showed us as we passed, the place where it had occurred.

On the land side all is forest—never ending, dense, and impenetrable—the only certain mode of access being by the river itself, from the interior, or along the sands and portages. But the river, with its deep black hue, looks more like Ancheron than any thing else, and is so encumbered with trees that have been swept into it by storms, that it is with much difficulty navigable in the canoes of the country.

R. H. BONNYCASTLE
The Canadas in 1841 1841

HAMPDEN MOODY after PHILIP JOHN BAINBRIGGE
Ice-boating at Penetanguishene on Lake Huron, Upper Canada   ca. 1840
Water-colour, 6½ × 9¾ inches

ANONYMOUS
The mouth of the Nottawasaga River, Lake Huron, Upper Canada   1824
Water-colour, 9 × 11 inches

Early on Saturday morning we passed Silver Islet, that mine of wealth to our neighbours across the line. It lies in an island-dotted bay, and is so covered with mining works that it looks like a pile of buildings rising out of the water. The crushing-mills are on the mainland close by. Silver Islet first belonged to a Canadian company; but from the lack of enterprise or capital it was sold to an American company for a nominal sum, and, as is often the case, the sanguine nature of Cousin Jonathan, acting on the motto, "Nothing ventured nothing won," has been successful, and the company is now (1879) shipping $20,000 worth of silver ore a day. The islet can be visited only by those who have especial permission to see the mines and works, or friends among the officials, neither of which had we.

M. FITZGIBBON
A Trip to Manitoba   1880

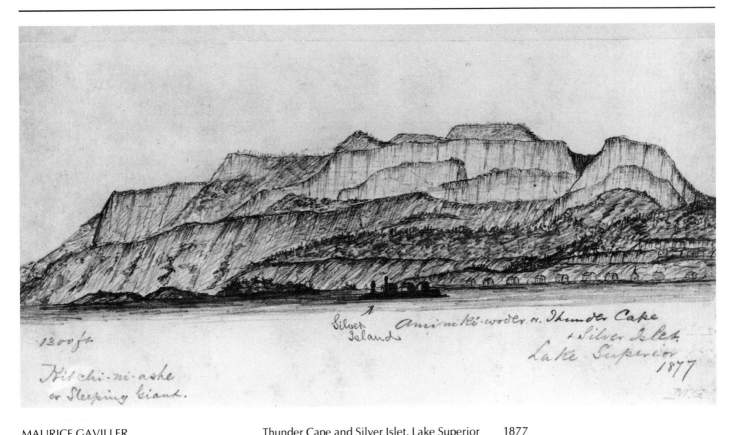

MAURICE GAVILLER

Thunder Cape and Silver Islet, Lake Superior   1877
Pencil drawing, 5¼ × 10½ inches

At four o'clock in the morning we were running down the bay under full steam, and at eleven arrived at

SILVER ISLET,

where there is one of the richest silver mines in the world, belonging to the American Silver Mining Company. Every ton of quartz taken in 1874 was worth over £4,000, most of it being sent to England or the States packed in casks, a large number of which we took on board. The population at the works was from 1,500 to 2,000 comprising English, Scotch, and Irish, the captain being a native of Belfast. As far as I could see from a three hours' visit everything was in apple pie order.

P. O'LEARY
Travels and Experiences in Canada   no date

We next arrive at Silver Islet, the most profitable silver mine in the world for a time. This island is a mere speck, 70 or 80 feet square, distant from the shore 3,000 or 4,000 yards; yet from this little island probably two millions of dollars in silver have already been extracted, at an outlay of one million dollars. Breakwaters have been made, shafts sunk, and precious metal taken out many hundred feet below the water. A village of considerable size sprang up as if by magic, on the shore just opposite, but it is now deserted for a time at least. When litigation ceases with the company and stock is concentrated and held by a few this mine may yet flourish. A large number of the miners removed to Manitoba, where they will no doubt find that it is safer and more profitable to work on the surface than under ground.

J. TROW
Manitoba and North West Territories   1878

WILLIAM H. E. NAPIER

The Hudson's Bay Company post at Fort William, Lake Superior, Canada West   1857
Water-colour, 6¾ × 9¾ inches

Wednesday, 24th. — Early this morning we left the encampment, and after two hours' paddling, Fort William burst upon our enraptured gaze, mirrored in the limpid waters of that immense freshwater sea, Lake Superior, whose rocky shores and rolling billows vie with the ocean in grandeur and magnificences.

Fort William was once one of the chief posts in the Indian country; and, when it belonged to the North-West Company, contained a great number of men. Now, however, much of its glory has departed. Many of the buildings have been pulled down, and those that remain are very rickety-looking affairs. It is still, however, a very important fishing station, and many hundreds of beautiful whitefish, with which Lake Superior swarms, are salted there annually for the Canada markets. These whitefish are indeed ex-

cellent, and it is difficult to say whether they, or the immense trout, which are also caught in abundance, have the most delicate flavour. These trout, as well as whitefish, are caught in nets, and the former sometimes measure three feet long, and are proportionately broad. The one we had to breakfast on the morning of our arrival, must have been very nearly this size.

The fur trade of the post is not very good, but the furs traded are similar to those obtained in other parts of the country.

A number of *canôtes de maître,* or very large canoes, are always kept in store here, for the use of the Company's travellers. These canoes are of the largest size, exceeding the north canoe in length by several feet, besides being much broader and deeper. They are used solely

for the purpose of travelling on Lake Superior, being much too large and cumbersome for travelling with through the interior. They are carried by four men instead of two, like the north canoe, and, besides being capable of carrying twice as much cargo, are paddled by fourteen or sixteen men. Travellers from Canada to the interior generally change their *canôtes de maître* for north canoes at Fort William, before entering upon the intricate navigation through which we had already passed; while those going from the interior to Canada, change the small for the large canoe. As we had few men, however, and the weather appeared settled, we determined to risk coasting round the northern shore of the lake in our north canoe.

R. M. BALLANTYNE
Hudson's Bay   1848

Three hours' steaming brought our flotilla to the west end of the lake. A portage of three quarters of a mile intervenes between it and Lake Kashaboiwe. The Indians emptied the canoes in a trice; two shouldered a canoe, weighing probably three hundred pounds, and made off at a rapid trot across the portage. The others loaded the waggon of the station with the luggage, and carried on their backs, by a strap passed over their foreheads, what the waggon could not take. This portage strap is three or four inches broad in the middle, where it is adjusted to the forehead; its great advantage to the voyageur is that it leaves him the free use of his arms in going through the woods. A tug has been placed on Kashaboiwe, but as the machinery was out of gear the Indians paddled over the lake, doing the ten miles of its length in two hours. The wood on this lake is heavier than on Shebandowan: poplars, white birch, red, white and scrub pine, all show well. The second portage is between Kashaboiwe and Lac de Mille Lacs, and is the Height of Land where the water begins to run north and west instead of east and south. The lakes, after this, empty at their west ends. At the east end of Lac des Mille Lacs, a little stream three yards wide, that flows in a tortuous channel with gentle current into the lake, eventually finds its way to Hudson's Bay. The Height of Land is about a thousand feet above Lake Superior....

The second half was to be by waggons and canoes; — waggons at the beginning and end; and, in the middle, canoes paddled by Indians or tugged by steam launches over a chain of lakes, extending like a net work in all directions along the watershed that separates the basin of the great Lakes and St. Lawrence from the vast Northern basin of Hudson's Bay.

G. M. GRANT
Ocean to Ocean 1873

Thus we finished our journey, from Lake Superior to Red River, by the Dawson road, of which all had previously heard much, in terms of praise or disparagement. The total distance is about five hundred and thirty miles; forty-five at the beginning and a hundred and ten at the end by land; and three hundred and eighty miles between, made up of a chain of some twenty lakes and lacustrine rivers, separated from each other by spits, ridges, or short traverses of land or granite rocks, that have to be portaged across. Over those three hundred and eighty miles the only land suitable for agriculture is along Rainy River, and, perhaps, around the Lake of the Woods. North and south the country is a wilderness of lakes, or tarns on a large scale, filling huge holes scooped out of primitive rock. The scenery is picturesque, though rather monotonous, owing to the absence of mountains; the mode of travelling, whether the canoes are paddled or tugged, novel and delightful; and, if a tourist can afford a crew of Indians, and three or four weeks' time, he is certain to enjoy himself, the necessity of roughing it adding zest to the pleasure.

The road has been proved on two occasions to be a military necessity for the Dominion, until a railway is built farther back from the boundary line. If Canada is to open up her North-west to all the world for colonization, there must be a road for troops, from the first: there are sufficient elements of disorder to make preparedness a necessity. As long as we have a road of our own, the United States would perhaps raise no objection to Canadian volunteers passing through Minnesota; were we absolutely dependent, it might be otherwise.

In speaking of this Dawson road it is only fair to give full credit for all that has been accomplished. Difficulties have been overcome, insomuch that, whereas it took Colonel Wolseley's force nearly three months to reach Fort Garry from Thunder Bay, a similar expedition could now do the journey in two or three weeks.

But, as a route for trade, for ordinary travel or for emigrants to go west, the Dawson road is far from satisfactory. Only by building a hundred and fifty-five miles or so of railway at the beginning and the end, and by overcoming the intervening portages in such a way that bulk would not have to be broken, could it be made to compete even with the present route by Duluth and the railway thence to Pembina.

G. M. GRANT
Ocean to Ocean 1873

WILLIAM ARMSTRONG
Building the Dawson Road at
Kashabowie Station, Ontario   1869
Water-colour, 9 × 13 inches

WILLIAM ARMSTRONG
Red Rock, looking south on the Nipigon River from near
the Hudson's Bay Company post, Ontario   1867
Water-colour, 19¾ x 27½ inches

The scenery of Nepigon Bay is of the grandest description. There is nothing like it elsewhere in Ontario. Entering from the east we pass up a broad strait, and can soon take our choice of deep and capacious channels, formed by the bold ridges of the islands that stud the Bay. Bluffs, from three hundred to one thousand feet high, rise up from the waters, some of them bare from lake to summit, others clad with graceful balsams. On the mainland, sloping and broken hills stretch far away, and the deep shadows that rest on them bring out the most distant in clear and full relief. The time will come when the wealthy men of our great North-west will have their summer residences on these hills and shores; nor could the heart of man desire more lovely sites.

G. M. GRANT
Ocean to Ocean   1873

PHILIP JOHN BAINBRIGGE
Fort Niagara from Fort Mississauga, Upper Canada
1840
Water-colour, 6½ x 9¾ inches

The town occupies a pretty situation on the margin, and about twenty feet higher than the lake, which has so much encroached upon it by the waves undermining the banks, that batteries which were thrown up but a few years since, as near as possible to the margin of the water, for the laudable purpose of annoying the enemy's fort on the opposite peninsula, have now nearly disappeared. The common above the town is intersected with the breastworks and redoubts of the English and Americans, as each party alternately had possession. The most extensive of them, dignified with the appellation of Fort George, contains some low wooden decayed barracks; and another below the town, in a still more mouldering state, is named Fort Mississagua, from a tribe of Indians, the original possessors of the tract of country between it and Fort Erie, thirty miles distant. These works, which are now rapidly crumbling into dust, and possess but the shadow of their former greatness, might with some trifling expense be again rendered formidable. At the present time they are only put to shame by the neat, white appearance of the American fort Niagara, which being built exactly opposite the English town, and not 800 yards distant, might annoy it by a very effective bombardment. During the late war it was rendered almost useless, being surprised by Colonel Murray during the night, when the officer in command of the garrison had retired to his private residence two miles distant, and the royal salute fired for the capture first conveyed to him the news of the loss of his post. It was built by the French so far back as 1725, passed into the hands of the British by the conquest of Canada in 1759, was ceded by treaty to the United States in 1794, and restored to them after the peace of 1814. A long spit or bar of sand, running out from it into the lake, compels vessels bound up the river to pass under the guns of Fort Mississagua, which completely commands the entrance.

E. T. COKE
A Subaltern's Furlough 1833

GEORGE HERIOT   Queenston, Upper Canada   1805
                                Water-colour, 5 x 7 inches

From the brow of one of the hills in this ridge, which overhangs the little village of Queenston, the eye of the traveller is gratified with one of the finest prospects that can be imagined in nature: you stand amidst a clump of large oaks, a little to the left of the road, and looking downwards perceive, through the branches of the trees with which the hill is clothed from the summit to the base, the tops of the houses of Queenston, and in front of the village, the ships moored in the river; the ships are at least two hundred feet below you, and their masts appear like slender reeds peeping up amidst the thick foliage of the trees. Carrying your eye forward, you may trace the river in all its windings, and finally see it disembogue into Lake Ontario, between the town and the fort: the lake itself terminates your view in this direction, except merely at one part of the horizon, where you just get a glimpse of the blue hills of Toronto. The shore of the river, on the right hand, remains in its natural state, covered with one continued forest; but on the opposite side the country is interspersed with cultivated fields, and neat farm houses down to the water's edge. The country beyond the hills is much less cleared than that which lies towards the town of Niagara, on the navigable part of the river.

I. WELD
Travels Through the States of North America and the Provinces of Upper and Lower Canada 1799

The scenery from Niagara to Queenstown is highly pleasing, the road leading along the summit of the banks of one of the most magnificent rivers in the universe; and on ascending the mountain, which is rather a sudden elevation from one immense plain to another, where the river becomes lost to the view, the traveller proceeds through a forest of oak-trees, until he becomes surprised, and his attention is arrested by the falls presented to the eye through openings now cut in the woods, on the steep banks by which they are confined.

Queenstown is a neat and flourishing place, distinguished by the beauty and grandeur of its situation. Here all the merchandise and stores for the upper part of the province are landed from the vessels in which they have been conveyed from Kingston, and transported in waggons to Chippawa, a distance of ten miles, the falls, and the rapid and broken course of the river, rendering the navigation impracticable for that space. Between Niagara and Queenstown the river affords, in every part, a noble harbour for vessels, the water being deep, the stream not too powerful, the anchorage good, and the banks on either side of considerable altitude.

G. HERIOT
Travels Through the Canadas 1807

JAMES PATTISON COCKBURN   Brock's Monument, Queenston, Upper Canada   ca. 1830
Water-colour, 6 x 9½ inches

It is worth while to stop at Queenston, and, having scaled the mountain, as it is called, which is exactly three hundred and forty-six feet above the Niagara, to mount the lofty monument, under which Brock, and M'Donell, his aid-de-camp, repose. From this lofty station, a panoramic view of a most singular kind is obtained, the eye ranging for miles over forest and fell, over mountain, towns, and river, and over the broad and unlimited expanse of the blue Ontario. Beneath you, at the back of the village of Queenston, and under the heights, is a meadow with a solitary tree; here fell Brock, in the arms of Victory.

It must have been a proud day when your officers met under the disfigured and disjointed column erected on Queenston heights, to the memory of the leader whom the militia of Upper Canada loved as a father — the gallant, the victorious Brock; and the soul of the miscreant, whose unholy hand despoiled that shrine, must have been "disquieted within him," if he witnessed, as probably he did, that noble scene. Rebuild it on sure foundations! Guard it, as the apple of your eye, and inscribe upon it Navy Island, Point Pelée, Amherstburgh, Hickory Island, Prescott! Yes, all those places where invaders dared to show themselves, where "treason looked so giant like," but where it could "but peep at what it would," and acted "little of its will."

In the evening several officers and gentlemen assembled at the hotel to be in readiness to attend the ceremony of laying the foundation-stone of the monument to be raised to the memory of General Brock, on Queenston heights, in lieu of the one destroyed by the American sympathiser of the name of Lett, one of the rebel Mackenzie's rag-tag followers.

R. H. BONNYCASTLE
The Canadas in 1841   1841

R. H. BONNYCASTLE
The Canadas in 1841   1841

W. H. G. KINGSTON
Western Wanderings   1856

WASHINGTON FRIEND   The Horseshoe Falls, Niagara Falls   ca. 1845
                          Water-colour, 22 x 30½ inches

To leave out Niagara when you can possibly bring it in would be as much against the stock-book of travel as to omit the duel, the steeple-chase, or the escape from the mad bull in a thirty-one-and-sixpenny fashionable novel. What the pyramids are to Egypt–what Vesuvius is to Naples–what the field of Waterloo has been for fifty years to Brussels, so is Niagara to the entire continent of North America.

W. F. BUTLER
The Great Lone Land   1872

The falls of Niagara surpass in sublimity every description which the powers of language can afford of that celebrated scene, the most wonderful and awful which the habitable world presents. Nor can any drawing convey an adequate idea of the magnitude and depth of the precipitating waters. By the interposition of two islands, the river is separated into three falls, that of the Great Horse-shoe on the west or British side, so denominated from its form, and those of Fort Slausser and Montmorenci, on the eastern or American side. The larger island is about four hundred yards in width, and the small island about ten yards. The three falls, with the islands, describe a crescent, and the river beneath becomes considerably contracted. The breadth of the whole, at the pitch of the waters, including the curvatures which the violence of the current has produced in the Horse-shoe, and in the American falls, may be estimated at a mile and a quarter, and the altitude of the Table Rock, from whence the precipitation commences, is one hundred and fifty feet.

G. HERIOT
Travels Through the Canadas   1807

It was early in the month of September, three years prior to the time I now write of, when I first visited this famous spot. The Niagara season was at its height: the monster hotels were ringing with song, music, and dance; tourists were doing the falls, and touts were doing the tourists. Newly-married couples were conducting themselves in that demonstrative manner characteristic of such people in the New World. Buffalo girls had apparently responded freely to the invitation contained in their favourite nigger melody. Venders of Indian beadwork; itinerant philosophers; camera-obscura men; imitation squaws; free and enlightened negroes; guides to go under the cataract, who should have been sent over it; spiritualists, phrenologists, and nigger minstrels had made the place their own. Shoddy and petroleum were having "a high old time of it," spending the dollar as though that "almighty article had become the thin end of nothing whittled fine": altogether, Niagara was a place to be instinctively shunned.

W. F. BUTLER
The Great Lone Land   1872

JAMES BUCKNALL   The camp of the 43rd regiment at Niagara Falls, Upper Canada   1838
BUCKNALL ESTCOURT   Water-colour, 7½ x 10¼ inches

While at a field-day at 6 o'clock A.M. of 30th June, a sudden order reached the 43rd directing their immediate removal to Upper Canada. Precisely as the clock struck nine they left their barracks. The left wing proceeded by the Ottawa and the Rideau Canal, while the right took the line of the St. Lawrence, making a sort of amphibious march — by steam where the river was navigable, by land where the rapids rendered it impassable — and reached Kingston on Lake Ontario on the 3rd of July. On the 6th an order came to advance on the Niagara frontier, to occupy a line of country hitherto almost entirely defended by militia and volunteers. With the despatch which had lately characterised their movements the right wing, accompanied by Sir John Colborne, was embarked the same evening. A detachment of artillery with two guns, and a party of sappers and miners with camp equipage for 1000 men, were also shipped. . . .

The route from Queenstown to Niagara was beautiful and exciting; the foliage of the solemn forests contrasting artistically with the luxuriance of the lower vegetation. Within a mile of their destination Lundy's Lane was crossed — a sandy ravine leading up to an elevation which formed the key of the British position in the battle of 1814. Reaching the pretty little village of Drummondville, and debouching from a straggling grove of chestnuts, a verdant plateau extended, scarped by a precipitous bank some 300 feet in depth, thickly clothed with magnificent trees. Far above their topmost boughs the mists and sunbow of the Falls spanned the heavens, and through the foliage sparkled the first glitter of the world's greatest wonder. The word passed to form open column of companies, the right wing 43rd reached the greensward just above the table rock; arms were piled and all rushed to the edge of the soul-stirring and stupendous cataract — "that 'almighty' fall of waters."

A few weeks later, all hands were put on the qui vive by the arrival of Lord Durham and household. Old Niagara probably never did, and never will again, see such a gathering of cocked hats and radiant uniforms as on this occasion, when His Excellency was met by Sir John Colborne and Sir George Arthur with their respective staffs. The Governor-General adopted the soothing system, and was most liberal in his hospitalities. Willing, perhaps, first to astonish, and afterwards to mollify the Yankees, he issued public notice of a review on the 17th of July — in which the 43rd were the principal actors — and cards for two hundred persons to dinner in the evening. An immense concourse, chiefly Americans, attended; the ground was kept by two companies of the 24th Regiment, and 'a troop of Her Majesty's Niagara Lancers—a most excellent and efficient corps.

The spectators had the enjoyment of a rapid field-day in Colonel Booth's best style, with a liberal allowance of blank cartridge. In the evening, all the invités betook themselves to the banquet — a feast chiefly remarkable for the strange mélange of guests, among whom were a considerable proportion of ladies.

R. G. A. LEVINGE
Historical Records of the Forty-third Regiment, Monmouthshire Light Infantry   1868

JAMES BUCKNALL BUCKNALL ESTCOURT   Near Lundy's Lane at Niagara Falls, Upper Canada   1838
Water-colour, 5½ x 7¾ inches

The Field of Battle of Lundy's Lane is in the vicinity of a small village one mile from the Falls, and was the scene of the hardest contested action during the late war. A burial ground has been formed and a church is in meditation upon the rising eminence where the British artillery was posted, and where the bodies of those who fell were buried. The remaining portion of the field was purchased after the conclusion of the peace by an officer who was present in the action, and who now resides there.

The whole of this part of the frontier is a fine and fertile country; but, owing to its long settlement and sad misman-agement, the soil has become nearly exhausted. I did not see any part of America which I should prefer as a resi-dence to that which lies between Lakes Erie and Ontario. It is much sought after by retired officers, and better class of emigrants. The majority of the company at the hotel during my stay there consis-ted of families lately arrived, who were making purchases in the vicinity. If the

settler seeks society, he may meet a con-tinued stream of his countrymen on their pilgrimage to the most stupendous natu-ral curiosity in the world; and, if he wish retirement, he may have it in perfection, for the attention of all travellers is so en-tirely engrossed by the one grand object that they trouble not themselves with making visits, or intruding upon those who have settled down within hearing of the roar of the cataract.

E. T. COKE
A Subaltern's Furlough   1833

I afterwards got into conversation with a most intelligent negro, and commenced a series of questions, which I put to a great number of his race, to ascertain if they themselves had ever thought of suggesting any plan by which the eman-cipation of their brethren in the Southern States could be brought about without the ruin of their masters and the utter demoralisation of the negroes them-

selves. . . . He told me there are twenty-five thousand negroes in Upper Canada, a large number of whom are either emancipated, or have taken "French leave" of their masters. My friend acted as ostler at the inn. He was contented and happy, though, as he told me, he was alone in the world—no wife, nor children, nor brothers, nor sisters—yet he had known them, but they were all

dead. Providence has kindly implanted a contented, uncomplaining disposition in the bosom of the negro, enabling him to bear up against misfortunes which would break the spirits of his white-skinned fellow-mortals.

W. H. G. KINGSTON
Western Wanderings   1856

CAROLINE BUCKNALL ESTCOURT   The good "woman of colour" of Lundy's Lane, Upper Canada   1838
Water-colour, 10½ x 8½ inches

HENRY JAMES WARRE   Brantford, Canada West   1840
Pencil drawing, 8½ x 10½ inches

BRANTFORD

A Town in the township of Brantford, situated on the Grand River, 23½ miles from Hamilton. It was laid out by the crown in 1830, and is a place of considerable business. A canal, two miles and a-half in length, has been constructed from Brantford to below the falls of the Grand River, which will be capable of admitting and allowing vessels drawing three feet and a-half water to reach the town. The fall in the river between the town and the termination of the canal, is about twenty-three feet, which has been overcome by means of three locks. During the last two seasons, a steamer ran regularly three times a-week from the entrance of the canal to Dunnville (fare $1½). The Western road runs through the town. Brantford contains eight churches and chapels, viz., Episcopal, Presbyterian, Catholic, two Methodist, Baptist, Congregationalist, and one for coloured people; also a Fire Company with an engine, and a Mechanics' Institute. A weekly newspaper is published here, the "Brantford Courier."

Population about 2,000. Post Office, post daily.

Professions and Trades. — Three physicians and surgeons, four lawyers, three grist mills, carding machine and fulling mill, foundry, two surveyors, two breweries, four distilleries, twenty-one stores, one soap and candle factory, fourteen taverns, two druggists, one printer, twelve groceries, two watchmakers, three tinsmiths, seven tailors, ten shoemakers, five painters, five cabinet makers, two livery stables, one gunsmith, one tobacconist, one marble factory, three barbers, two ladies' schools, two do. for boys, three bank agencies — "B. N. America," "Montreal," and "Gore."

Principal Taverns. — "Clements," "Irish's," and "Matthews."

Land Agent. — Jas. R. Buchanan.

W. H. SMITH
Smith's Canadian Gazetteer   1846

Woodstock.
u.c. 1840

HENRY JAMES WARRE   Woodstock, Canada West   1840
                                     Pencil drawing, 8½ x 10½ inches

WOODSTOCK

The District Town of the Brock District, in the south-west corner of the township of Blandford, thirty-two miles from London, and forty-six miles from Hamilton, pleasantly situated on a rising ground in the midst of a rolling country. It forms one long street of about a mile in length, and is divided into East Woodstock, and West Woodstock. It became the district town in the year 1840, (before which time the county of Oxford formed a portion of the London District). It contains six churches and chapels, viz. Episcopal, (of brick, and in which is a tolerable organ), Presbyterian, Baptist, British Wesleyan, Canadian Wesleyan, and Christian. There is a jail and court house, built partly of brick, and partly framed.

Two newspapers are published here weekly, the "Monarch," and "Herald." There is a Mechanics Institute, and a cricket club.

Population, 1,085.

Post Office, post every day.

The following Government and district offices are kept in Woodstock: — Judge of district court, sheriff, clerk of peace, judge of surrogate court, registrar of ditto, treasurer, inspector of licenses, district clerk, clerk of district court, deputy clerk of crown, district superintendent of schools.

Professions and Trades. — Two grist mills, one saw mill, carding machine and fulling mill, brewery, distillery, two tanneries, four physicians and surgeons, two lawyers, one foundry, ten stores, seven groceries, one bookseller and stationer, five taverns, five cabinet and chair makers, four waggon makers, two watchmakers, one soap and candle factory, two livery stables, one glover, one turner, six blacksmiths, ten shoemakers, three bakers, four butchers, four saddlers, two coopers, one tinsmith, one barber, three painters, eight tailors, one printers, one school, one bank agency "Gore."

Principal Tavern. — "Woodstock Hotel."

Land Agent. J. F. Rogers.

W. H. SMITH
Smith's Canadian Gazetteer 1846

*near London
UC 1840*

*the Gaol at London UC
from the River.
1840*

HENRY JAMES WARRE   On the Thames River showing the jail at London, Canada West   1840
Pencil drawing, 8½ x 10½ inches

The removal of the seat of government from Niagara to Toronto, according to the plan laid down, was only to have been a preparatory step to another alteration: a new city to have been named London, was to have been built on the river formerly called La Trenche, but since called the Thames, a river running into Lake St. Clair; and here the seat of government was ultimately to have been fixed. The spot marked out for the site of the city possesses many local advantages. It is situated in a healthy, fertile country, on a fine navigable river, in a central part of the province, from whence the water communication is extensive in every direction. A few settlements have already been made on the banks of the river, and the tide of emigration is setting in strongly towards that quarter; at a future day, therefore, it is by no means improbable but that this spot may be deemed an eligible one for the capital of the country; but to remove the seat of government immediately to a place little better than a wilderness, and so far from the populous parts of the province, would be a measure frought with numberless inconveniencies to the public, and productive apparently of no essential advantages whatsoever.

I. WELD
Travels Through the States of North America and the Provinces of Upper and Lower Canada 1799

CHATHAM

The County Town of the County of Kent; pleasantly and advantageously situated on the River Thames, at the junction of the townships of Chatham, Raleigh, Harwich, and Dover East; and at the entrance of McGregor's Creek into that river: the portion of it situated on the north shore of the river being called Chatham North. This town was originally laid out by Governor Simcoe, who, while examining the valley of the Thames, on arriving at the spot on which Chatham now stands, was so much struck with its great natural advantages, that he immediately reserved 600 acres for a town plot. The town, however, may be said to have commenced only about fifteen years ago; since which time it has progressed rapidly, and now contains about 1500 inhabitants; and property has greatly increased in value, so much so, that a small town lot, which at the first

PHILIP JOHN BAINBRIGGE   6th Street, Chatham, Upper Canada   1838
Water-colour, 6 x 8¾ inches

settlement could have been worth but a mere trifle, was sold a short time since to a merchant at the enormous advance of 750 dollars.

This place was a garrison town during the rebellion, and contains barracks, but they are at present unoccupied.

The new road from London to Amherstburgh passes through the town. Four-horsed stages, going eastward and westward, leave Chatham every day.

The steamboat "Brothers," Captain Eberts, is owned here, and, during the season, leaves Chatham for Detroit and Amherstburgh every Monday, Wednesday and Friday, returning on the alternate days. The "London," Captain Van Allen (the fastest boat on the upper lakes) meets the "Brothers" at Detroit and continues the route to Buffalo, touching at the intermediate ports on the Canadian side. The "London" is a beautiful boat;

and, during the winter of 1844-5, the "Brothers" was overhauled, enlarged and refitted.

Chatham contains four churches and chapels; viz;, Episcopal, Presbyterian, Secession, and Methodist: also, a Theatre, which is well attended, the performers being amateurs; and a cricket club.

A newspaper, the "Chatham Gleaner," is published here every Tuesday. Town lots of a quarter of an acre, and park lots varying from three to ten acres, are still to be purchased, the price varying according to situation. . . .

List of Professions and Trades. — Five physicians and surgeons, one lawyer, one dentist, one steam grist mill, one water do., two saw mills, two breweries, three distilleries, one tannery, ten stores, four groceries, one pottery, one maltster, six tailors, two saddlers, three shoemak-

ers, ten taverns, one printing office, one watchmaker, one gunsmith, eight blacksmiths, three cabinet makers, one hatter, one tinsmith, two carriage makers, one foundry, two bakers, one tallow chandler, two asheries, one livery stable, one bookseller and stationer, two bank agencies (Gore and Upper Canada), one land agency, three schools.

Principal tavern and stage house, the "Royal Exchange," at which is a reading and news room.

Land Agent, Abraham Steers.

Stage fare from Chatham to London, $3½; to Detroit, $2½. Steamboat fare from Chatham to Detroit, $2; to Amherstburg, $2½.

Chatham is thirty-six miles from London, and fifty miles from Detroit.

W. H. SMITH
Smith's Canadian Gazetteer 1846

PHILIP JOHN BAINBRIGGE   On a bush farm near Chatham, Upper Canada   1838
                                Water-colour, 6 x 10 inches

OPPOSITE
ANONYMOUS   An oil well at Bothwell, Ontario   1870
                                Water-colour, 8¼ inches diameter

I must now tell you what my husband is doing on our land. He has let out ten acres to some Irish choppers who have established themselves in the shanty for the winter. They are to receive fourteen dollars per acre for chopping, burning, and fencing in that quantity. The ground is to be perfectly cleared of every thing but the stumps: these will take from seven to nine or ten years to decay; the pine, hemlock, and fir remain much longer. The process of clearing away the stumps is too expensive for new beginners to venture upon, labour being so high that it cannot be appropriated to any but indispensable work. The working season is very short on account of the length of time the frost remains on the ground. With the exception of chopping trees, very little can be done. Those that understand the proper management of uncleared land, usually underbrush (that is, cut down all the small timbers and brushwood), while the leaf is yet on them; this is piled in heaps, and the windfallen trees are chopped through in lengths, to be logged up in the spring with the winter's chopping. The latter end of the summer and the autumn are the best seasons for this work. The leaves then become quite dry and sear, and greatly assist in the important business of burning off the heavy timbers. Another reason is, that when the snow has fallen to some depth, the light timbers cannot be cut close to the ground, or the dead branches and other incumbrances collected and thrown in heaps.

We shall have about three acres ready for spring crops, provided we get a good burning of that which is already chopped near the site of the house,–this will be sown with oats, pumpkins, Indian corn, and potatoes: the other ten acres will be ready for putting in a crop of wheat. So you see it will be a long time before we reap a harvest. We could not even get in spring-wheat early enough to come to perfection this year.

We shall try to get two cows in the spring, as they are little expense during the spring, summer, and autumn; and by the winter we shall have pumpkins and oat-straw for them.

C. P. TRAILL
The Backwoods of Canada   1836

For many years to come Ontario, will require emigration, for that, and that only will level her forests and open her mines which are as yet in their infancy,

THE OIL WELLS

alone being almost an inexhaustible source of wealth to a young country. In 1870, the Enniskillen Oil Company, at their wells in Petrolia, 51 miles north west of London, employed 5,825 men, and 750 horses, and since then other wells have been opened in the locality. The total number of men engaged in mining operations in 1871, being 6,495, and 820 horses. Ontario possesses almost all the most useful minerals except coal, but that is found in abundance in Nova Scotia and in Manitoba, and when the Canada Pacific Railway is built it will be brought through from both places without difficulty.

P. O'LEARY
Travels and Experiences in Canada   no date

The East Branch of the Sydenham would lead us up to Strathroy, a prosperous manufacturing town of Middlesex, on the highway of commerce between London and Sarnia. The North Branch takes us into the heart of Lambton, a rich champaign, dotted over with cosy villages. Threading our way through groves of derricks, we reach in Enniskillen the heart of Petroleum Land. This Township, in 1860, became famous by the discovery of a flowing well, the first in Canada. By some dark alchemy the marine animals and plants embedded in the shales and encrinal limestone that form the base of the "Hamilton" formation, have distilled out the complex mixture of things that we gather up in the single word, Petroleum. Crude oil is drawn chiefly from the wells around Petrolea, Oil Springs, and Oil City, and wafted — with a very considerable whiff — to the refineries in Petrolea and London. There the "Crude" is decanted from tank-carts into a vast subterranean rotunda of boiler plate, and the sand and water subside to the bottom. By treatment with acid and alkali, "sweetness" is divorced from "light." Distillation at carefully regulated temperatures yields a series of valuable products — thigoline, naptha, kerosene, lubricating oil, etc. Heavier Canadian petroleums are rich in paraffine; the snowy whiteness of this beautiful substance contrasts strongly with the black, garlicky fluid from which it is extracted.

G. M. GRANT (ED.)
Picturesque Canada   1882

PHILIP JOHN BAINBRIGGE

Ruins of the old naval depot at the mouth of the Grand River, Lake Erie, Upper Canada 1840
Water-colour, 6½ x 9½ inches

The lake, the banks, the grouping of the trees, were all more beautiful than before; and so far from the ride seeming long, we dropped into the quiet little naval establishment at the mouth of the Grand River — our ultimate object — long before it appeared that we had come nearly to the journey's end.

The flag-staff was struck, the works gone to decay, the store-house nearly empty. Every thing we saw, in short, bespoke the stillness and neglect of peace, as contradistinguished from the rattling activity of iron war.

A small military party were stationed here, under the command of an officer, whose unhappiness at this moment interested our feelings not a little. All things, it is said, are judged of by comparison; but surely it required some elasticity in the imagination to understand how such a wretched abode as the Grand River station could be deemed a desir-able residence. Yet so it seemed to this worthy officer, and his poor family, who were in great distress at the necessity of leaving it. . . .

Some months previous to our visit, a party of soldiers had been ordered from Quebec to this remote station, and our friend, who considered himself fortunate in getting the appointment, set off accordingly with his family, in high spirits. The proverbial miseries of a protracted voyage across Lake Ontario, in a badly found sloop, and the ten times more harassing journey through the forest; were submitted to with patience. Not far from the Grand River, the party were benighted, and such was the jolting of the carriage over the Corduroy roads, that to save the little life of one of their children, only three weeks old, it was lifted out of the carriage and carried in one of the men's arms in the dark, through the woods, though at every third step the honest soldier-nurse plunged up to his knees in the mud; while the poor urchin was unconsciously augmenting the miseries of the night by crying with cold and hunger. . . . The arrival of the baggage waggons brought fresh cares in the shape of a miserable account of broken crockery — an irreparable misfortune in the back woods! But as I said before, they were far too happy to feel themselves fixed at last, to worry one another with unavailing complaints, but turned about cheerfully to make the most of their situation for the next few years. On the very morning we arrived, however, counter orders reached the station; the regiment, it seems, was ordered from Canada to England, and another officer was of course appointed to supersede our afflicted host.

B. HALL
Travels in North America in the Years 1827 and 1828 1829

The Royal Navy played an important part in bringing to public notice the farther reaches of the eighteenth and nineteenth century world. When Captain James Cook sailed into Nootka Sound on the Pacific Northwest coast in 1778, the English artist John Webber was on board to make a visual record. When Sir John Franklin set out overland for the polar coast, the expedition's official artist was Robert Hood. But when he was killed by a guide in the Barrens, George Back took over his official duties.

The Hudson's Bay Company had since 1670 been successfully challenging the Arctic ice floes to supply its outposts in the northern interior. Peter Rindisbacher, who, with other Swiss colonists, travelled on one such supply ship, has left us unique water-colours of these isolated HBC trading posts. As master of half a continent, the HBC controlled the Canadian West until the middle of the nineteenth century, by which time the pressures of American expansion had begun to threaten its interests. In response

to this threat in Oregon, the British government sent Henry James Warre and a fellow officer across the continent to the mouth of the Columbia River in 1845-6. The government was persuaded to establish a garrison at Fort Garry in 1846 and 1857; Hampden Moody and George Seton were both personally involved as officers.

In 1846, with the loss of the Oregon Territory, the Hudson's Bay Company was forced to concentrate its activities in what became the colony of British Columbia. The discovery of gold on the Fraser River in 1858 and the Cariboo in 1862 attracted worldwide attention. The ensuing rush of prospectors and adventurers, which included W.G.R. Hind, could not help but be harmful to the interests of the company.

Adventurers were not the only people interested in the West; it was attracting the attention of the Canadian government as an area of settlement, and they sent exploratory expeditions in 1857 and 1858 to report back on the potential of

the region west of Lake Superior. It was as a member of the 1857 expedition that W.H.E. Napier had the opportunity to see St. Boniface cathedral. After Confederation, the official interest in the West increased. British Columbia was invited to join the eastern provinces, and was visited by Lord and Lady Dufferin to impress upon the people the advantages of Canadian connections. These same advantages were promoted by G.M. Grant in Ocean to Ocean.

With the settlement of the West and the turning over of Rupert's Land to the Canadian government in 1869, the old economy of the interior dwindled, and the already tenuous position of the Indian was once again threatened. Lord Lorne's attempts to placate the Indians of the Far West in 1881 are ironic when we consider that the expressed purpose of his trip was to attract immigrants from the Old Country, who would put the entire West under the plough at the expense of the original inhabitants' way of life.

During the time I was at this village, Mr. Webber, who had attended me thither, made drawings of every thing that was curious, both within and without doors. I had also an opportunity of inspecting, more narrowly, the construction of the houses, household furniture, and utensils, and the striking peculiarities of the customs and modes of living of the inhabitants.

J. COOK
A Voyage to the Pacific Ocean   1785

JOHN WEBBER
Indian women weaving at Nootka on the Northwest coast of North America
April 1778
Water-colour, 7½ x 5¾ inches

Their common dress is a flaxen garment, or mantle, ornamented on the upper edge by a narrow strip of fur, and, at the lower edge, by fringes or tassels. It passes under the left arm, and is tied over the right shoulder, by a string before, and one behind, near its middle; by which means both arms are left free; and it hangs evenly, covering the left side, but leaving the right open, except from the loose part of the edges falling upon it, unless when the mantle is fastened by a girdle (of coarse matting or woollen) round the waist, which is often done. Over this, which reaches below the knees, is worn a small cloak of the same substance, likewise fringed at the lower part. In shape this resembles a round dish cover, being quite close, except in the middle, where there is a hole just large enough to admit the head; and then, resting upon the shoulders, it covers the arms to the elbows, and the body as far as the waist. Their head is covered with a cap, of the figure of a truncated cone, or like a flower-pot, made of fine matting, having the top frequently ornamented with a round or pointed knob, or bunch of leathern tassels; and there is a string that passes under the chin, to prevent its blowing off.

Besides the above dress, which is common to both sexes, the men frequently throw over their other garments the skin of a bear, wolf, or sea-otter, with the hair outward, and tie it, as a cloak, near the upper part, wearing it sometimes before, and sometimes behind. In rainy weather, they throw a coarse mat about their shoulders. They have also woollen garments, which, however, are little in use. The hair is commonly worn hanging down loose; but some, when they have no cap, tie it in a bunch on the crown of the head. Their dress, upon the whole, is convenient, and would by no means be inelegant, were it kept clean. But as they rub their bodies constantly over with a red paint, of a clayey or coarse ochry substance, mixed with oil, their garments, by this means, contract a rancid offensive smell, and a greasy nastiness. So that they make a very wretched dirty appearance; and what is still worse, their heads and their garments swarm with vermin, which, so depraved is their taste for cleanliness, we used to see them pick off with great composure, and eat.

J. COOK
A Voyage to the Pacific Ocean   1785

JOHN WEBBER
Members of Captain James Cook's
Expedition hunting sea lions on
the Northwest coast of America
1778

Water-colour, 6½ x 12 inches

I have chosen to refer to this class the sea-otter, as living mostly in the water. It might have been sufficient to have mentioned, that this animal abounds here, as it is fully described in different books, taken from the accounts of the Russian adventurers in their expeditions Eastward from Kamtschatka, if there had not been a small difference in one that we saw. We, for some time, entertained doubts, whether the many skins which the natives brought, really belonged to this animal; as our only reason for being of that opinion, was founded on the size, colour, and fineness of the fur; till a short while before our departure, when a whole one, that had been just killed, was purchased from some strangers who came to barter. . . . It was rather young, weighing only twenty-five pounds; of a shining or glossy black colour; but many of the hairs being tipt with white, gave it a greyish cast at first sight. The face, throat, and breast were of a yellowish white, or very light brown colour, which, in many of the skins, extended the whole length of the belly. It had six cutting teeth in each jaw; two of those of the lower jaw being very minute, and placed without, at the base of the two middle ones. In these circumstances, it seems to disagree with those found by the Russians; and also in not having the outer toes of the hind feet skirted with a membrane. There seemed also a greater variety in the colour of the skins, than is mentioned by the describers of the Russian sea-otters. These changes of colour certainly take place at the different gradations of life. The very young ones had brown hair, which was coarse, with very little fur underneath; but those of the size of the entire animal, which came into our possession, and just described, had a considerable quantity of that substance; and both in that colour and state the sea-otters seem to remain, till they have attained their full growth. After that, they lose the black colour, and assume a deep brown or sooty colour; but have then a greater quantity of very fine fur, and scarcely any long hairs. Others, which we suspected to be still older, were of a chestnut brown; and a few skins were seen that had even acquired a perfectly yellow colour. The fur of these animals, as mentioned in the Russian accounts, is certainly softer and finer than that of any others we know of; and, therefore, the discovery of this part of the continent of North America, where so valuable an article of commerce may be met with, cannot be a matter of indifference.

J. COOK
A Voyage to the Pacific Ocean 1785

PETER RINDISBACHER

The meeting of the Hudson's Bay Company ships, the *Prince of Wales* and the *Eddystone*, carrying the Swiss immigrants, and Captain W.E. Parry's ships, the *Hecla* and the *Griper*   July 16, 1821
Water-colour, 8½ x 12¼ inches

On the 13th, both ships' companies were exercised in firing at a target on the ice, as well for the purpose of giving them occupation, as of finding out who were our best shots. On the same afternoon, we saw two ships beset to the northward, which we supposed to be those bound to the Hudson's Bay factories. They were joined the next day by a third ship, which afterwards proved to be, as we conjectured, the Lord Wellington, having on board settlers for the Red River. The ice being somewhat more slack about the ships on the 15th, we cast off and made sail at nine P.M.; but after running with difficulty about a mile to the W.bN., we were obliged to make fast to a small berg near us. Here we remained till eleven P.M., the wind blowing a gale from the N.E., when the ice closing in suddenly and violently to leeward of the berg, forced the ships against it, and was near carrying away the Hecla's bowsprit by

the pressure. The Fury also received a heavy "nip," which, lifting her abaft, made her timbers crack a good deal about the quarters, but no material injury was sustained. To avoid, however, a repetition of this occurrence, we cast off, and allowed the ships to take their chance among the loose ice for the rest of the night, which was dusky about midnight.

The ice being rather less close on the morning of the 16th, we made sail to the westward, at 7.45 A.M., and continued "boring" in that direction the whole day, which enabled us to join the three strange ships. They proved to be, as we had supposed, the Prince of Wales, Eddystone, and Lord Wellington, bound to Hudson's Bay. I sent a boat to the former, to request Mr. Davidson, the master, to come aboard, which he immediately did. From him we learned that the Lord Wellington, having on board one

hundred and sixty settlers for the Red River, principally foreigners, of both sexes and every age, had now been twenty days among the ice, and had been drifted about in various directions at no small risk to the ship. Mr. Davidson considered that he had arrived here rather too early for advancing to the westward, and strongly insisted on the necessity of first getting to the northward, or in-shore, before we could hope to make any progress;—a measure, the expediency of which is well known to all those accustomed to the navigation of icy seas. By the Prince of Wales we sent our last letters for our friends in England; and I took the same opportunity to acquaint the Secretary of the Admiralty with the proceedings of the Expedition up to this date.

W. E. PARRY
Journal of a Second Voyage for the Discovery of a North-West Passage 1824

ROBERT HOOD

The first Franklin overland expedition making a
portage at Trout Fall   September 27, 1819
Water-colour, 10 x 15 inches

Knee Lake towards its upper end becomes narrower, and its rocky shores are broken into conical and rounded eminences, destitute of soil, and of course devoid of trees. We slept at the western extremity of the lake, having come during the day nineteen miles and a half on a S.W. course.

We began the ascent of Trout River early in the morning of the 27th, and in the course of the day passed three portages and several rapids. At the first of these portages the river falls between two rocks about sixteen feet, and it is necessary to launch the boat over a precipitous rocky bank. This cascade is named *Trout-Fall,* and the beauty of the scenery afforded a subject for Mr. Hood's pencil. The rocks which form the bed of this river are slaty, and present sharp fragments, by which the feet of the boatmen are much lacerated. The second portage, in particular, obtains the the expressive name of *Knife Portage.* The length of our voyage to-day was three miles.

J. FRANKLIN
Narrative of a Journey to the Shores of the Polar Sea,
in the Years 1819, 20, 21, and 22 1823

GEORGE BACK

Fort Franklin, the headquarters of the second Franklin expedition overland to the Polar Sea, showing Bear Lake   Autumn 1825

Water-colour, 5¼ x 8¼ inches

TRANSACTIONS AT FORT FRANKLIN, 1825-26

Mr. Dease, having passed the winter of 1824-25 at the Big Island of Mackenzie, arrived here with fifteen Canadian voyageurs, Beaulieu, the interpreter, and four Chipewyan hunters, on the twenty-seventh of July, 1825; which, on account of the drifting of the ice, was as soon as he could, with safety, ascend the Bear Lake River. Several of the Dog-Rib Indians were on the spot, which enabled him to take immediate steps towards procuring a supply of dried meat for our winter use, as well as of fresh meat for present consumption. It having been ascertained that the Rein-deer are most abundant in the north-east quarter of the lake, during the months of August and September, a select party of Indians was despatched to hunt thereabout, under the direction of the interpreter, who took a large canoe for the purpose of bringing home the produce of their hunt. Other men were sent to inform the Hare Indians of our wish to purchase any meat they might bring to the establishment. Our principal subsistence, however, was to be derived from the water, and Mr. Dease was determined in the selection of the spot on which our residence was to be erected, by its proximity to that part of the lake where the fish has usually been most abundant. The place decided upon was the site of an old fort belonging to the North-West Company, which had been abandoned many years; our buildings being required of a much larger size, we derived very little benefit from its materials. The wood in the immediate vicinity having been all cut down for fuel by the former residents, the party was obliged to convey the requisite timber in rafts from a considerable distance, which, of course, occasioned trouble and delay. We found, however, on our arrival, all the buildings in the habitable state, but wanting many internal arrangements to fit them for a comfortable winter residence. They were disposed so as to form three sides of a square, the officers' house being in the centre, those for the men on the right, with a house for the interpreter's family, and the store on the left. A blacksmith's shop and meat store were added, and the whole was inclosed by the stockading of the original fort, which we found highly serviceable in skreening us from the snow-drift, and wintry blasts. The officers' dwelling measured forty-four feet, by twenty-four, and contained a hall and four apartments, beside a kitchen. That of the men was thirty-six feet by twenty-three, and was divided into three rooms. These buildings were placed on a dry sandy bank, about eighty yards from the lake, and twenty-five feet above it; at the distance of half a mile in our rear, the ground rose to the height of one hundred and fifty feet, and continued in an even ridge, on which, though the timber had been felled, we found plenty of small trees for fuel. This ridge bounded our view to the north; and to the west, though confined to less than two miles, the prospect was pretty, from its embracing a small lake, and the mouth of a narrow stream that flowed in at its head. Our southern view commanded the south-west arm of Bear Lake, which is here four miles wide, and not deeper than from three to five

Etsahwalna

GEORGE BACK
Etsahwalna, one of the native retainers of the Franklin party   1826
Water-colour, 5¼ x 8¼ inches

fathoms, except in the channel of the river, which conveys its waters to the Mackenzie. We had also, in front, the Clark-hill, a mountain about thirty-six miles distant, which was always visible in clear weather. When the refraction was great, we saw the tops of some other hills, belonging to the range that extends from Clark-hill to the rapid in Bear Lake River.

Immediately under the sandy soil on which the house stood, there is a bed of tenacious bluish clay, of unknown thickness, which, even in the months of August and September, was firmly frozen at the depth of twenty-one inches from the surface. No rocks were exposed in any part, and wherever the surface had been torn up, a clayey soil appeared. Many boulder stones of granite, limestone, sand-stone, and trap rocks, were scattered about the lake, not far from the shore.

The trees at some distance from our fort consisted of black and white spruce, and larch, generally small, though a few of the better grown measured from four to five feet in girth, and were from fifty to fifty-five feet high. Dr. Richardson ascertained, by counting the annual rings, that some of them, in a sound state, were upwards of one hundred and thirty years old; while others, which were not much greater in size, had two hundred and fifty rings, but these were decayed at the heart.

The officers had done me the honour, previous to my arrival, of giving the name of Franklin to the fort, which I felt a grateful pleasure in retaining at their desire, though I had intended naming it Fort Reliance. The number of persons belonging to the establishment amounted to fifty: consisting of five officers, including Mr. Dease; nineteen British seamen, marines, and voyagers; nine Canadians; two Esquimaux; Beaulieu, and four Chipewyan hunters; three women, six children, and one Indian lad; besides a few infirm Indians, who required temporary support. This party was far too large to gain subsistence by fishing at one station only; two houses were, therefore, constructed at four and

seven miles distance from the fort, to which parties were sent, provided with the necessary fishing implements; and not more than thirty persons were left to reside at the principal establishment. From fifteen to twenty nets were kept in use, under the superintendence of Pascal Coté, an experienced fisherman, who had two assistants. These were placed opposite the house, and towards the end of summer, and in autumn, they yielded daily from three to eight hundred fish, of the kind called "the Herring Salmon of Bear Lake," and occasionally some trout, tittameg, and carp. Four Dog-Rib Indians, who were engaged to hunt the Rein-deer in the neighbourhood of the fort, from want of skill, contributed very little fresh meat to our store. Augustus and Ooligbuck employed themselves in the same service, but from not being accustomed to hunt in a woody country, they were not more successful.

J. FRANKLIN
Narrative of a Second Expedition to the Shores of the Polar Sea in the Years 1825, 1826, and 1827
1828

GEORGE BACK

ABOVE   A ceremonial dance of the Hare Indians, Rupert's Land   1826
RIGHT   Egheechololle, one of the native retainers of the Franklin party
BELOW   Cokwonayea-bethah, one of the native retainers of the Franklin party
        Water-colours, 5¼ x 8¼ inches

OWEN STANLEY
H.M.S. *Terror* at sunrise   July 14, 1837
Water-colour, 4¼ x 6¼ inches

July 13th. Though there was ice in every direction, we continued to drift about a quarter of a mile an hour. Some small calves found their way from beneath our clog, and it was with great satisfaction that we contemplated the increased breadth of the saw line—a satisfaction not lessened by the discovery that the ship had settled more down, her draught now being abaft thirteen feet eight inches, and forward twelve feet eight. Neither, with the incessant working of one pump, had the water accumulated in the well beyond eleven inches. At 9ʰ A.M. there was a moderate breeze from the westward with a thin mist, and, to our unaccustomed eyes a sight almost marvellous, a gentle swell on an apparently unbroken surface. It was thought the agitation, slight as it was, might crack or break the ice alongside; but as it proved otherwise, two warps fixed to ice anchors, and leading to either extremity of the ship, were firmly attached at a favourable angle for separating and entirely disuniting the entire mass; however, while we were in the act of heaving a powerful strain on the warps, it suddenly split diagonally from a hummocky point about fifteen paces from the starboard bow, along its outer edge, to somewhere near the after part of

the main chains. The detached portion, on which were two men, (a third being in the dingy, close to them), was instantaneously splintered into three pieces, two of which, singularly enough, were separately occupied by the persons just mentioned, who, standing steadily on the whirling and heaving ice, thus violently discarded, gave a hearty cheer, while their companion, having lost his balance from the sudden jerking of the dingy, lay stretched at full length, and grasping the gunwhale on each side. The cheering however was turned to astonishment, as they watched the ship slowly rising and heeling over to port. We on board had been surprised that no counter action occurred, and were beginning to wonder that the vessel did not recover her equilibrium, but were now startled by the conviction that she was gradually going over; and the great inclination rendering it impossible to stand on deck, every one clung on to windward as he best could. Then it was we beheld the strange and appalling spectacle of what may be fitly termed a submerged berg, fixed low down with one end to the ship's side, while the other, with the purchase of a long lever, advantageously placed at a right angle with the keel, was slowly rising towards

the surface. Meanwhile, those who happened to be below, finding every thing falling, rushed or clambered on deck, where they saw the ship on her beamends, with the lee boats touching the water, and felt that a few moments only trembled between them and eternity. Yet in that awful crisis there was no confusion; the sails were clewed up and lowered; fresh men from former crews were stationed in the boats, which again were rather unhooked than lowered; the barge was hoisted out; and with a promptitude and presence of mind which I shall ever remember with admiration, the whole five were provisioned and filled with arms, ammunition, and clothing, and veered astern clear of danger. The pumps were never quitted, and though expecting that the ship might capsize, yet the question of "Does the leak gain on us?" was asked, and when answered in the negative, there was still a manifestation of hope. Our fate, however, yet hung in suspense, for not in the smallest degree did the ship right; happily for us there was a dead calm, which permitted us to examine the berg.

G. BACK
Narrative of an Expedition in H.M.S. Terror...
1836-37   1838

THOMAS MITCHELL
The return of the sun at Discovery Bay,
Ellesmere Island
March 1, 1876
Water-colour, 10 x 18¾ inches

The long arctic winter, with its un-paralleled intensity and duration of darkness produced by an absence of sunlight for 142 days, was passed by each individual on board with much cheerfulness and contentment. Owing to the sameness in the daily routine, which, when looking into futurity, is thought to entail a long duration of dreary monotony, the time, in reality, passed with great rapidity, and in January, when the first glimmering increase in the mid-day twilight began to lengthen sensibly day by day, the want of light was scarcely noticed by anyone; and not until the sun actually returned on the 1st March did we in any way realize the intense darkness.

G. S. NARES
Arctic Expedition 1875-76   1877

PETER RINDISBACHER

York Factory, the Hudson's Bay Company post on Hudson's Bay   1821
Water-colour, 6¼ x 8½ inches

York factory is the principal depôt of the Northern department, from whence all the supplies for the trade are issued, and where all the returns of the department are collected and shipped for England. As may be supposed, then, the establishment is a large one. There are always between thirty and forty men resident at the post, summer and winter; generally four or five clerks, a postmaster, and a skipper for the small schooners; and the whole is under the direction and superintendence of a chief factor, or chief trader.

As the winter is very long, nearly eight months, and the summer consequently very short, all the transport of goods to, and returns from, the interior, must necessarily be effected as quickly as possible. The consequence is, that great numbers of men and boats are constantly arriving from inland, and departing again during the summer; and, as each brigade is commanded by a chief factor, trader, or clerk, there is a constant succession of new faces, which, after a long and dreary winter, during which the inhabitants never see any stranger, renders the summer months at York factory the most agreeable part of the year. The arrival of the ship from England, too, delights them with letters from *home*, which can only be received twice a year.

The fort (as all establishments in the Indian country, whether small or great, are called) is a large square, I should think about six or seven acres, inclosed within high stockades, and built on the banks of Hayes River, nearly five miles from its mouth. The houses are all of wood, and of course have no pretension to architectural beauty; but their clean white appearence, and regularity, have a very pleasing effect on the eye. Before the front gate stand four large brass field-pieces; but these warlike instruments are only used for the purpose of saluting the ship with blank cartridge, on her arrival and departure, the decayed state of the carriages rendering it dangerous to load the guns with a full charge.

R. M. BALLANTYNE
Hudson's Bay   1848

PETER RINDISBACHER   Norway House, a Hudson's Bay Company post on Lake Winnipeg   1821
Water-colour, 6¼ x 8½ inches

Nearly eighteen days after we left York Factory, we arrived in safety at the depôte of Norway House.

This fort is built at the mouth of a small and sluggish stream, known by the name of Jack River. The houses are ranged in the form of a square; none of them exceed one storey in height, and most of them are whitewashed. The ground on which it stands is rocky, and a small garden, composed chiefly of sand, juts out from the stockades like a strange excrescence. A large, rugged mass of rocks rises up between the fort and Playgreen Lake, which stretches out to the horizon on the other side of them. On the top of these rocks stands a flag-staff as a beacon to guide the traveller; for Norway House is so ingeniously hid in a hollow that it cannot be seen from the lake till the boat almost touches the wharf.

On the left side of the building extends a flat, grassy park, or green, upon which, during the summer months, there is often a picturesque and interesting scene. Spread out to dry in the sun, may be seen the snowy tent of the chief factor, lately arrived; a little farther off, on the rising ground, stands a dark and almost imperceptible wigwam, the small wreath of white smoke issuing from the top proving that it is inhabited; on the river bank, three or four boats and a north canoe are hauled up; and just above them a number of sunburnt voyageurs and a few Indians amuse themselves with various games, or recline upon the grass, basking in the sunshine.

Behind the fort stretches the thick forest, its outline broken here and there by cuttings of firewood or small clearings for farming. . . .

Norway House is also an agreeable and interesting place, from its being in a manner the gate to the only route to Hudson's Bay; so that, during the spring and summer months, all the brigades of boats and canoes from every part of the northern department must necessarily pass it on their way to York Factory with furs; and as they all return in the autumn, and some of the gentlemen leave their wives and families for a few weeks till they return to the interior, it is at this sunny season of the year quite a gay and bustling place; and the clerk's house in which I lived was often filled with a strange and always noisy collection of human beings, who rested here awhile ere they started for the shores of Hudson's Bay, the distant regions of M'Kenzie's River, or the still more distant land of Oregon.

R. M. BALLANTYNE
Hudson's Bay   1848

Fort Ellice near the Assineboine River

HENRY JAMES WARRE   The Hudson's Bay Company post Fort Ellice near the Assineboine River   1845
Pen and ink drawing, 4¼ x 7½ inches

Of the two great monopolies which the impecuniosity of Charles II gave birth to, the Hudson Bay Company alone survives, but to-day the monopoly is one of fact, and not of law. All men are now free to come and go, to trade and sell and gather furs in the great Northern territory, but distance and climate raise more formidable barriers against strangers than law or protection could devise. Bold would be the trader who would carry his goods to the faraway Mackenzie River; intrepid would be the *voyageur* who sought a profit from the lonely shores of the great Bear Lake. Locked in their fastnesses of ice and distance, these remote and friendless solitudes of the North must long remain, as they are at present, the great fur preserve of the Hudson Bay Company. Dwellers within the limits of European states can ill comprehend the vastness of territory over which this Fur Company holds sway. I say holds sway, for the north of North America is still as much in the possession of the Company, despite all cession of title to Canada, as Crusoe

was the monarch of his island, or *the man* must be the owner of the moon. From Pembina on Red River to Fort Anderson on the Mackenzie is as great a distance as from London to Mecca. From the King's Posts to the Pelly Banks is farther than from Paris to Samarcand, and yet to-day throughout that immense region the Company is king. And what a king! no monarch rules his subject with half the power of this Fur Company. It clothes, feeds, and utterly maintains nine-tenths of its subjects. From the Esquimaux at Ungava to the Loucheaux at Fort Simpson, all live by and through this London Corporation. The earth possesses not a wilder spot than the barren grounds of Fort Providence; around like the desolate shores of the great Slave Lake. Twice in the year news comes from the outside world—news many, many months old—news borne by men and dogs through 2000 miles of snow; and yet even there the gun that brings down the moose and the musk-ox has been forged in a London smithy; the blanket that covers the wild Indian in his cold

camp has been woven in a Whitney loom; that knife is from Sheffield; that string of beads is from Birmingham. Let us follow the ships that sail annually from the Thames bound for the supply of this vast region. It is early in June when she gets clear of the Nore; it is mid-June when the Orkneys and Stornaway are left behind; it is August when the frozen Straits of Hudson are pierced; and the end of the month has been reached when the ship comes to anchor off the sand-barred mouth of the Nelson River. For one year the stores that she has brought in lie in the warehouses of York factory; twelve months later they reach Red River; twelve months later again they reach Fort Simpson on the Mackenzie. That rough flint-gun, which might have done duty in the days of the Stuarts, is worth many a rich sable in the country of the Dogribs and the Loucheaux, and is bartered for skins whose value can be rated at four times their weight in gold; but the gun on the banks of the Thames and the gun in the pine woods of the Mackenzie are two widely different ar-

HENRY JAMES WARRE   The Hudson's Bay Company post Carleton House   1846
Pencil drawing, 4½ x 7¼ inches

ticles. The old rough flint, whose bent barrel the Indians will often straighten between the cleft of a tree or the crevice of a rock, has been made precious by the long labour of many men; by the trackless wastes through which it has been carried; by winter-famine of those who have to vend it; by the years which elapse between its departure from the workshop and the return of that skin of sable or silver-fox for which it has been bartered. They are short-sighted men who hold that because the flint-gun and the sable possess such different values in London, these articles should also possess their relative values in North America, and argue from this that the Hudson Bay Company treat the Indians unfairly; they are short-sighted men, I say, and know not of what they speak. That old rough flint has often cost more to put in the hands of the Dogrib hunter than the best finished central fire of Boss or Purdey. But that is not all that has to be said about the trade of this Company. Free trade may be an admirable institution for some nations—making them,

amongst other things, very much more liable to national destruction; but it by no means follows that it should be adapted equally well to the savage Indian. Unfortunately for the universality of British institutions, free trade has invariably been found to improve the red man from the face of the earth. Free trade in furs means dear beavers, dear martens, dear minks, and dear otters; and all these "dears" mean whisky, alcohol, high wine, disease, smallpox, and death. There is no use to tell me that these four dears and their four corollaries ought not to be associated with free trade, an institution which is so pre-eminently pure; I only answer that these things have ever been associated with free trade in furs, and I see no reason whatever to behold in our present day amongst traders, Indian, or, for that matter, English, any very remarkable reformation in the principles of trade. Now the Hudson Bay Company are in the position of men who have taken a valuable shooting for a very long term of years or for a perpetuity, and who therefore are desirous of

preserving for a future time the game which they hunt, and also of preserving the hunters and trappers who are their servants. The free trader is as a man who takes his shooting for the term of a year or two and wishes to destroy all he can. He has two objects in view; first, to get the furs himself, second to prevent the other traders from getting them. "If I cannot get them, then he shan't. Hunt, hunt, hunt, kill, kill, kill; next year may take care of itself." One word more. Other companies and other means have been tried to carry on the Indian trade and to protect the interests of the Indians, but all have failed; from Texas to Saskatchewan there has been but one result, and that result has been the destruction of the wild animals and the extinction, partial or total, of the Indian race.

W. F. BUTLER
The Great Lone Land   1872

HENRY JAMES WARRE
The Bay of Fort Victoria and a corner of the Fort, Vancouver Island   1846
Pencil drawing, 4½ x 7 inches

Carlton stands on the edge of the great forest region whose shores, if we may use the expression, are washed by the waves of the prairie ocean lying south of it; but the waves are of fire, not of water. Year by year the great torrent of flame moves on deeper and deeper into the dark ranks of the solemn-standing pines; year by year a wider region is laid open to the influences of sun and shower, and soon the traces of the conflict are hidden beneath the waving grass, and clinging vetches, and the clumps of tufted prairie roses. But another species of vegetation also springs up in the track of the fire; groves of aspens and poplars grow out of the burnt soil, giving to the country that park-like appearance already spoken of. Nestling along the borders of the innumerable lakes that stud the face of the Saskatchewan region, these poplar thickets sometimes attain large growth, but the fire too frequently checks their progress, and many of them stand bare and dry to delight the eye of the traveller with the assurance of an ample store of bright and warm

firewood for his winter camp when the sunset bids him begin to make all cosy against the night.

W. F. BUTLER
The Great Lone Land   1872

Victoria is very beautifully situated on the shores of a small rocky bay — an indentation in the promontory which is formed by the sweeping round of the sea into the land-locked harbour of Esquimalt. The site was originally chosen by Sir James (then Mr.) Douglas, Governor of the Hudson's Bay Company's territories west of the Rocky Mountains, for the establishment of head-quarters, in place of Fort Vancouver, when Oregon passed into the possession of the United States in the year 1844. Fourteen years afterwards, when the news of the discovery of gold

on the Fraser caused such excitement in California, the only buildings were the Company's Fort, and one or two houses inhabited by their employés. In the course of a few weeks 30,000 people were collected there, waiting for the flooded Fraser to subside, and allow them to proceed to the diggings.

Amongst this immense assemblage of people — the majority of them the most desperate and lawless of the Californian rowdies — Governor Douglas, without the aid of a single soldier or regular police-force, preserved an order and security which contrasted most forcibly with the state of things in San Francisco and Sacramento under similar circumstances. The city wore a very thriving aspect when we visited it, and could already boast of several streets. The whole traffic to and from British Columbia passing through it, has rapidly enriched its merchants, and handsome brick stores are fast replacing the original wooden buildings.

VISCOUNT MILTON AND W. B. CHEADLE
The North-West Passage By Land   1865

From that day, until recently, the colony has been going back, or as some gloomily say, getting into its normal condition. Within the last ten years, millions of dollars in solid gold have been taken out of the colony. No one thought of remaining in it except to make a fortune; no one was interested in its political life; no one of the thousands of foreign immigrants became a subject of the Crown. It was a mere finger-joint separated from its own body. But all this is now changing. With Confederation came the dawn of a brighter future; and, although British Columbia may never have the population of California or Oregon, an orderly development is commencing that will soon make it rank as a valuable Province of the Dominion. It has the prospect of being no longer a dissevered limb, but of being connected by iron, as well as sympathetic, hands with its trunk; and it is already receiving the pulses of the larger life. Had the Columbia River, instead of the 49th parallel been made its Southern boundary instead of a purely artificial one, it could compete with California in cereals as well as in gold mining. But in this, as in every case of disputed lines in America, U.S. diplomatists knew the value of what they claimed, and British diplomatists did not. Every one in the Province believes that they lost the Columbia, because the salmon in it would not take a fly. At the time of the dispute, when the Secretary for War was using brave words in the House of Commons, the brother of the Prime Minister happened to be stationed on the Pacific coast, and fished in the Columbia without success, because the salmon were too uneducated to rise to a fly. He wrote home that "there was no use making a fuss about the country for it wasn't worth a _____." And so the worthless region, now considered the most valuable on the Pacific, was gracefully given up. And why not, when it was the privately if not publicly announced aim of a school of British politicians to get rid of the whole of British America, and thus gradually work out Benjamin Franklin's problem of how "a great nation may be made into a very little one." But enough of this. We still have more good land than we know what to do with.

G. M. GRANT
Ocean to Ocean 1873

HENRY JAMES WARRE
The settlement and Father Belcourt's Church
at White Horse Plains near the Red River
June 17, 1845
Pen and ink drawing, 4¼ x 7¼ inches

The Fort of White Horse Plains is situated near the Assiniboine and the settlement extends itself along the banks of that river. For twenty miles, almost without a break, small farms run outwards from the river-side into the uncultivated but grass-clad prairies. The soil seems rich, a belt of large, fine elm-trees borders the course of the stream, and young poplars grow in masses here and there; the ground undulates considerably in many parts, and altogether this settlement looks warmer and more home-like than that on the Red River near Fort Garry.

'The settler' houses are generally plain square boxes, devoid of the smallest attempt at ornament; without a chimney even, unless a short projecting iron stove-pipe may be called so. Wood is the material invariably employed – placed horizontally in long logs about a foot square. Neither gardens nor surrounding fences are in favour, and the cottages stand all raw and bare-faced, as boulders are strewn by a flood, or meteor-stones dropped from the sky.

THE EARL OF SOUTHESK
Saskatchewan and the Rocky Mountains 1875

Shortly after starting we passed the Roman Catholic church, just as the congregation was coming out. There seemed to be about two hundred people, mostly men, and more or less of French-Canadian blood. They have one almost invariable type of dress, which, though handsome in itself, looks rather sombre in a crowd, — capots of dark blue, leggings of the same, caps either of the same or of some dark fur. The only relief to this monotony is given by a scarlet, crimson or variegated scarf round the waist, and red stripes embroidered with various coloured ribbons down the outside of the leggings. The female costume is generally dark also, and not remarkable, though with much picturesqueness about the head-dress, which is sometimes a dark shawl or blanket worn as a hood, sometimes a crimson or yellow silk handkerchief, which forms a rich contrast to the glossy black hair it partly conceals.

THE EARL OF SOUTHESK
Saskatchewan and the Rocky Mountains 1875

ABOVE

HENRY JAMES
WARRE

Hunting buffalo on
the Western prairies
1846

Water-colour,
7 x 11½ inches

WILLIAM GEORGE
RICHARDSON HIND

Cutting up the buffalo
1862

Water-colour,
3¼ x 6 inches

Too soon will the last of them have vanished from the great central prairie land; never again will those countless herds roam from the Platte to the Missouri, from the Missouri to the Saskatchewan; chased for his robe, for his beef, for sport, for the very pastime of his death, he is rapidly vanishing from the land. Far in the northern forests of the Athabasca a few buffaloes may for a time bid defiance to man, but they, too, must disappear and nothing be left of this giant beast save the bones that for many an age will whiten the prairies over which the great herds roamed at will in times before the white man came.

W. F. BUTLER
The Great Lone Land 1872

Thursday [July] 17 [1845]. — Rain had descended during the whole night, and so drenched our things that we were unable to start till 12oC taking advantage of the delay to dry them. We went on for a few miles, crossing a small, but deep Creek, also Battle River; when the Rain again came down in such torrents, accompanied by the most vivid Lightening, wind & Thunder, we were obliged again to encamp, having hardly advanced 6 miles. — The lightening was so near to us, that at one time, we jumped on our legs, fancying the tent itself had been struck. We were very miserable the whole day cold & wet to the skin — The Rain continued almost the whole night and sleep was next to impossible — At 4 oC. am on Friday 18th we again got under way through the same kind of impenetrable bush down a small River, called Prince's, from the circumstance of a Man of that name having been killed by the Blackfeet on the borders of it, and crossed and recrossed this River 3 different times, at

our crossing we were obliged to carry every thing over on the Mens shoulders, so deep was it in Mud & Water; on through the swamp, round a small Lake where we breakfasted after which we crossed a chain of Hills and again found ourselves surrounded by swamps, Fir & Poplar Trees, having the greatest possible difficulty to get through Horses & Men stumbling & sticking in the Mire. Ogden from his great weight is always worse off, falling frequently but always managing to escape uninjured. I was fairly carried off my horse by a Tree, which in endeavouring to avoid found myself lying on the flat of my back in the mud. Passed a very large lake called Gull Lake, and through magnificient Pine Forest, some of the trees of which were of great size; camped on a small stream completely knocked up, with 11 hours ride and a perfect fever from the bites of the persevering little Tormentors the Mosquitoes. Nor did the horses escape, but were attacked by large Horse Flies

called Bull dogs, which drove them almost mad. — We made about 28 miles SSW course. — The night was very cold & on the Morning of Saturday July 19th we found the whole ground covered with a thick White Frost which was followed by a lovely day. — off at 5oC. through the same kind of thick wood & over swamp till 11oC when we reached a chain of very high hills and much clearer & more practicable country — with beautiful views on all sides of the distant Prairies. Passing over this range we came to a second, on surmounting which we came in sight of the magnificent Range of the Rocky Mountains, in all the irregularity of Mountain Scenery and stretching far away into the blue distance North & South. From the height of the Hills on which we stood the intervening country appeared like an extreme plain, and made the Mountains appear very large. Snow covered several, and had accumulated in the Valleys; but I was disappointed at seeing so little — nor will

HENRY JAMES WARRE/The mountains from near the Bow River, British Columbia   1845/Water-colour, 4¼ x 14½ inches

the Rocky Mountains bear comparison with the Alps either in size or magnificence of outline. Had I not seen Switzerland I should have been much more struck, but I had allowed my imagination too much scope & as is frequently the case, I was on the whole disappointed. — We breakfasted in full view of the Mountains and descended afterwards to an immense plain, which proved to be a deep swamp which we were obliged to pass to a River called by the Indians Medicine Lodge River — The tumbles crossing the swamp were very laughable, but the unfortunate horses suffered and many a Saddle Bag got wet — damaging our goods and chattels. We encamped on the River and dried our things & killed several Grouse which are now of a very good size and made a change in our usual Meal — We have been living on bad Buffaloe Meat dried & made into "Pemican" Hams, and Biscuit. — We passed over the fresh trail of Indians which put us all on the qui vive but we saw none, made about 32 miles W.S.W. Course. —

Tuesday 20th — Leaving our Camp at 5 oC. we traversed a fine extent of open Prairie Country, covered with a kind of brush dog Wood & Artemesia that we had seen. Cross up the M. Lodge River 3 times & from thence crossing to little Elk River, into which I tumbled head over heels down the steep bank the saddle sliding over the horses head — from thence we came to the Main Stream of Elk River a broad & very rapid Stream at which we had to unload all the horses to enable them to cross. The Hunter of the party fortunately killed a Red Deer which was fat & gave us fresh meat, a very acceptable addition to our scanty stores — we also killed several Geese & Grouse. — Ascending the River for some distance we camped on its banks making about 20 miles only, in consequence of the delays in traversing the numerous streams.

H. J. WARRE   *Diaries*   1845

Before us, at times, a grove of dark green spruce, and beyond the sombre wood, the infinitely more sombre grey of the mountains; where the wood had been burnt, the bare blackened poles seemed to be only a screen hung before, half revealing, half concealing, what was beyond. The mountains dwarfed and relieved everything else. There was less snow than had appeared yesterday, the explanation being that the first and least elevated mountain range only was before us now that we were near, whereas, when at a greater distance, many of the higher summits beyond had been visible.

G. M. GRANT
Ocean to Ocean   1873

HENRY JAMES WARRE
An Indian Chief's tomb on the Cowelitz River, Oregon Territory   1846
Water-colour, 6½ x 10 inches

We did not reach our Camp, wet & cold, till ½ past 8oC. an old Indian Village afforded us some shelter. but the fleas & insects were dreadful. — Leaving early each morning & camping late each Evening we did not reach Fort Vancouver till ½ past 9oC on the Evening of the 6th. March [1846]. after an unusually long & very wet passage up the River. — without any object to interest one except on the ascent of Mount Coffin about 5 miles below the Cowlitz River an Isolated and very high Rock (said to be 700 feet) perfectly perpendicular towards the Country & sloping more gradually to the River being also difficult to ascend from that quarter. — This Rock was formerly the grave Yard for Hundreds of Indians. whose Canoes covered the face of the Rocks, but Capt. Wilkes' of the U.S. Exploring Squadron boat Crew having camped on the foot accidentally or designedly, left their fire which spread and burnt the whole of the Graves. which are formed of Canoes, supported on Trestles. — We ascended to the top and were repaid by a beautiful view of the surrounding Country but almost driven back by the numbers of Snakes & serpents 26 of which we killed on one progress. —

The number we saw is incredible, and only to be accounted for, from the fact of this having been the Indian burying ground for Centuries. — I witnessed a fight between a large white headed Eagle & a Fish Hawk. The Hawk caught a fish from the Water & no sooner had he risen with the prey than the Eagle rushed at him, to force him to drop the prey. — This however the hawk was not inclined to do. Such a screaming & flapping of wings when another Eagle came to the assistance of her mate, and obliged the poor hawk to make another dive for his breakfast. —

H. J. WARRE
Diaries 1846

Our pedestrian labors now commenced. For three days we continued the ascent of the valley of the Canoe river, wading twenty times in the course of each day through this mountain torrent, landing on the snow, which covered the whole country, and over the half thawed surface of which, we dragged the heavy lumbering, but well adapted, shoe, that prevented our being submerged at every step; at night we formed our couch on the snow, without an opportunity being afforded to us of drying our saturated garments, or being able to pitch our tent to guard against the cold. On the fourth day we ascended the "Grand Cote" to the height of land on which are situated two small lakes, from whence flow two rivers, the waters of which fall into different oceans — the Columbia into the Pacific, and the Athabasca into the Frozen ocean. The fatigue of mounting nearly 5000 feet on the soft snow, which sank, even with the snow shoes, nearly to the knees at every step, can hardly be conceived. We were obliged to follow one another in file, and relieve the leading file every ten minutes, by which means the road was formed for the carriers, whose endurance, under their heavy burdens, was wonderful.

We were now in the very heart of the mountains, which rose several thousand feet on every side of us. "Avalanches" of snow and rock were detached under the influence of the mid-day sun, and rolled across our path into the valley beneath, threatening to engulph us in their overwhelming course.

H. J. WARRE

Sketches in North America and the Oregon Territory 1848

HENRY JAMES WARRE
Ascending the Rocky Mountains on the return of Warre's party to Canada
Spring 1846

Water-colour, 10 x 6¾ inches

En route to Red River July 1846.

HAMPDEN MOODY

En route to the Red River Settlement   July 1846
Pen and ink drawing, 3¾ x 9¾ inches

The sun rose bright but was soon clouded. Ten good miles were made and then the halt called for breakfast at a beautiful headland, just as it commenced to rain. Now we got some idea of what a rainy day in these regions means. After breakfast we put on our water-proofs, covered up our baggage and moved ahead, under a deluge of rain that knew no intermission for four hours. Most of the water-proofs proved to be delusions; they had not been made for these latitudes. The canoes would have filled, had we not kept bailing, but, without a word of complaint, the Indians stuck to their paddles.

G. M. GRANT
Ocean to Ocean   1873

'Had "berry-pemmican" at supper. (That is to say, the ordinary buffalo pemmican, with Saskootoom berries sprinkled through it at the time of making, — which acts as currant jelly does with venison, correcting the greasiness of the fat by a slightly acid sweetness. Sometimes wild cherries are used instead of the Meesasskootoom-meena. Berry-pemmican is usually the best of its kind, but poor is the best. Take scrapings from the driest outside corner of a very stale piece of cold roast beef, add to it lumps of tallowy rancid fat, then garnish all with long human hairs (on which string pieced, like beads, upon a necklace), and short hairs of oxen, or dogs, or both, — and you have a fair imitation of common pemmican, though I should rather suppose it to be less nasty.

Pemmican is most endurable when uncooked. My men used to fry it with grease, sometimes stirring-in flour, and making a flabby mess, called "rubaboo," which I found almost uneatable. Carefully-made pemmican, such as that flavoured with the Saskootoom berries, or some that we got from the mission at St. Ann, or the sheep-pemmican given us by the Rocky Mountain hunters, is nearly good, — but, in two senses, a little of it goes a long way.)

THE EARL OF SOUTHESK
Saskatchewan and the Rocky Mountains   1875

WILLIAM H. E. NAPIER   Slave Falls on the Winnipeg River, Rupert's Land   1857
Water-colour, 7 x 10½ inches

The Slave Falls! who that has ever beheld that superb rush of water will forget it? Glorious, glorious Winnipeg! it may be that with these eyes of mine I shall never see thee again, for thou liest far out of the track of life, and man mars not thy beauty with ways of civilized travel; but I shall often see thee in imagination, and thy rocks and thy waters shall murmur in memory for life. . . .

Thus the great Slave Fall tells by its name the fate of two Sioux captives taken in some foray by the Ojibbeway; lashed together in a canoe, they were the only men who ever ran the Great Chute. The rocks around were black with the figures of the Ojibbeways, whose wild triumphant yells were hushed by the roar of the cataract; but the torture was a short one; the mighty rush, the wild leap, and the happy hunt-ing-ground, where even Ojibbeways cease from troubling and Sioux warriors are at rest, had been reached.

W. F. BUTLER
The Great Lone Land 1872

GEORGE SETON   The men's barracks from the window of the officer's mess, Fort Garry   1857
Water-colour, 6¼ x 9¾ inches

Miss Rye's place is about a couple of miles from the village, across a very fine common, on which at the time of my visit there were three thousand

CANADIAN VOLUNTEERS

under canvas. These troops are a kind of compromise between English militia and volunteers, being men of a better social position than the one, and not so good as the other. They certainly are stalwart and wiry-looking fellows, and some of the regiments were in excellent trim; particularly an Artillery one which showed to great advantage. The troops are called out in the summer of each year, to drill for about a month, as the Canadian Government keeps no standing army, except a few men in Quebec and Fort Garry, and there are no British troops, with the exception of

a half regiment at Halifax. What a lesson is here taught to despots, who govern their subjects by the strength of their armies, and thus convert men into human butchers. Ireland takes 14,000 military police, and between 20,000 and 30,000 regulars to keep five millions of people in subjection, and we are gravely told, it is to protect society; yet, I venture to say, that if Ireland were governed on the same enlightened principles as Canada, the country would not require these hordes of military mercenaries; for the Irish are naturally a law-loving and law-abiding people. A soldier of the rank and file in the European armies, is a mere machine without a mind or reasoning powers of his own, he is taught two duties—and two only—namely, to kill his

fellowmen and pay almost divine honours to the chief engineers who work the machine. How differently are things managed in Canada, where over four millions of people are kept in order without a regular soldier from Quebec to Fort Garry, except a handful of stately old fellows at Ottawa, called the Governor General's Guards, who, perhaps, are as useful in amusing the citizens as in any other capacity; yet, Canada is a country of law and order, as much as any other, and more so than some where armies are kept to prevent the people getting justice, or, in other words, a good Government.

P. O'LEARY
Travels and Experiences in Canada   no date

WILLIAM H. E. NAPIER
St. Boniface Cathedral, Red River Settlement
1857
Water-colour, 3½ x 7¼ inches

The Scottish settlers are a considerable and very thriving body. Their farms (in this quarter at least) are entirely on the western side of the Red River, where also stand the Fort and the Protestant churches; the French and French half-breeds occupy the eastern side, and their large cathedral, with its two horn-like little steeples, and the comfortable-looking adjacent establishment of the nuns, are as conspicuous as Fort Garry itself, opposite to which they hold their place, close beside the farther bank of the stream.

In population the whole settlement, including White Horse Plains, does not much exceed 7000 — the common estimate, 10,000, being a great exaggeration — and this number is almost equally divided between Protestants and Roman Catholics, with a trifling majority of the former. This calculation, I am informed, shows also with much accuracy the division of the races, those of British origin belonging to the Protestant churches, those of French origin to the church of Rome.

THE EARL OF SOUTHESK
Saskatchewan and the Rocky Mountains 1875

WILLIAM ARMSTRONG
Fort Garry   1857
Water-colour, 8 x 16 inches

Now, had the country bordering on Red River been an unpeopled wilderness, the plan carried out in effecting the transfer of land in the North-West from the Hudson's Bay Company to the Crown, and from the Crown to the Dominion of Canada, would have been an eminently wise one; but, unfortunately for its wisdom, there were some 15,000 persons living in peaceful possession of the soil thus transferred, and these 15,000 persons very naturally objected to have themselves and possessions signed away without one word of consent or one note of approval. Nay, more than that, these straggling pioneers had on many an occasion taunted the vain half-breed with what would happen when the irresistible march of events had thrown the country into the arms of Canada: then civilization would dawn upon the benighted

country, the half-breed would seek some western region, the Company would disappear, and all the institutions of New World progress would shed prosperity over the land; prosperity, not to the old dwellers and of the old type, but to the new-comers and of the new order of things. Small wonder, then, if the little community, resenting all this threatened improvement off the face of the earth, got their powder-

horns ready, took the covers off their trading flint-guns, and with much gesticulation summarily interfered with several anticipatory surveys of their farms, doubling up the sextants, bundling the surveying parties out of their freeholds, and very peremptorily informing Mr. Governor M'Dougall, just arrived from Canada, that his presence was by no means of the least desirability to Red River or its inhabi-

tants. The man who, with remarkable energy and perseverance, had worked up his fellow-citizens to this pitch of resistance, organizing and directing the whole movement, was a young French half-breed named Louis Riel—a man possessing many of the attributes suited to the leadership of parties, and quite certain to rise to the surface in any time of political disturbances.

W. F. BUTLER
The Great Lone Land   1872

WILLIAM GEORGE RICHARDSON HIND
The Overlanders setting out from Fort Garry   June 1862
Water-colour, 2¼ x 3½ inches

Then, in 1862 the Cariboo mines were discovered, and the second rush was greater than the first; but again, not an emigration of sober, steady householders, whose aim was to establish homes, and live by their own industry, but of fever-heated adventurers from all parts of the world—man without a country and without a home. San Francisco was deserted for a time. Thousands sold their lots there, and bought others in Victoria or claims in Cariboo. Cariboo was four hundred miles from the sea, and there was no road but an old Indian trail, winding up and down mountains and precipices, across deep gorges and rivers, through thick woods without game; but the obstacles that would have stopped an army were laughed at by miners. Of course the wave soon spent itself.

G. M. GRANT
Ocean to Ocean   1873

WILLIAM GEORGE RICHARDSON HIND
The Overlanders Jones and Carpenter playing cards   1862
Water-colour, 3¼ x 6 inches

The caravan is not more needed in the East, across the deserts, than it is in the West, across the fertile but uninhabited prairies. Provisions for the whole party and for the return journey of the men must be carried—unless you make frequent delays to hunt. Your tents and theirs, in other words, house and furniture; kitchen, larder and pantry; tool-chest and spare axle-trees; clothes, blankets, water-proofs, arms and ammunition, medicine-chest, books, paper boxes for specimens to be collected on the way, and things you never think of till you miss them, all are or may be required.

G. M. GRANT
Ocean to Ocean   1873

It was a marvel how well those Red River carts stood out all the jolting they got. When any part broke before, a thong of shaganappi or buffalo raw-hide thong had united the pieces. Shaganappi in this part of the world does all that leather, cloth, rope, nails, glue, straps, cord, tape, and a number of other articles are used for elsewhere. Without it the Red River cart, which is simply a clumsy looking but really light box cart with wheels six or seven feet in diameter, and not a bit of iron about the whole concern, would be an impossibility. These small-bodied high-wheeled carts cross the miry creeks, borne up by the grass roots, and on the ordinary trail the horses jog along with them at a steady trot of four or five miles an hour. Ordinary carts would stick hopelessly in the mud at the crossings of the creeks and marshes, and travel slowly on a good trail. A cart without an ounce of iron was a curiosity to us at first, but we soon found that it was the right thing in the right place.

G. M. GRANT
Ocean to Ocean   1873

WILLIAM GEORGE RICHARDSON HIND   St. Ann's Lake on the prairies   1862
Pen and ink drawing, 3¼ x 6 inches

On our arrival at St. Ann, we proceeded to the mission-house, where we met with a most cordial reception. — 'Had the pleasure of dining with Pères Lacome and Le Frain at the Roman Catholic mission-house — agreeable men and perfect gentlemen. What an advantage Rome has in this respect — Protestants constantly send vulgar, underbred folk to supply their missions, Rome sends polished, highly-educated gentlemen. Then how much the best is her mode of addressing the Indian mind; — for example, every Indian who joins the Mission Temperance Society is given a handsome medal to wear.' (This appeals to their pride or vanity, and is far more effectual than mere dry exhortations.)

On the pressing invitation of my kind hosts, I remained for the night at the mission house. — 'Everything there is wonderfully neat and flourished, it is a true oasis in the desert. The cows fat and fine, the horses the same, the dogs, the very cats, the same. A well-arranged and well-kept garden, gay with many flowers — (some of them the commonest flowers of the woods and plains, brought to perfection by care and labour.) The house beautifully clean; the means served up as in a gentleman's dining-room. Excellent preserves of service-berries and wild raspberries; — everything made use of and turned to account.'

Surrounded by such comfort and refinement, and in the society of such agreeable entertainers, I passed a most pleasant evening, one that often recalled itself to my memory amidst the experiences of later times.

The rooms were decorated with religious prints, and there was likewise a good library of books of a similar character. In my own bedroom were several of the latter, which I looked through with interest, among them, however, was one which it surprised me to find in such honourable company — a cheap Dublin publication called *The Life of the Virgin Mary*, a pamphlet, 'full of falsehoods as gravely told and reasoned on as any chapter in Baron Munchausen's travels.' (Such childish fables, though possibly attractive to simple-minded people in other lands, seemed to me ill adapted to impress the Indians, who are not wanting in shrewdness, and whose own supernaturalism is of a grave and sombre character. But the success of the mission convinces one that this foolish book could not have been in general use, whatever accident had brought it all the way from Ireland.)

'Lake St. Ann is a sheet of water about seven miles long. The Indians call it Great Spirit Lake; it is also known by the name of God's Lake.' (It was sometimes designated Manito Lake, which merely means *Spirit* Lake, a prefix being required to denote whether a good or an evil spirit is intended.)

THE EARL OF SOUTHESK
Saskatchewan and the Rocky Mountains   1875

There are three ways of dealing with the less than half-million of red men still to be found on the continent of America, each of which has been tried on a smaller or larger scale. The first cannot be put more clearly or badly than it was in a letter dated San Fransisco, Sept. 1859, which went the round of the American press, and received very general approval. The writer, in the same spirit in which Roebuck condemned the British Government's shilly-shally policy towards the Maories, condemned the Federal Government for not having ordered a large military force to California when they got possession of it, "with orders to hunt and shoot down all the Indians from the Colorado to the Klamath." Of course the writer adds that such a method of dealing with the Indians would have been the cheapest, "and probably the most humane." With regard to this policy of no nonsense, thorough-going as selfishness itself, it is enough to say that no Christian nation would now tolerate it for an instant.

The second way is to insist that there is no Indian question. Assume that the Indian must submit to our ways of living and our laws because they are better than his; and that, as he has made no improvement on the land, and has no legal title-deeds, he can have no right to it that a civilized being is bound to recognize. Let the emigrants, as they pour into the country, shove the old lords of the soil back; hire them if they choose to work; punish them if they break the laws, and treat them as poor whites have to be treated. Leave the struggle between the two races entirely to the principle of natural selection, and let the weaker go to the wall. This course has been practically followed in many parts of America. It has led to frighful atrocities on both sides, in which the superior vigour of the civilized man has outmatched the native ferocity of the savage. The Indian in such competition for existence, soon realizing his comparative weakness, had resource to the cunning that the inferior naturally opposes to the strength of the superior. This irritated even the well-disposed white, who got along

PETER RINDISBACHER
The Sioux war chief Wuana-tea
ca. 1822
Water-colour, 8¼ x 6½ inches

honestly, and believed that honesty was the best policy. It was no wonder that, after a few exchanges of punishment and vengeance, the conviction became general that the presence of the Indian was inconsistent with public security; that he was a nuisance to be abated; and that it was not wise to scrutinize too closely, what was done by miners who had to look out for themselves, or by the troops who had been called in to protect settlers. The Indians had no newspapers to tell how miners tried their rifles on an unoffending Indian at a distance, for the pleasure of seeing the poor wretch jump when the bullet struck him; or how, if a band had fine horses, a charge

PETER RINDISBACHER
A Saulteau Indian in winter dress
ca. 1822
Water-colour, 8¾ x 6½ inches

paternal, is to go down to the Indian level when dealing with them; go at least half-way down; explain that, whether they wish it or not, immigrants will come into the country, and that the Government is bound to seek the good of all the races under its sway, and do justly by the white as well as by the red man; offer to make a treaty with them on the principles of allotting to them reserves of land that no one can invade, and that they themselves cannot alienate, giving them an annual sum per family in the shape of useful articles, establishing schools among them and encouraging missionary effort, and prohibiting the sale of intoxicating liquors to them. When thus approached, they are generally reasonable in their demands; and it is the testimony of all competent authorities that, when a treaty is solemnly made with them that is according to Indian ideas of solemnity, they keep it sacredly. They only break it when they believe that the other side has broken faith first. . . .

It may be said that, do what we like, the Indians as a race, must eventually die out. It is not unlikely. Almost all the Indians in the North-west are scrofulous. But on the other hand, in the United States and in Canada, they exist, in not a few cases, as christianized self-supporting communities, and have multiplied and prospered. These are beginning to ask for full freedom. It was all right, they argue, to forbid us to sell our lands, when we did not know their value, and to keep us as wards when we could not take care of ourselves; but it is different now; we are grown men; and it is an injustice to prevent us from making the most we can out of our own.

At all events, there are no Indian difficulties in our Northwest. For generations the H.B. Company governed the tribes in a semi-paternal way, the big children often being rude and noisy, sometimes plundering a fort, or even maltreating a factor, but in the end always returning to their allegiance, as without the Company, they could not get tea or tobacco, guns or powder, blankets or trinkets.

G. M. GRANT *Ocean to Ocean* 1873

was trumped up against them, that the band might be broken up and the horses stolen; or how the innocent were indiscriminately slaughtered with the guilty; or how they were poisoned by traders with bad rum, and cheated till left without gun, horse, or blanket. This policy of giving to the simple children of the forest and prairie, the

blessings of unlimited free-trade, and bidding them look after their own interests, has not been a success. The frightful cruelties connected with it and the expense it has entailed, have forced many to question whether the fire and sword plan would not have been "cheaper and, perhaps, more humane."

The third way, called sometimes the

SYDNEY PRIOR HALL   An Indian chief in British finery, Fort Ellice
1881
Pencil drawing, 6¾ x 4½ inches

The universal passion for dress is strangely illustrated in the Western Indian. His ideal of perfection is the English costume of some forty years ago. The tall chimney-pot hat with round narrow brim, the coat with high collar going up over the neck, sleeves tight-fitting, waist narrow. All this is perfection, and the chief who can array himself in this ancient garb struts out of the fort the envy and admiration of all beholders. Sometimes the tall felt chimney-pot is graced by a large feather which has done duty in the turban of a dowager thirty years ago in England. The addition of a little gold tinsel to the coat collar is of considerable consequence, but the presence of a nether garment is not at all requisite to the completeness of the general get-up.

For this most ridiculous-looking costume a Blackfeet chief will readily exchange his beautifully-dressed deer-skin Indian shirt—embroidered with porcupine quills and ornamented with the raven locks of his enemies—his head-dress of ermine skins, his flowing buffalo robe: a dress in which he looks every inch a savage king for one in which he looks every inch a foolish savage. But the new dress does not long survive—bit by bit it is found unsuited to the wild work which its owner has to perform; and though it never loses the high estimate originally set upon it, it, nevertheless, is discarded by virtue of the many inconveniences arising out of running buffalo in a tall beaver, or fighting in a tailcoat against Crees. . . .

Money-values are entirely unknown in these trades. The values of articles are computed by "skins"; for instance, a horse will be reckoned at 60 skins; and these 60 skins will be given thus: a gun, 15 skins; a capote, 10 skins; tobacco, 15 skins—total, 60 skins. The Bull Ermine, or the Four Bears, or the Red Daybreak, or whatever may be the brave's name, hands over the horse, and gets in return a blanket, a gun, a capote, ball and powder, and tobacco. The term "skins" is a very old one in the fur trade; the original standard, the beaver skin—or, as it was called, "the made beaver"—was the medium of exchange, and every other skin and article of trade was graduated upon the scale of the beaver; thus a beaver, or a skin, was reckoned equivalent to 1 mink skin, one marten was equal to 2 skins, one black fox 20 skins, and so on; in the same manner, a blanket, a capote, a gun, or a kettle had their different values in skins. This being explained, we will now proceed with the trade. Sapoomaxica, or the Big Crow's Foot, having demonstrated the bigness of his heart, and received in return a tangible proof of the corresponding size of the trader's, addresses his braves, cautioning them against violence or rough behaviour—the braves, standing ready with their peltries, are in a high state of excitement to begin the trade. Within the fort all the preparations have been completed, communication cut off between the Indian room and the rest of the buildings, guns placed up in the loft overhead, and men all get ready for anything that might turn up; then the outer gate is thrown open, and a large throng enters the Indian room. Three or four of the first-comers are now admitted through the narrow passage into the trading-shop, from the shelves of which most of the blankets, red cloth, and beads have been removed, for the red man brought into the prescence of so much finery would unfortunately behave very much after the manner of a hungry boy put in immediate juxtaposition to bath-buns, cream-cakes, and jam-fritters, to the complete collapse of profit upon the trade to the Hudson Bay Company. The first Indians admitted hand in their peltries through a wooden grating, and receive in exchange so many blankets, beads, or strouds. Out

Ugly Customers at Smart's Store, Battleford. Aug. 30. S.R.Hall

SYDNEY PRIOR HALL   Ugly customers at Smart's Store, Battleford   August 30, 1881
Pencil drawing, 4½ x 7¼ inches

they go to the large hall where their comrades are anxiously awaiting their turn, and in rush another batch, and the doors are locked again. The reappearance of the fortunate braves with the much-coveted articles of finery adds immensely to the excitement. What did they see inside? "Oh, not much, only a few dozen blankets and a few guns, and a little tea and sugar"; this is terrible news for the outsiders, and the crush to get in increases tenfold, under the belief that the good things will all be gone. So the trade progresses, until at last all the peltries and provisions have changed hands, and there is nothing more to be traded; but sometimes things do not run quite so smoothly. Sometimes, when the stock of pemmican or robes is small, the braves object to see their "pile" go for a little parcel of tea or sugar. The

steelyard and weighing-balance are their especial objects of dislike. "What for you put on one side tea or sugar, and on the other a little bit of iron?" they say; "we don't know what that medicine is—but, look here, put on one side of that thing that swings a bag of pemmican, and put on the other side blankets and tea and sugar, and then, when the two sides stop swinging, you take the bag of pemmican and we will take the blankets and the tea: that would be fair, for one side will be as big as the other." This is a very bright idea on the part of the Four Bears, and elicits universal satisfaction all round. Four Bears and his brethren are, however, a little bit put out of conceit when the trader observes, "Well, let it be as you say. We will make the balance swing level between the bag of pemmican and the blankets, but we will

carry out the idea still further. You will put your marten skins and your otter and fisher skins on one side, I will put against them on the other my blankets, and my gun and ball and powder; then, when both sides are level, you will take the ball and powder and the blankets, and I will take the marten and the rest of the fine furs." This proposition throws a new light upon the question of weighing-machines and steelyards, and, after some little deliberation, it is resolved to abide by the old plan of letting the white trader decide the weight himself in his own way, for it is clear that the steelyard is a great medicine which no brave can understand, and which can only be manipulated by a white medicine-man.

W. F. BUTLER
The Great Lone Land 1872

E. D. PANTER-DOWNES

Nanaimo, the coaling station for the British Navy on Vancouver Island, British Columbia
1859
Water-colour, 7 x 9 inches

At Nanaimo proper is a population of seven or eight hundred souls — all depending on the old or Douglas mine. The manager informed us that they would probably ship fifty thousand tons this season, while last year they shipped less than thirty thousand; and that, next year, they would be in a position to ship an hundred thousand or more. They could give employment to fifty or sixty additional men at once, at wages averaging from two to three dollars a day. A new seam, nine feet thick, had lately been discovered below the old one; and we went down the shaft three hundred feet to see it. The coal was of the same excellent quality as that of the old mine, which is the best for gas or steam purposes on the Pacific coast. But the miners had come upon a fault in the seam, caused by the dislocation of the strata, immediately above and below, intruding a tough conglomerate rock that they were now cutting away in the hope of its soon giving out. The coal measures, which these few seams now worked represent, extend over the whole eastern coast of Vancouver Island, and, like those on the east of the Rocky Mountains, are cretaceous or of tertiary age. They are considered as valuable as if they were carboniferous.

G. M. GRANT
Ocean to Ocean   1873

LADY DUFFERIN   Metlakatla, British Columbia   1876
                               Water-colour, 4¾ x 6¾ inches

Tuesday, [August] 29th. — There is very little to tell of to-day, for the weather has been desperately bad — pouring rain, and much fog. We have seen nothing in the way of scenery, and had it not been for having our tender to pilot us into Metlacatlah, we should have spent the night at sea; however, here we are safe at anchor. I saw one little sea-beast to-day; it jumped clear of the water several times, and showed itself plainly — a sea-otter.

Metlacatlah is one of the most successful of Indian missions. It is entirely the work of a Mr. Duncan, who when he came here found the Indians in a most savage condition. He has lived entirely among them, and is regarded by them as their father and their friend. I hear that the influence he has, and the real good he has done, is wonderful.

Wednesday, [August] 30th. — It was delightful, after yesterday's rain, to find a lovely morning, and to see the beautiful scenery of this place to perfection; but I must tell you to-day about our visit to the Indian village of Metlacatlah.

We started in boats directly after breakfast, our Staff being dressed in red, to please the Indians. As we approached the shore they (the Indians) fired ready to present arms; a boarded place had been prepared on the grass for us to stand on, and round it were all the inhabitants of the village. . . .

We next saw the "Council Room," and in it a peculiar fireplace, which they have in all the cottages, and which D. [Lord Dufferin] would like to put into some large hall somewhere. It is a good sized square, in the center of the room, with the chimney directly over it. Every one in the room is thus able to get an equal share of the fire, and it looks most cheerful with people sitting all round it.

In this room Mr. Duncan and his Indian colleagues carry on the business of the place. Outside, there are gymnastics for the boys.

The Prison stands opposite; it is a funny little tower, painted black below and white above. It is divided into two rooms, the "black" prison being more disgraceful than the "white." On the top of this building there is a stand for the band! The Church comes next, and is quite new, having been built entirely by Mr. Duncan and the Indians. . . .

The School is another very good building, and round its walls there are texts and pictures. The pupils all learn to read English, which they prefer for reading to their native tongue — their own words are so very long. They translate what they read into Tschimshyau.

MARCHIONESS OF DUFFERIN AND AVA *My Canadian Journal, 1872-78* 1891

LADY DUFFERIN

The Indians serenading the Governor-General,
Lord Dufferin, at Metlakatla, British Columbia   1876
Water-colour, 5¾ x 7¾ inches

The Governor-General expressed a great desire to hear the men sing one of their national melodies (Heaven save the mark!) but they begged to be excused on the ground that they would be ashamed to sing it before him on shore as they were, but that they would follow the ship and sing it in their canoes, which they did on his return from Fort Simpson. I don't think Mr. Duncan encourages reminiscences of their former life, which these war songs are, and it struck me that he threw, and successfully threw, cold water on the Governor-General's bestowing any special mark of recognition on the chief. He has to conduct his operations in a peculiar way, and it can easily be understood that much of his advice and direction would be thrown away, were there a recognized authority over the Indians other than himself. He strives to make industry and merit the standards by which the men of the village are measured, and in presenting an address to the Governor-General, which was done immediately after the singing was concluded, there was no apparent priority or distinction amongst them. . . .

He [Lord Dufferin] then ordered the distribution of a few presents that he had brought for them, and re-embarking sailed away for Metlakahtla, where he arrived in the evening, and was met by the promised national howl from the crews of Tsimpsean canoes that had been waiting for him. Their song was the dirge for the dead sung by a returning war party. It appears to be the principal relic of their former minstrelsy and is hardly worth preserving. It is, as it is intended to be, extremely melancholy, filled with spasmodic exclamations, and calling upon the dead, but is calculated to defeat its own end by leaving it open to doubt whether the greater anguish should be felt for the loss of the slain, or in view of the fact that some had been still left alive to sing.

M. ST. JOHN
The Sea of Mountains 1877

LADY DUFFERIN

The Indian totem poles at Skidegate,
Queen Charlotte Islands, British Columbia   1876
Water-colour, 5 x 6¾ inches

Thursday, 31st. — We were to have started at daybreak, but there was a thick fog, which only lifted at 9:30; after that the day was beautiful, and we had a splendid passage over to Queen Charlotte's Islands. I suppose this is the wildest place I shall ever be at. It is solely inhabited by Indians, and as yet there is no missionary among them; but Mr. Collinson is coming here from Metlacatlah.

We anchored opposite a village which, in the distance, looked like a forest of bare poles. These poles are heraldic, and are the monuments to chiefs that I told you of before. Every house seems to have one — and, as I think I said, they are highly valued — as symbols of rank. Some are carved the whole way up with grotesque figures and faces, some are painted; and in many houses the door is a part of the pattern of the pillar, and is an oval hole, through which you see the picturesque Indian figures appearing. When a man dies, his friends destroy his house, leaving the framework and the pillar, and make a little hut for the dead body to lie in, with a blanket nailed before it. We saw one with two canoes outside, ready to take the owner across the "silent lake." On one house were two figures with tall hats and frock-coats — missionaries evidently.

MARCHIONESS OF DUFFERIN AND AVA
My Canadian Journal, 1872-78   1891

It grieves the heart of a lover of trees to travel through America. For hundreds and thousands of miles his eyes behold nothing but wholesale destruction of those noblest ornaments of the earth. Fire everywhere, the axe everywhere, the barking-knife and the bill-hook — joint ravagers with the storm, the lightning, and the flood — all busy in pulling down nature's forest handiwork — and who builds up anything in its stead?

THE EARL OF SOUTHESK
Saskatchewan and the Rocky Mountains   1875

The delay gave us time to walk round Yale and up the river. The village itself has a neat, clean, thriving appearance, as if its inhabitants had settled down to live in the country. The scenery in the neighbourhood is of the grandest kind, varying with every bend of the river. Hills rise in gradual wooded slopes for five, six or eight hundred feet; and above, bald rocks shoot up plumb for ten or twelve hundred feet higher. The valley is narrow, affording but little room for the farmer.

G. M. GRANT
Ocean to Ocean   1873

E. SANDY
Logging on Vancouver Island,
British Columbia
Water-colour, 16¾ x 24 inches

F. WHYMPER

Fort Yale, British Columbia   ca. 1865
Water-colour, 6¾ x 8¾ inches

We arrived at Yale about four o'clock in the afternoon, and immediately ordered the best dinner they could give us at the Colonial Hotel. The house was kept by a Frenchman, who excelled himself on this occasion, and provided a meal which to us, who had not eaten anything deserving the name of a dinner for at least eighteen months, appeared perfection. The champagne, however, and sundry drinks with fraternising miners, caused us to wake with most tremendous headaches next morning. Some of the visitors to the bar amused us greatly. One tall Yankee, considerably intoxicated, was possessed with the idea that he was Lord Nelson, and associating the great admiral in some way with cucumbers, ate several in succession, to prove his identity.

The little town of Yale is merely a single row of houses facing the river, which, having just escaped through the Canons, here sweeps to the west, a broad and noble river. The town is built on a small flat, backed on the north by lofty hills, and looking down the widening valley to the south, where the receding mountains still tower up grand and high. The situation is exceedingly picturesque, and the clean, white, wooden buildings were as gay with flags as any Yankee could desire. Gold may be obtained in the street of Yale, and a couple of Indians were working with a "rocker" opposite the Hotel when we were there.

VISCOUNT MILTON AND W. B. CHEADLE
The North-West Passage By Land   1865

ANONYMOUS

Yale in construction days, British Columbia
Pencil drawing, 16¾ x 28½ inches

At various points on the river, all down the road, miners are still to be found. These are chiefly Siwashes and Chinese, who take up abandoned claims, and wash the sand over again, being satisfied with smaller wages than what contents a white man. Their tastes are simple and their expenses moderate. None of them dream of going to the wayside hotels, and paying a dollar for every meal, a dollar for a bed, a dollar for a bottle of ale, or twenty cents for a drink. The Chinaman cultivates vegetables beside his claim; these and his bag of rice suffice for him, greatly to the indignation of the orthodox miner. The Siwash catches salmon in his scoop net from every eddy of the river, and his wife carries them up to the house and makes his winter's food. These two classes of the population, the one representing an ancient civilization, the other scattered nomads with almost no tribal relationships, resemble each other in appearance so much that it would be difficult to distinguish them, were it not for the long tail or queue into

which the Chinaman braids his hair, and which he often folds at the back of his head, instead of letting it hang down his back. The Pacific Indian is Mongolian in size and complexion, in the shape of the face, and the eyes. He has neither the strength of limb, the manly bearing, nor the dignity so characteristic of the Indians on the east side of the Rocky Mountains, but he is quite as intelligent, and takes more readily to civilized ways.

Gold was and is found in every sandbar of the river and in every creek; but it had to be found in large quantities to enable a man to live. A pound of flour cost a dollar and a half, and everything else sold at proportional prices. The gold was in largest quantities near the bed rock, and this was generally covered with a deposit of silt from five to forty feet thick, containing but little of the precious metal near the surface. The country presented every obstacle to prospecting. Range upon

range of stern hills wooded from base to summit, through which a way could be forced only with incredible toil, and at the daily risk of starvation; it is little wonder that the way to Cariboo, and the country itself proved to be the grave of many an adventurous gold seeker. A few made fortunes, in a week or a month, which as a rule they dissipated in less than a year; hundreds gathered moderately large sums, which they took away to spend elsewhere; thousands made wages; and tens of thousands, nothing. It had been the same in California, when gold was discovered there, but then the masses who were unsuccessful could not get out of the country, and they had — fortunately for themselves — to hire out as farm servants and herdmen. In British Columbia they could get back to Oregon and California, and back they went, poorer than they had come, but leaving the Province little the better for their visit.

G. M. GRANT
Ocean to Ocean   1873

EDWARD ROPER   The boardwalk at New Westminster, British Columbia   1887
Water-colour, 12¼ x 20¼ inches

I was seated during that afternoon by a road-side, amongst ferns and rose-bushes, making a sketch up the river, and while there I was much amused with the strange diversity of people who passed by me along a side-walk across the road. First came by some ladies, dressed in the latest style, fit for Bond Street. Then two Celestials, with their pig-tails, their poles, and swinging baskets. After them came along, laughing and shouting, a number of school children—regular young Britishers, I was sure. Then two smug, well-dressed Chinese gentlemen, in complete Chinese dress, but wearing straw hats like ours, and each carrying an English silk umbrella neatly furled. By and by there passed by me some Indian men, followed by a party of gaily-shawled klootchmans, with their tenas (young ones). Then some more ladies, then some Indians; afterwards some white labourers, and so on—a continual procession of all kinds of people, but all looked well-to-do. I did not see in all that place one specimen of pauper humanity, such as you will see in a town at home so frequently.

E. ROPER
By Track and Trail 1891

The city of New Westminster, the capital of British Columbia, stands in a commanding position, on ground gradually rising from the river, which is here three-quarters of a mile broad. The town has been beautifully laid out by Col. Moody, R.E., the late Commissioner of Lands and Works, and several streets of good wooden houses already exist.

The great drawback to its situation is the dense forest of timber of the largest size by which it is shut in. The little clearing which has been already done has been effected with great labour by the help of the engineers quartered there for several years; but, although the land is fertile enough, the expense of clearing it is so heavy that but little farming has been carried out. The place is still unsightly, from the stumps of trees sticking up on every side. The river is navigable to this point for vessels drawing eighteen or twenty feet of water, and, should direct communication be established with England, it may eventually rival Victoria. As yet, however, it is completely eclipsed by that more favoured city.

VISCOUNT MILTON AND W. B. CHEADLE
The North-West Passage By Land 1865

LUCIUS RICHARD O'BRIEN   The Rocky Mountains of British Columbia   1887
Water-colour, 21¼ x 29¾ inches

But there is no sharp line dividing vegetation from the naked rock. A belt of harder rock intervening breaks the forest; one or two hundred feet above, the trees may reappear in a long thin streak along the side of the mountain, like a regiment in line, or in a dense grove, like a column; and a different stratification above stops them again. The same change of strata probably accounts for the absence of snow from belts which have snow above and beneath them; far away these bare belts look like highways winding round the mountain. Behind, Myette reared his head over us, seemingly as near as ever;

the Pyramid Mountain supported by a great rampart of rock, from which his lofty head rose gracefully, still closed the view; and a cluster of snow-clad peaks surrounded him at a respectful distance. From time to time we passed through woods growing along the sides of burns rushing down into the lake. The woods prepared us for fresh prospects beyond, so that the eye had a perpetual feast. . . .

There is a wonderful combination of beauty about these mountains. Great masses of boldly defined bare rock are united to the beauty that variety of form, colour, and vegetation give. A noble river with many tributaries, each defining a distinct range, and a beautiful lake ten miles long, embosomed three thousand three hundred feet above the sea, among mountains twice as high, offer innumerable scenes, seldom to be found within the same compass, to the artist.

G. M. GRANT
Ocean to Ocean 1873

EDWARD ROPER
San Juan Island and Mount Baker
from Vancouver Island, British Columbia
1887

Water-colour, 14¾ x 29¾ inches

Mount Baker was the great feature in the landscape all day. We could hardly help feeling envious that the United States instead of ourselves possessed so glorious a landmark; especially as it still bears the name of the British Naval Officer in Capt. Vancouver's ship who first saw it, and is in the country that was formally taken possession of for the British Crown in 1792, and that had been, up to 1846, held by a British Company. Indeed, it is difficult to conceive of any plausible excuse that the United States could have brought forward, in claiming the country round Puget's Sound. They knew its value, and the British Premier, not only did not, but his brother had said that the whole country was not worth much; for the salmon wouldn't take a fly.

Before noon we entered the Haro Strait that separates San Juan from Vancouver's Island. Between the northern part of the Haro Channel and Vancouver's Island, are several islets and two narrow channels, that ships going to Victoria may take. South of these, there is nothing between San Juan and the southern extremity of Vancouver, but the Haro Strait, six or seven miles wide. It is therefore evident that while San Juan would be useless to Britain for military purposes, its possession by the United States is a menace to us; for it commands the entrance to British waters, British shores, a British river, and British Province. There is a hill on San Juan about a thousand feet high, a battery on which would command the whole Strait.

G. M. GRANT
Ocean to Ocean 1873

A. E. BOULTBEE
Our camp on Mosquito Creek, Yukon   1898
Water-colour, 7¾ x 10¾ inches

It is a great mistake to take anything except what is necessary; the trip is a long arduous one, and a man should not add one pound of baggage to his outfit that can be dispensed with. I have known men who have loaded themselves up with rifles, revolvers and shot-guns. This is entirely unnecessary. Revolvers will get you into trouble, and there is no use of taking them with you, as large game of any character is rarely found on the trip. I have prospected through this region for some years and have only seen one moose. You will not see any large game whatever on your trip from Juneau to Dawson City, therefore do not take any firearms along. . . .

The miners here are a very mixed class of people. They represent many nationalities and come from all climates. Their lives are certainly not enviable.

The regulation miner's cabin is 12 by 14 with walls six feet high and gables eight feet in height. The roof is heavily earthed and the cabin is generally kept very warm. Two, or sometimes three or four men will live in a house of this size. The ventilation is usually bad, the windows being very small. Those miners who do not work their claims during the winter confine themselves to these small huts most of the time. Very often they become indolent and careless, only eating those things which are most easily cooked or prepared. During the busy time in summer when they are shovelling in, they work hard and for long hours, sparing little time for eating and much less for cooking.

This manner of living is quite common amongst beginners, and soon leads to debility and sometimes to scurvy. Old miners have learned from experience to value health more than gold, and they therefore spare no expense in procuring the best and most varied outfit of food that can be obtained.

In a cold climate such as this, where it is impossible to get fresh vegetables and fruits, it is most important that the best substitutes should be provided. Nature helps to supply these wants by growing cranberries and other wild fruits in abundance, but men in summer are usually too busy to avail themselves of these.

The diseases met with in this country are dyspepsia, anaemia, scurvy caused by improperly cooked food, sameness of diet, overwork, want of fresh vegetables, overheated and badly ventilated houses; rheumatism, pneumonia, bronchitis, enteritis, cystitis and other acute diseases, from exposure to wet and cold; debility and chronic disease due to excesses.

J. LADUE
Klondyke Facts   1897

A. E. BOULTBEE
A group of cabins at the upper end
of Klondike City, Yukon   1898
Water-colour, 7¾ x 10¾ inches

Friend George: Don't pay any attention
to what any one says, but come in at your
earliest opportunity. My God! it is appalling to hear the truth, but nevertheless
the world has never produced its equal
before. Well, come. That's all. Your
friend,

"Casey"

From a letter quoted in
J. LADUE
Klondyke Facts   1897

EPILOGUE

The Dominion of Canada stretched from the Atlantic to the Pacific, from the Arctic shores to the 49th parallel. Its fertile centre was empty of people, but would soon be crossed by a thin steel ribbon that bound the East to the West.

Looking fairly at all the facts, admitting all the difficulties — and what country has not drawbacks — it is impossible to avoid the conclusion that we have a great and fertile North-west, a thousand miles long and from one to four hundred miles broad, capable of containing a population of millions. It is a fair land; rich in furs and fish, in treasures of the forest, the field, and the mine; seamed by navigable rivers, interlaced by numerous creeks, and beautiful with a thousand lakes; broken by swelling uplands, wooded hill-sides, and bold ridges; and protected on its exposed sides by a great desert or by giant mountains. The air is pure, dry, and bracing all the year round; giving promise of health and strength of body and length of days. Here we have a home for our own surplus population and for the stream of emigration that runs from northern and central Europe to America. Let it be opened up to the world by rail and steamboat, and in an incredibly short time the present gap between Manitoba and British Columbia will be filled up, and a continuous line of loyal Provinces extend from the Atlantic to the Pacific.

G. M. GRANT
Ocean to Ocean   1873

There was a steady campaign to encourage emigration from the British Isles. Lord Lorne, Queen Victoria's son-in-law and Governor-General of Canada, encouraged emigration from the Old Country by commissioning correspondents like S.P. Hall from the British newspapers to come to Canada and report back on the magnificent opportunities that existed. Immigration from Continental Europe was encouraged. The Mennonites, suffering from persecution in Czarist Russia, were invited to take up lands specially set aside for them. Americans from the South and Canadians from the Eastern provinces also left their established homes and set out to farm the incredibly rich soil of the Canadian West with often outstanding results. The West did fill up, but not at the rate expected. The vagaries of Nature and the world economic situation impeded the Canadian government's attempts to settle the West almost from the outset. However, the potential was there and is still being tapped in the Northwest by a hardy breed of twentieth-century pioneers. The Prairies became characterized by the sparse population, the space, the acres of grain, the grain elevators reaching skyward from the flat plain, and the railway — a narrow band of uniting steel.

We know that we have a great Northwest, a country like old Canada — not suited for lotus-eaters to live in, but fitted to rear a healthy and hardy race. The late Hon. W.H. Seward understood this when he declared that "Vigorous, perennial, evergrowing Canada would be a Russia behind the United States." Our future is grander than even that conceived by Mr. Seward, because the elements that determine it are other than those considered by him. We shall be more than an American Russia, because the separation from Great Britain to which he invites us is not involved in our manifest destiny. We believe that union is better than disunion, that loyalty is a better guarantee for true growth than pulling down. The ties that bind us to the Fatherland must be multiplied, the connection made closer and politically complete. Her traditions, her forms, her moral elevation, her historic grandeur shall be ours forever. And if we share her glory, we shall not shrink even at the outset from sharing her responsibilities."

G. M. GRANT
Ocean to Ocean   1873

THE STEERAGE PASSENGERS
consisted of nearly all the nationalities in Europe, but, of course, the majority were from the United Kingdom, a large number being English agricultural labourers, members of the Union, who were emigrating through the lock-out in the Eastern Counties, the Union assisting to pay their passage. When I saw so many fine stalwart workmen in a state of destitution, leaving the wealthiest country in the world because they could not get sufficient remuneration for their labour to live decently, I could not help exclaiming with Shakespeare, there is

"SOMETHING ROTTEN IN
THE STATE OF DENMARK."

Being a working man, I had no difficulty in making myself a home among them, and I was sorry to see that many were illiterate, a strong evidence of the poverty of their early years; the richly endowed and state-paid educational establishments, religious and secular, had entirely neglected those poor slaves, for they were nothing else; the reader may raise a technical objection to this remark, and say that no man is bought or sold in England, but I reply, that if not sold they are starved and brutalised.

P. O'LEARY
Travels and Experiences in Canada no date

Sunday, June 23rd
We have attended a meeting in the steerage, where some of the Canadian passengers talked to the emigrants about the country they are going to. D. [Lord Dufferin] also spoke, and told them that in Canada they need never complain, as he had heard one of them do, 'that he had too many children,' for that there the more they had the better. An enthusiastic young man on hearing this slapped D. on the back and said, 'That is just what I have been telling Emily.'

MARCHIONESS OF DUFFERIN AND AVA
My Canadian Journal, 1872-78 1891

THE DISCIPLINE
of the "Scandinavian" was everything that could be desired, the crew and passengers being prohibited as far as possible from intermingling. The male steerage passengers slept in hammocks slung from the decks, the women and children in bunks along the sides, the single females having a place partitioned off away from the others; the children sent out by

MISS MCPHERSON
were taken excellent care of, every one trying to do them some little kindness; they were under the charge of two young ladies and a gentleman, who paid every

attention to their little childish fancies, Captain Smith himself setting the example. Those little creatures sung delightfully every morning and evening to as appreciative an audience as ever listened, even to a prima donna at Covent Garden; they were well clad, and bore evidence of good care in every way.

P. O'LEARY
Travels and Experiences in Canada   no date

SYDNEY PRIOR HALL

Immigrants on board ship   1878
Pencil drawing, 8¾ x 14 inches

How Mr Norquay (the Premier) raised a mountain in Manitoba.

SYDNEY PRIOR HALL
How Mr. Norquay
raised a mountain
in Manitoba
1881

Pencil drawing,
6¾ x 4¼ inches

Society at Winnipeg is very pleasant; composed chiefly of the old families who formed the Hudson Bay Company and their descendants, many of whom have Indian blood in their veins. Their education, carefully begun by their parents, is often completed in Scotland, and they are well-read, intelligent people, as proud of their Indian as of their European descent. Many of them are handsome and distingué-looking. Their elegant appearance sometimes leads to awkward mistakes. One of these ladies, meeting a young Englishman fresh from the old country, and full of its prejudices, was entertained by him with reflections on race, and condolences, at having to associate with half-castes. At last he inquired how long she had been in the country? Making him a stately curtsy, she answered—

"All my life! I am one of these despised half-breeds," and instantly left him. She said afterwards she was sorry for the poor fellow's discomfiture; but he brought it upon himself by disregarding all her efforts to change the conversation.

M. FITZGIBBON
A Trip to Manitoba   1880

SYDNEY PRIOR HALL
Mr. Cauchon's garden party on
the occasion of Lord Lorne's
visit to Winnipeg, Manitoba
1881
Pencil drawing, 4¼ x 8½ inches

LORNE'S RECEPTION

need not occupy much space, as the telegraph despatches sent from time to time have doubtless given all the leading facts connected therewith. On arriving on Saturday night, His Excellency and party went straightway to Silver Heights, which had been very handsomely fitted up for them by Donald A. Smith. Unfortunately just about the time of Lord Lorne's arrival a telegram brought the melancholy announcement that Mrs. Smith was dangerously ill in the old country, and of course Mr. Smith was obliged to hurry away.

The Winnipeg welcome to His Excellency was very enthusiastic, but the decorations fell considerably short of what I had been led to expect. One of the mottoes at least was extremely silly, while another and prominent one was simply a "cheap and nasty" advertisement of some sort of dry-goods or grocery house. The arches were both rather pretty, but that is about the best that can be said of the decorations. An address by the civic authorities was presented to His Excellency and appropriately responded to.

On Tuesday His Excellency and some of his party attended a picnic at Bird's Hill, which was given by the members of the Local Government. Later in the afternoon they waited for some time waiting to witness the launch of the steamer *Princess*, but she caught on the ways and delayed the ceremony so long that the distinguished visitors were obliged to leave before it had been concluded. In the evening His Excellency attended a banquet given in his honour by Lieutenant Governor Cauchon.

On Wednesday, the civic holiday, His Excellency attended a cricket match at Dufferin Park, and the Caledonian games at the racecourse. While in the racecourse His Excellency was presented with an address by the members of the St. Andrew's Society, to which His Excellency replied.

On Thursday afternoon His Excellency and suite attended a garden party at Government House, where they were met by the Chancellor and members of the University of Manitoba, by whom an address was presented, and the usual reply given. In the evening His Excellency gave a dinner party at Silver Heights.

On Friday Lord Lorne visited the penitentiary at Horny Mountain, and the Historical Society's rooms at Winnipeg.

On Saturday (to-day) His Excellency visited St. Mary's Academy at Winnipeg, the Archepiscopal Palace, the Orphanage of the Grey Nuns, and the College at St. Boniface in the forenoon, and went to Emerson in the afternoon.

TORONTO
Globe   August 20, 1881

SYDNEY PRIOR HALL   The last of the line near Portage la Prairie, Manitoba   1881
Pencil drawing, 4¼ x 6¾ inches

We will move westward, and take the line of the Canadian Pacific Railway. Excellently laid over flat or rolling prairie, a train can proceed at almost any speed; but as we proceed along the solidly-laid track we can take some notes. As we again take the "cars" and until we reach the Assiniboine, on the frontiers of the province of Manitoba, we see on our horizon-line, and usually nearer to us, clumps and bands of poplar wood. There are also many lakes and lakelets — pretty ponds, for few are so large as to be worthy of the name of lake; ponds where numerous wild fowl seem to be for ever swimming about among the rich reeds on the margin, ponds around which deep rank grass rises higher than anywhere else on the level summer meadows. There is many a tract where the meadow appears still untouched by the hand of man; yet it has long ago, depend upon it, been bought, and bought for a good round sum, and is now being held for a further advance in price. Why should a further advance be expected? The answer is simple. You need only look north, east, south, and west, and everywhere you will see the wooden-planked house of the emigrant. Often a great patch of yellow wheat-field is bowing in the breezes; each train along the line you are following has, during the summer months, been carrying hundreds into Winnipeg, and hundreds away from Winnipeg to the west.

Hundreds more have taken the trails over the prairie for points to which railway companies are already directing their attention, and to which lines are already projected or in process of completion. The arrival of yet more and yet more, and the consequent rise in the value of the lands, is looked upon as a certainty. Last year 40,000 to 50,000 entered this land of promise, and this year it is probable that the number has been yet greater. Never was a railway better endowed for the purposes of its existence, for the Canadian Pacific Railway has about 25,000,000 of acres in this fertile belt, and of this vast amount they still at the present moment hold at least 17,000,000; and having the power to choose the good lands, and being able to reject those which may be inferior, they became possessed, when they undertook the line, of a land-fortune which, with the $25,000,000 in cash, was one of the greatest dowers ever granted. The line is the shortest from Europe to Asia by at least 1,000 miles. There are 2,700 miles of track from Montreal to the Pacific. Truly a stupendous and most essential enterprise!

MARQUIS OF LORNE
Canadian Pictures 1884

SYDNEY PRIOR HALL
Lord Lorne interviewing
an 18-month settler on the prairies
1881
Pencil drawing, 4¼ x 11 inches

The settlers came to see the governor. I have their names, but it is enough to say that their statements tallied exactly with those already recorded. One of them gave thirty-five bushels of wheat to the acre, seventy-five of oats, and said that the potatoes were an enormous crop. I have learned that hail-storms, though very limited in their range, were very destructive. They are one of the worst evils that settlers have to contend with. I could not find any who had suffered from locusts. Next day found us in a rolling plain, the view in all directions interrupted by clumps of poplar. M. R., a typical farmer, had come from Ontario fourteen months before. He came in June; broke in twelve acres from the sod, and eighteen in the spring, all now under crop; expects thirty bushels of wheat and seventy of oats from this new-turned land. I measured his oats, and they had strong straw four and a half feet high, with well-filled ears. His house, and especially steading, which was formed of logs piled one on the other, and covered with his winter store of hay, were certainly plain enough. But they served his purpose, and his house was commodious enough to be used as a sort of run. He built them both with his own hands at a cost of $30. He gets water at twelve feet, likes the climate, and thinks it better than that of Ontario. He says that the heights are warmer and more fertile than the hollows. The settler can dispose of all the grain he grows for seed to the newcomer.

MARQUIS OF LORNE
Canadian Pictures 1884

SYDNEY PRIOR HALL
The prairie   1881
Pencil drawing,
8¾ x 13¾ inches

This was a prairie country of sand and crisp grass, of level tracts varied with hills and bluffs and undulations, of many little lakes and swamps scattered about here and there. Flowers of the gayest colour enlivened the landscape. The most common were the small tiger-lilies and the roses, and next came blue-bells and white strawberry blossoms. Sometimes acres and acres were covered with intermingled masses of the orange lily and the pendulous blue-bell, the whole of them so short of stem that the glory of the flowers combined with the rich greenness of their leaves, and it seemed as if a vast carpet had been thrown upon the plain. . . .

June 23rd. — A fine day, but spoiled by two or three thunderstorms, one especially heavy while it lasted. After breakfast I walked on before the carts and shot ducks till dinner time. I only bagged four, though double that number fell, and even for these I was obliged to wade in hip-deep every time, for the useless retriever as usual refused to bring them out. The country was of the prairie sort, and rather flat than undulating, but every small hollow had its swamp or lake, in which innumerable ducks made their abode.

THE EARL OF SOUTHESK
Saskatchewan and the Rocky Mountains   1875

SYDNEY PRIOR HALL/The beginnings of Calgary, Alberta   1881/Pencil drawing, 4¼ x 8½ inches

GOVERNOR-GENERAL'S CAMP,
FORT CALGARY, SEPT. 12

This morning we were early on the move, Col. Irvine having decided that with the aid of the fresh horses Calgary could be reached in one hitch. We rattled along at a lively pace, the fresh horses hauling the ambulance and some of the loaded waggons in grand style. Blanch and Touchwood kept up to them without difficulty and Mr. Dewdney's buckboards were also well to the fore, but the waggons drawn by horses brought through by Battleford made but sorry progress. Five or six miles east of the Fort I overtook Captain Perceval and Mr. Sidney Hall walking beside their buckboard and doing their best to keep their thoroughly "played out" Broncho on the move. Luckily I had Punch tied by the halter to the back of my waggon, and having harnessed him to the buckboard in the place of the tired Broncho, they they were enabled to jog along for the remainder of the distance in company with the rest of the party. Late in the forenoon we reached the verge of the high prairie bluff over-looking Fort Calgary, and of all the charming pictures we have seen on the journey this was generally admitted to be by far the most beautiful. The valley of the river at this point is much wider and the stream more tortuous than at Blackfoot crossing; indeed,

the valley of Bow River and that of one of its chief tributaries, the Elbow, unite in a broad, low plain, and the great rich valley, studded with grey poplars or cottonwood, wild cherries, and willows, looked like some fancifully arrayed plantation. A slight frost had nipped the leaves of many of the trees, so that the lovely autumnal shades of lemon and gold and orange and crimson contrasted …with the fresh summer verdure of the untouched trees. But

THE CAMP

here is nearly or quite a mile and a half from the ford, and in a beautiful plateau on the Elbow River. The camp commands a charming view of the Rocky Mountains, and is in all respects the most beautiful that we have had on the whole journey from Winnipeg. The rows of tents and waggons are laid out so as to enclose a parallelogram with mathematical precision, and the little raised plateau, the whole of which is thus enclosed, is almost as smooth and level as a billiard table. In this whole region, so far as I have been able to observe,

THE SOIL

consists of a very pliable rich black loam, extremely productive, and deep enough to be practically inexhaustable. We are now almost 1,000 miles west of Winnipeg, and after having carefully noted the character of every mile of country

through which we have travelled, I can only say that I have not seen an acre of land anywhere along the route that is not likely sooner or later to be of value either for agricultural or grazing purposes. The lack of fuel is for the present a serious drawback, but unless I am much mistaken coal will be found in such quantities and so distributed throughout the country as to make fuel easily obtainable in any part of the North-west, while the construction of railways will ere long make the cost of building material very much less than it is at present . . . .

FORT CALGARY

was once one of the regular posts of the Mounted Police, but it has since been reduced to an outpost, and only a non-commissioned officer and two constables reside within the stockade. The Hudson Bay Company Bow River Post is located here, and the American traders J. G. Baker & Co., do an extensive trade here with the ranchers and Indians. The ford being both deep and swift it was deemed advisable to ferry the passengers and baggage in the boats which had been built for the use of His Excellency, when it was intended that he and his party should travel by water from here to the elbow of the South Saskatchewan instead of returning by the way of Helena as they have since determined to do.

TORONTO   *Globe*   October 10, 1881

SYDNEY PRIOR
HALL

ABOVE LEFT

Colonel Irvine,
North West
Mounted Police
1881

Pencil drawing,
3¾ x 3¼ inches

ABOVE RIGHT

Colonel Herchmer,
North West
Mounted Police
1881

Pencil drawing,
6½ x 4½ inches

Corporal Shaw,
North West
Mounted Police
1881

Pencil drawing,
13½ x 8¾ inches

A few hours before our arrival, Mr. Clark had received intelligence from Edmonton, that Yankee free-traders from Belly River had entered the country, and were selling rum to the Indians in exchange for their horses. The worst consequences were feared, as when the Indians have no horses they cannot hunt. When they cannot hunt they are not ashamed to steal horses, and horse-stealing leads to wars. The Crees and Blackfeet have been at peace for the last two or three years, but, if the peace was once broken, the old thirst for scalps would revive and the country be rendered insecure. Mr. Clark spoke bitterly of the helplessness of the authorities, in consequence of having had no force from the outset to back up the proclamation that had been issued. Both traders and Indians, he said, were learning the dangerous lesson that the Queen's orders could be disregarded with impunity. We comforted him with the assurance that the Adjutant-General was coming up to repress all disorders and see what was necessary to be done for the future peace of the country.

Making allowances for the fears of those who see no protection for life or property within five hundred or a thousand miles of them, and for the exaggerated size to which rumours swell in a country of such magnificent distances, where there are no newspapers and no means of communication except expresses, it is clear that if the government wishes to avoid worrying, expensive, murderous difficulties with the Indians, "something must be done." There must be law and order all over our Northwest from the first. Three or four companies of fifty men each, like those now in Manitoba, would be sufficient for the purpose, if judiciously stationed. Ten times the number may be required if there is long delay. The country cannot afford repetitions of the Manitoba rebellion. The Crees are anxious for a treaty. The Blackfeet should be dealt with firmly and generously; treaties made with both on the basis of those agreed upon in the east; a few simple laws for the protection of life and property explained to them, and their observance enforced; small annuities allowed; the spirit-traffic prohibited, and schools and missionaries encouraged.

G. M. GRANT
Ocean to Ocean 1873

SYDNEY PRIOR HALL

The foothills of the Rockies   1881
Pencil drawing, 4½ x 7¾ inches

An immense plain stretched from my feet to the mountain—a plain so vast that every object of hill and wood and lake lay dwarfed into one continuous level, and at the back of this level, beyond the pines and the lakes and the river-courses, rose the giant range, solid, impassable, silent—a mighty barrier rising midst an immense land, standing sentinel over the plains and prairies of America, over the measureless solitudes of this Great Lone Land. Here, at last, lay the Rocky Mountains.

W. F. BUTLER
The Great Lone Land   1872

EDWARD ROPER

Sulky ploughing near Carberry Mountain, Manitoba   1887
Water-colour, 12¼ x 20¼ inches

Very different implements are used there for farm-work; they are all much lighter and cheaper than in Britain. They use machinery wherever it is possible to do so; self-binders always. They thresh on the field; no barns are needed. The straw is practically worthless. "Sulky" ploughs are in common use. The man rides on it, guiding it with a lever. They appear to work perfectly, with very much less labour to the man, at any rate.

Everything is adapted to make work easy and quick. The horses used in Manitoba, and all through Canada, are not half so heavy as ours; they seemed to do very much more work with them, though.

Horses and men have to work there far harder than in England; but both seem to thrive on it.

Carberry and round it is merely a typical Manitoban village and locality —

north and south of the track the same prosperity prevails wherever there has been settlement. I could relate hundreds of instances of successful settlers, some who have gone there with money, some without. One man from Kent went out in 1881 with £200 and two sons, and in 1887 he had 960 acres, he had 8,000 bushels of wheat, he had 2,700 dollars worth of cattle, and his real estate was worth 8,000 dollars.

Another man from Ireland arrived in 1882 without a cent; now he owns 320 acres, has two teams of horses, eight cows, a wife and two children, and 9,000 bushels of wheat.

These are the sort of instances I heard of time and again. Why repeat them? They can be seen in print in any of the Government and Railway pamphlets.

They are nearly all true, these accounts, but, naturally, there may be

another set of incidents given quite opposite to them. I met many in other parts of Canada who had left Manitoba and the N.W.T. in disgust. Why?

The climate, they said, was unbearable, weather most terrible, summer heats, mosquitoes, awful cold of winter, no end of horrors; last year there was no crop at all, owing to the dry weather; the year before, early frosts ruined them, and so on, and so on. . . .

The conclusion I came to may be summed up in a very few words. It is a good enough country for those to go to who have a little money, and understand farm-work; it is a terrible country for people to go to who have no money, and do not know what real hard work is.

E. ROPER
By Track and Trail   1891

J. PEDDER

The railway station and corn elevators at Brandon, Manitoba   ca. 1889
Pen and ink drawing, 5¼ x 7½ inches

Sept. 26 [1890]. — Made a most interesting expedition to Mr. Sandison's farm, five or six miles from Brandon. Mr. S., a Scotchman, began without a cent seven years ago. Hired himself out at first, then took a small section, and has gradually added to this, either by purchase or hire, till he farms above 5,000 acres. He is still quite a young man — perhaps 30. He employs a great deal of labour, mostly Scotchmen, probably giving at this time of the year about $2½ a day. He has 33 teams of horses (66 horses), and three teams of driving horses. A team sometimes goes with grain into Brandon with loads three times in a day (total, 30 miles). His men's work hours are as follows; — Half-past 6 to half-past 11; rest, 2 hours; half-past 1 to half-past 6; total, 10 hours. He does not find it answers to do longer hours.

He threshes all his grain from the stooks, and leaves the straw in. Can thresh 312½ quarters (2,500 bushels) in a day! but straw is very short and much broken; it is used to fire the engine. The wheat is cleaned again at the elevator before being put on the railway. It goes direct there, and a certain percentage is charged for dirt — with Sandison probably about 5 per cent. The men get $35 a month, and board.

I saw some splendid black oats grown on the farm, about 80 or 90 bushels to acre (?), they said. I admired a stable well guarded with 3 feet of sods — almost the first of the kind I had seen in the country.

Mr. Sandison and his wife live in the most tumble-down old shanty, though his stables, barns, &c., are most excellent. I believe he frequently goes to Scotland, and brings out fresh men for his farm.

DEPARTMENT OF AGRICULTURE
The Visit of the Tenant-Farmer Delegates To Canada in 1890   1891

J. PEDDER

Salvation Army meeting at Calgary   ca. 1889
Pen and ink drawing, 6¼ x 9¼ inches

The Salvation Army was the great attraction yesterday. Early in the morning they commenced operations by a Hallelujah Feast at the Barracks. From 10 to 11 o'clock, they paraded the streets, led by Capt. Young and his concertina, and singing the "catchy" airs which are the chief feature of the Army's work. Crowds followed them around the streets and filled the hall at the meetings. There was no disorder and the Army were permitted to do just about as they liked. They will hold meetings every night this week.

Capt. Mercer of the Salvation Army arrived here from the east last night and will take charge of the station here. Capt. Mercer has earned quite a reputation in the work, and her presence will no doubt make the proceedings still more attractive. There was a large crowd at the meeting last night.

CALGARY
Herald   August 26, 1887

Capt. Young who is in command of the Salvation Army from Port Arthur to the coast, is in town. In conversation with him, he intimated that the work of the Army was to be begun here at once, Boynton Hall having been leased for a period of three years, to be used as a barracks. The post at Calgary will be in charge of Capt. Mercer, Lieut. Patterson and Cadet Iverich, all of them ladies, or as they are now more generally termed 'Salvation lasses.' They will be in town in a day or two and will hold their first service on Sunday next. Capt. Dawson, of Victoria, will arrive on Friday morning to assist at the inaugural meetings. After Sunday regular meetings will be held each evening at 8 o'clock prior to which there will be a parade through the streets. Sunday morning the 'hallelujah breakfast' will be discussed at 7 o'clock and generally the army will be in full swing and a fixed and permanent institution of the town. Capt. Young goes east to-morrow morning.

CALGARY
Tribune   August 19, 1887

Alexander, Sir J.E. *L'Acadie, or Seven Years' Exploration in British America.* 2 vols. Henry Colburn, London: 1849.

Anonymous. *The Case and Claim of the American Loyalists Impartially Stated and Considered.* London: 1783.

Back, G. *Narrative of an Expedition in H.M.S. Terror, Undertaken with a View to Geographical Discovery on the Arctic Shores in the Years 1836-37.* John Murray, London: 1838.

Ballantyne, R.M. *Hudson's Bay.* (2nd edition). William Blackwood and Sons, Edinburgh: 1848.

Bigsby, J.J. *By Shoe and Canoe.* 2 vols. Published privately, London: 1850.

Bishop, Isabella L. *The English Woman in America.* John Murray, London: 1856.

Bonnycastle, Sir R.H. *Canada As It Was, Is, and May Be.* 2 vols. Colburn & Co., London: 1852.

_____. *The Canadas in 1841.* 2 vols. Henry Colburn, London: 1841.

Bouchette, J. *A Topographical Description of the Province of Lower Canada.* W. Faden, London: 1815.

_____. *The British Dominions in North America.* 2 vols. Longman, Rees, Orme, Brown, and Green, London: 1832.

Brooke, F. *The History of Emily Montague.* T. Dodsley, London: 1769; McClelland and Stewart Ltd., Toronto: 1961.

Butler, W.F. *The Great Lone Land.* Sampson Low, London: 1872.

Calgary Herald, August 26, 1887.

Calgary Tribune, August 19, 1887.

Chappell, E. *Voyage of His Majesty's Ship Rosamond to Newfoundland and the Southern Coast of Labrador.* J. Mawman, London: 1818.

(Cockburn, J.P.) *Quebec and Its Environs.* Thomas Cary & Co., Quebec: 1831.

Cockloft, J. *Cursory Observations, Made in Quebec, Province of Lower Canada in the Year 1811.* Edward Ward, Bermuda: n.d.

Coke, E.T. *A Subaltern's Furlough.* Saunders and Otley, London: 1833.

Cook, J. *A Voyage to the Pacific Ocean.* (2nd edition). H. Hughs, London: 1785.

Cozzens, F.S. *Acadie; or, A Month with the Blue Noses.* Derby & Jackson, New York: 1859.

Department of Agriculture. *The Visit of the Tenant-Farmer Delegates to Canada in 1890.* McCorquodale & Co., London: 1891.

Dufferin and Ava, Marchioness of. *My Canadian Journal, 1872-78.* D. Appleton and Company, New York: 1891.

Ellice, K. J. *Diary.* Manuscript in the Public Archives of Canada.

Fergusson, A. *Practical Notes Made During a Tour in Canada.* William Blackwood, Edinburgh: 1831.

Fitzgibbon, M. *A Trip to Manitoba; or, Roughing on the Line.* Rose-Belford Publishing Company, Toronto: 1880.

Franklin, J. *Narrative of a Journey to the Shores of the Polar Sea in the Years 1819, 20, 21, and 22.* John Murray, London: 1823.

_____. *Narrative of a Second Expedition to the Shores of the Polar Sea in the Years 1825, 1826, and 1827.* J. Murray, London: 1828.

Goldie. J. *Diary of a Journey Through Upper Canada, 1819.* Privately published, 1967. (Original manuscript held in the Metropolitan Toronto Public Library, Central Branch).

Grant, G.M. *Ocean to Ocean.* James Campbell, Toronto: 1873.

_____. (ed). *Picturesque Canada.* Beldon Bros. Toronto: (1882).

Haliburton, T. C. *An Historical and Statistical Account of Nova Scotia.* 2 vols. Joseph Howe, Halifax: 1829.

Halifax *Evening Express.* September 12, 1859.

Hall, B. *Travels in North America in the Years 1827 and 1828.* 3 vols. Cadell and Company, Edinburgh; Simpkin and Marshall, London: 1829.

Hardy, Lieut. C. *Sporting Adventures in the New World.* 2 vols. Hurst & Blackett, London: 1855.

Hawkins, A. *Hawkins's Picture of Quebec; with Historical Recollections.* Neilson and Cowan, Quebec: 1834.

Hayman, R. *Quodlibets, Lately Come Over from New Britaniola, Old Newfoundland.* Robert Michell, London: 1628.

Heriot, G. *Travels Through the Canadas.* Richard Phillips, London: 1807.

Hind, H.Y. et al. *The Dominion of Canada.* L. Stebbins, Toronto: 1869.

Hunt, T.S. *The Gold Region of Nova Scotia.* Ottawa: 1868.

Jameson, A. *Winter Studies and Summer Rambles in Canada.* Saunders and Otley, London: 1838.

Kingston *Chronicle and Gazette,* November 17, 1838.

Kingston, W.H.G. *Western Wanderings.* 2 vols. Chapman & Hall, London: 1856.

Ladue, J. *Klondyke Facts.* Lovell, Montreal: 1897.

Lambert, J. *Travels Through Canada and the United States of North America.* L. Cradouc and W. Joy, London: 1814.

Landmann, G.T. *Adventures and Recollections of Colonel Landmann.* 2 vols. Colburn and Company, London: 1852.

Levinge, Capt. R.G.A. *Echoes from the Back-woods.* J. & D.A. Darling, London: 1849.

_____. *Historical Records of the Forty-third Regiment, Monmouthshire Light Infantry.* W. Clowes and Sons, London: 1868.

Lorne, Marquis of. *Canadian Pictures.* Religious Tract Society, London: 1884.

McGregor, J. *British America.* 2 vols. W. Blackwood, Edinburgh: 1832.

_____. *Historical and Descriptive Sketches of the Maritime Colonies of British America.* Longman, Rees, Orme, and Green, London: 1828.

Milton, Viscount, and W.B. Cheadle. *The North-West Passage By Land.* Cassell, Pelter and Galpin, London: (1865).

Montreal, *Canadian Illustrated News,* January 5, 1878.

(Morgan, H.J.) *The Tour of H.R.H. The Prince of Wales Through British America and the United States.* J. Lovell, Montreal: 1860.

Nares, Capt. G.S. *Arctic Expedition 1875-76.* London: 1877.

O'Leary, P. *Travels and Experiences in Canada.* J.B. Day, London: (1877).

Parry, Capt. W.E. *Journal of a Second Voyage for the Discovery of a North-West Passage.* John Murray, London: 1824.

Roper, E. *By Track and Trail: a Journey Through Canada.* W.H. Allen and Co. Ltd., London: 1891.

Rose, G. *The Great Country; or Impressions of America.* Tinsley Brothers, London: 1868.

Smith, W.H. *Smith's Canadian Gazetteer.* H. & W. Rowsell, Toronto: 1846.

Southesk, The Earl of. *Saskatchewan and the Rocky Mountains.* Edmonston and Douglas, Edinburgh: 1875.

St. John, M. *The Sea of Mountains.* 2 vols. Hurst & Blackett, London: 1877.

Toronto *Globe,* October 6, 1869; August 20, 1881; October 10, 1881.

Traill, C.P. *The Backwoods of Canada.* Charles Knight, London: 1836.

Trow, J. *Manitoba and North West Territories.* Department of Agriculture, Ottawa: 1878.

Warburton, G.D. *Hochelaga; or, England in the New World.* 2 vols. (E. Warburton, ed.) H. Coburn, London: 1846.

Warre, H.J. *Diaries.* Manuscript in the Public Archives of Canada. *Sketches of North America and the Oregon Territory, 1848.* Dickenson and Co., London: 1848.

Weld, I. *Travels Through the States of North America and the Provinces of Upper and Lower Canada.* John Stockdale, London: 1799.

Winslow, J. *Journal, 1755.* Nova Scotia Historical Society: 1883-84.

Ackermann, Robert (1816/7-after 1860)
106-07
This artist was possibly Robert Ackermann, a wood engraver in New York, who lists his place of birth as Canada. The similarity in style suggests a close relationship to George Ackermann, a drawing master at the School for Deaf and Dumb, Belleville, Ontario. No family connection has yet been traced.

Ainslie, Henry Francis (1803-1879)
48, 98, 103, 105, 108, 116, 117
Commissioned in the 83rd Regiment of Foot, he served in British North America in both Upper and Lower Canada from 1838-1843.

Armstrong, William, A.R.C.A., (1822-1914)
135, 142-43, 144, 184-85
Armstrong immigrated to Canada from Ireland in 1851, and pursued careers as a civil engineer, a photographer, and an artist in Toronto; and contributed to the Canadian Illustrated News. His works were exhibited widely, including the Paris Universal Exhibition of 1855. He was a founding associate member of the Royal Canadian Academy, and was widely known as a teacher in Toronto.

Back, George (1796-1878)
137, 138, 164, 165, 166
Back joined the Royal Navy as a first class volunteer in 1808. Most of his active career was spent in Arctic exploration. He was a member of Sir John Franklin's first (1819-22) and second (1825-26) overland expeditions to the shores of the Polar Sea. He led an overland expedition down what became known as the Back River in 1833-35 and a traditional but abortive sea voyage into the Arctic as commander of H.M.S. Terror (1836-37).

Bainbrigge, Philip John (1817-1881)
12, 83, 87, 94, 95, 113, 114, 134, 139, 145, 155, 156, 158
Bainbrigge attended the Royal Military Academy, Woolwich, from 1830 to 1833. Commissioned in the Royal Engineers, he served in Canada during the years 1836-42, and travelled from the Maritimes to Amherstburg. He returned to England to become instructor at Woolwich and editor of the Professional Papers for the Royal Engineers.

Bastide, J.H. (active 1745-1758)
31
Commissioned in the Royal Engineers, Bastide served at Louisbourg, Cape Breton, and Fort Anne at Annapolis, Nova Scotia, during the Seven Years' War.

Bayfield, Fanny Amelia (1814-1891)
127
Daughter of General Charles Wright, she married Henry Wolsey Bayfield, who was Admiralty surveyor for British North America in the years 1817-57. They lived in Quebec and Charlottetown.

Bland, James Fox (active 1846-1886)
37
Commissioned in the 76th Regiment of Foot, Bland served in British North America, mostly at Halifax from 1853-57. He was appointed Chief Instructor of Musketry, Madras, India in 1868.

Bouchette, Joseph (1774-1841)
43
The son of Jean Baptiste Bouchette, Joseph Bouchette was a topographer who worked with Samuel Holland, Surveyor-General of Lower Canada whom he succeeded. He published The Topographical Description of the Province of Lower Canada (1815, English and French) and The British Dominions in North America (1831).

Boultbee, Alfred E. (active 1875-1929)
203, 204
The son of Alfred Boultbee, Toronto lawyer and

M.P., he regarded himself as an architect and artist; worked in the office of Toronto architect W.G. Storm in 1886 and travelled to the Klondyke in 1898.

Cartwright, Harriet (active 1832-1843)
112
Daughter of Conway Dobbs, of Dublin, Harriet married Reverend R. D. Cartwright of Kingston in 1832.

Chaplin, Millicent Mary (active 1838-1842)
58, 77
The wife of Thomas Chaplin of the Coldstream Guards, she accompanied her husband on posting to Quebec in British North America 1838-1842.

Cockburn, James Pattison (1778-1847)
11, 52, 54-55, 61, 62, 63, 64-65, 72, 74, 83, 126, 147
Cockburn attended the Royal Military Academy, Woolwich, 1793-95, and was commissioned in the Royal Artillery. He served in British North America from 1822 to 1832. His works were published widely, including important aquatint views of Quebec and Niagara Falls, and a guide book to Quebec, Quebec and Its Environs (1831). He was a prolific water-colourist.

Cranstone, Lefevre James (active 1845-1867)
38
Cranstone was an English artist, who travelled to North America in 1859-60. His works were exhibited in the Royal Academy, the British Institution and Suffolk Street Gallery. Fugitive Etchings was published in 1849.

Dartnell, George Russell (1798-1878)
136
Commissioned as Surgeon, Medical Corps, First Royal Regiment, Dartnell served in British North America at Niagara and London in Upper Canada, and in Quebec in Lower Canada, 1836-1843.

Davies, Thomas (1737(?)-1812)
69, 88-89
Davies attended Royal Military Academy, Woolwich, 1755-56; and was commissioned in the Royal Artillery. He served in North America: 1757-62, 1764-66, 1776-78, and 1786-90. A fine but unusual water-colourist, he published views of North American waterfalls ca. 1768.

Denny, William (1804-1886)
121
Commissioned in the 71st Regiment of Foot, Denny served in British North America 1824-31 and 1838-48 at Quebec, Montreal, Kingston, and York. He married the daughter of the Honourable John Richardson of Montreal.

Lady Dufferin (1844-1936)
193, 194, 195
Born Hariot Hamilton, Lady Dufferin married in 1862 and took up residence at Clandeboye, Ireland. Lord Dufferin was appointed Governor-General of Canada 1872-1878; and they travelled to British Columbia in 1876.

Ellice, Katherine Jane (died 1864)
13, 96
Born Katherine Jane Balfour, she married Edward Ellice, whose family owned the Beauharnois seigniory, in 1834. In 1838, she accompanied her husband to Lower Canada when he was appointed secretary to Lord Durham. She was a celebrated beauty in her time.

Estcourt, Caroline Bucknall (1809?-1886)
151
Daughter of Right Honorable Reginald Pole-Carew, she married James B. B. Estcourt in 1837 and accompanied him to Canada.

Estcourt, James Bucknall Bucknall (1802-1855)
149, 150
Commissioned in the 43rd Regiment of Foot, he served in British North America at Montreal and Niagara 1837-39 and as Queen's Boundary Commissioner in the Maritimes 1843-1846. He was stricken by cholera in the Crimea in 1855.

Mr. Ford
120
This gentleman visited the Dufferins at Ottawa in ca. 1876.

Friend, Washington (ca. 1820-after 1886)
148
In 1849, he commenced a 5,000-mile trip in United States and Canada. His multi-media show-panoramic pictures, song, and poetry-was performed for Queen Victoria at Buckingham Palace.

Gaviller, Maurice (1842-1928)
140
Gaviller immigrated as a child to Bond Head, Canada West, 1844, and attended the University of Toronto and McGill University. He followed the professions of civil engineer and land surveyor, and was president of the Association of Ontario Land Surveyors, 1895.

Hale, Elizabeth Francis (1774-1826)
130-31
Elizabeth married John Hale in 1798 in London, England. He soon became an influential member of the provincial Legislature and Executive Councils of Lower Canada. The Hales had 12 children.

Hall, Sydney Prior (1842-1922)
10, 28, 33, 190, 191, 206-07, 208, 209, 210, 211, 212-13, 214, 215, 216
Hall was a "special artist" for the London Graphic magazine. He accompanied the Marquis of Lorne and Princess Louise to Canada in 1878, and was commissioned by Lorne to accompany him on a trip to Western Canada in 1881. His works were exhibited in the Royal Academy.

Hamilton, John (active 1753, died 1777)
30
Commissioned in the 40th Regiment of Foot, Hamilton served in British North America in the Maritimes, 1753-59, and at Montreal in 1760 during the Seven Years' War.

Heriot, George (1766-1844)
39, 53, 56-57, 78-79, 146
Educated in Scotland, Heriot attended the Royal Military Academy, Woolwich, and served in the British Army paymaster's department at Quebec from 1791. He was appointed Deputy Post-Master General of British North America 1800-16. Travels Through the Canadas was published in 1807.

Hind, William George Richardson (1833-1889)
15, 175, 186, 187
Hind immigrated to Canada about 1852, where he joined his brother Henry Youle Hind. He taught at the Toronto Normal School in 1856, made illustrations for Explorations in the Interior of Labrador Peninsula (H. Y. Hind, 1861), and joined the Overlanders of '62 to the Cariboo.

Hood, Robert (1796-1821)
162
A member of Franklin's first overland expedition to the Polar Sea, Hood was murdered on the Barrens by the guide.

Hope, The Honourable James (1807-1854)
68, 91, 92
Commissioned in the Coldstream Guards, Hope was active in British North America in 1838-42,

ON THE MAKING OF THIS BOOK

type was set by *Mono Lino Typesetting Co. Ltd.,*

the book was prepared for lithography by *Herzig Sommerville Ltd.,*

printed by *Sampson Matthews Ltd.,*

and bound by *T.H. Best Printing Company Ltd.,*

the book was planned and designed by *Frank Newfeld*